OWAC

D0734687

PRAISE FOR
BRAINWASHED

"*Brainwashed* is a must-read for any parent who has a young kid who wants to play football or is playing football already. Having two young boys who are already talking about playing football, we are always trying to gain knowledge and educate ourselves on the head issues involving football. Merril really opened our eyes to the truth of head injuries and CTE.

As a professional football player, combined with my wife's medical background as a physician assistant, we realize there is still so much unknown in the realm of head injuries and concussions. We both feel more educated after reading Merril's book."

— Ben Roethlisberger and Ashley Roethlisberger
Pittsburgh Steelers quarterback; physician assistant

"Merril Hoge and Dr. Peter Cummings have produced a detailed, well-documented, first-hand account of the issues that surround the sport of football and the potential for brain injury. Based on their experiences, they give the reader an excellent review of the social, athletic, and scientific aspects of football, which should help parents and athletes decide what sport is best for them."

— Dr. Julian Bailes
Director of neurosurgery and codirector of the NorthShore HealthSystem Neurological Institute

"Merril Hoge has written an important book regarding the issues of concussions in sports, with particular emphasis on football. Whatever your position on the subject of CTE may be, you should read this book. It contains information every parent and athlete should carefully review."

— **Bill Polian**
  Former NFL general manager

"If you are a parent grappling with whether or not you should allow your child to play youth football, I urge you to read *Brainwashed*. Thank you, Merril, for presenting us with perspective and taking to task the people who have owned the narrative of CTE. They have played on our fears, but with *Brainwashed*, we are armed with comprehensive and compelling arguments for why diet and lifestyle are as big a part of the equation as playing a contact sport.

As one of the first little girls to ever play youth football, I agree with Merril that the sport's positives greatly outweigh the negatives. The strength I gained from just stepping out on that field helped pave the way for my future. Perhaps it will for your child as well."

— **Suzy Kolber**
  Host of ESPN's Monday Night Countdown

"Reading *Brainwashed* was an eye-opening experience. It exposes the hidden agendas at play and bad science at work. We are thankful to Dr. Cummings and Merril for their research."

— **Trent Dilfer and Cassandra Dilfer**
  Super Bowl champion; former collegiate athlete

"In a climate where misinformation has led to misunderstanding, the game of football has come under attack. Through careful analysis, Merril Hoge has emerged as a strong defender of this great game that has given so much to so many."

— **Solomon Wilcots**
  Former NFL defensive back

"My wife and I have discussed the articles on head trauma many times. It seemed to us that the press had jumped the gun on the subject of head trauma and that the reported science on the subject did not follow the scientific method. Because we love football, we yearned for an authentic explanation. Merril Hoge and Dr. Peter Cummings have provided that in *Brainwashed*."

— **Bruce Arians**
  Former head coach of the Arizona Cardinals

"As a football family, we've been looking for reliable information on the topic of head trauma and treatment. Merril Hoge and Dr. Peter Cummings have delivered just that in *Brainwashed*."

— **Walter "Bubby" Brister and Bonnie Brister**
  Former Pittsburgh Steelers quarterback; football mom

"Merril does a fantastic job of exposing the biased science and half-truths that capture the headlines and dominate the media in regard to CTE. *Brainwashed* is a must-read if you want the real story and unbiased science behind CTE."

— **Mark Schlereth**
  Former NFL offensive lineman

"*Brainwashed* is a game changer. Merril and his experts ask all the right questions about the conflicts of interest and ulterior motives behind the CTE media machine that's quick to vilify and slow to verify. As a parent questioning the real risks behind football and other contact sports, I was amazed at the lack of controlled scientific best practices applied to the research that people use to make real decisions about their children's lives. This book is a must-read for anyone who believes in balancing educated risk against our kids' rights to explore, have access to opportunity, and find out who they are truly meant to be."

— **Debra Mirabile**
  CEO of DSM Properties

"Merril Hoge and Dr. Peter Cummings have opened a long overdue dialogue on the topic of CTE, concussions, and brain health. *Brainwashed* enlightened me, demonstrating that we cannot take everything we read or hear at face value. This story and the science behind it are just the beginning of shifting the dialogue and research in a direction that is real and honest so we can properly diagnose and treat brain trauma."

— **Kyla Zalapski**
  Owner of Fitness Evolution

"Merril, thank you so much for your passion and energy and mission to help keep our kids safe! I greatly appreciate the actual facts, science, and information that will help me make a sound decision as a parent and support my son in what he loves: football.

Brainwashed was hard to put down. The stories of athletes were amazing and helpful. As a single mom, I want to raise my son with great values and morals and provide him with an amazing footing for life. I have always been supportive of football, and this book answered many of the questions I had, as well as provided me with more information because I always believe safety comes first."

— **Nicole Middendorf**
CEO of Prosperwell Financial

BRAINWASHED

BRAINWASHED

The Bad Science Behind CTE
and the Plot to Destroy Football

Merril Hoge

Contributions by
Peter Cummings, MD
Board-Certified Forensic Neuropathologist

www.amplifypublishing.com

Brainwashed: The Bad Science Behind CTE and the Plot to Destroy Football

Editor's Note: The interviews in this book have been lightly edited for clarity.

For more information, please contact:
Mascot Books
620 Herndon Parkway #320
Herndon, VA 20170
info@mascotbooks.com
www.mascotbooks.com

Jacket design by Danny Moore
Interior design by Ricky Frame

Library of Congress Control Number: 2018909523

CPSIA Code: PRFRE0918A
ISBN-13: 978-1-68401-865-9

Printed in Canada

To the kids who play sports,
and to the families who support them.

CONTENTS

SIGNIFICANT PLAYERS

- **Julian Bailes, MD,** director of neurosurgery and codirector of the NorthShore University HealthSystem Neurological Institute

- **Robert Cantu, MD,** clinical professor, Department of Neurosurgery at the Boston University School of Medicine; cofounder of the Boston University CTE Center; and cofounder of the Concussion Legacy Foundation

- **Micky Collins, PhD,** director of the University of Pittsburgh Medical Center (UMPC) Sports Medicine Concussion Program

- **Brooke de Lench,** journalist, author, filmmaker, youth sports safety activist, and cofounder of the MomsTEAM Youth Sports Safety Institute and Teams of Angels

- **Kevin Guskiewicz, PhD,** director of the Matthew Gfeller Sport-Related Traumatic Brain Injury Research Center at the University of North Carolina

- **Mark Lovell, PhD,** former director of the UPMC Sports Medicine Concussion Program and codeveloper of the ImPACT cognitive test

- **Joseph Maroon, MD,** clinical professor and vice chairman of the Department of Neurological Surgery at UPMC, Heindl Scholar in neuroscience, codeveloper of the ImPACT cognitive test, and Pittsburgh Steelers team neurosurgeon

- **Ann McKee, MD,** chief neuropathologist for the BU CTE Center

- **Bennet Omalu, MD,** the neuropathologist who first identified CTE in a football player (Mike Webster) and the main character in the film *Concussion*

- **Elliot Pellman, MD,** former NFL chief medical officer and director of the league's Mild Traumatic Brain Injury Committee

- **Robert Stern, PhD,** director of clinical research and cofounder of the BU CTE Center

A CTE TIMELINE

1990: Pittsburgh Steelers quarterback Bubby Brister sustains a concussion; coach Chuck Noll demands objective data to justify keeping him from returning to play

Dr. Joseph Maroon and Dr. Mark Lovell develop the pencil-and-paper version of the ImPACT cognitive test

1994: Merril Hoge sustains two concussions in five weeks and is forced to retire from the NFL due to post-concussion syndrome

The NFL creates the Mild Traumatic Brain Injury (MTBI) Committee

1996: The Boston University Chronic Traumatic Encephalopathy Center (BU CTE Center) is formed

1997: The NFL adopts return-to-play guidelines for players who have suffered concussions

2000: Merril Hoge wins lawsuit against Chicago Bears team physician Dr. John Munsell

2002: Mike Webster dies

2005: Dr. Bennet Omalu publishes a paper claiming that Webster had CTE

2006: Former Philadelphia Eagles safety Andre Waters commits suicide; the Waters family grants permission for Omalu to examine his brain

2007: The NFL holds its first concussion summit

Omalu announces that Waters had severe CTE

The Sports Legacy Foundation, later called the Concussion Legacy Foundation, is founded; the foundation quickly partners with BU to obtain the brains of deceased athletes

2009: Merril Hoge and numerous medical experts—including Boston University's Dr. Ann McKee—testify before Congress about football and brain trauma

The NFL implements its concussion protocol

2011: The NFL Players Association files a class action lawsuit against the league for damages related to brain injury

2012: The documentary *Head Games* is released

Former San Diego Chargers star Junior Seau commits suicide and is determined to have had CTE

USA Football launches the Heads Up Football youth football safety program

2013: The NFL announces new concussion safety measures, which include having a neurologist present at every game

League of Denial, which tells the story of Mike Webster and attacks the NFL's approach to brain injury, is published

2015:   The feature film *Concussion* is released

49ers linebacker Chris Borland retires, becoming the first player to publicly quit because of fear of head trauma and progressive brain damage

A consensus panel of CTE experts, led by Boston University, publishes diagnostic and staging criteria for CTE

2016:   NFL executive vice president Jeff Miller acknowledges a link between football and CTE before a congressional committee

2017:   Former New England Patriots player Aaron Hernandez commits suicide in prison and is later found to have had severe CTE

A *New York Times* story announces that the BU CTE Center has found that 110 out of 111 brains of former NFL players have CTE

INTRODUCTION

BACK IN 1994, I DIED for a few seconds.

It was my eighth season in the NFL. I was sitting on the training table in the Chicago Bears' locker room when I went into cardiac arrest. The next thing I remember, I was lying in a bed in intensive care. A few weeks later, I was done with pro football.

I had suffered two concussions in five weeks.

Back then, nobody was talking about brain injuries in football. Sure, you got hit in the head, but every guy on the field had been getting hit in the head since he was eight years old, so it just wasn't a big deal. Nobody used the word *concussion*. If you took a knock to the head, you "got your bell rung" or "saw stars." My attitude was that I wore a helmet to keep from getting my brain turned to tapioca, so what was the big deal?

We just didn't know then what we know now about brain trauma and how to treat it. Yes, I did sue Dr. John Munsell, the team doctor for the Chicago Bears, for improperly managing my concussions and prematurely ending my career by clearing me to play over the phone when an in-person office exam (which should have been common sense) would have told him that I wasn't ready. But this is not a book about blaming the NFL. It's also not about defending the NFL.

It's already been well-documented that the NFL did a lot wrong in dealing with what happens when two powerful men smash their brains into their skulls at one hundred times the force of gravity. For years, the league had no input on how teams or trainers should care for head injuries. Teams came up with their own protocols, if they had any. The team owners, then-NFL chief medical officer Dr. Elliot Pellman, then-commissioner Paul Tagliabue, and others have to answer for that, and they have.

The Steelers, my first team, were the pioneers in bringing neurology into football, largely thanks to the vision of team owner Mr. Dan Rooney and the skill of experts like Dr. Joe Maroon and Dr. Mark Lovell. The Steelers started doing cognitive testing with pencil and paper in 1991, and in 1997 they switched to computerized testing. That same year, the National Hockey League was the first major sports league to make neurocognitive testing mandatory. It took the NFL ten more years to get there.

But after I left the NFL, I wasn't concerned about all that. Instead, I worked for ESPN; raised my kids, Beau and Kori; got involved with USA Football; and survived open-heart surgery and a bout with cancer. I stayed involved with the league and consulted with Commissioner Roger Goodell from time to time, but mostly I lived my life.

Then came the death of my ex-teammate Mike Webster in 2002.

When Mike died and neuropathologist Dr. Bennett Omalu (the doctor Will Smith played in the movie *Concussion*) announced in 2005 that his brain showed signs of a severe case of the neurodegenerative disease chronic traumatic encephalopathy (CTE), the caution about football and brain trauma got dialed all the way up to exploitation.

HYSTERIA IS OUTRUNNING THE FACTS

Now you can barely pick up a newspaper, watch TV, or go online without finding another story about CTE. The average person on the street might not know what CTE stands for, but they've heard the letters and they're convinced that playing football causes a terrible, insidious brain disease that's threatening adults—and worse, children—with futures of depression, rage, memory loss, and suicide.

The trouble is that hysteria is outrunning facts. In about thirteen years, we've gone from Mike Webster to NFL representatives (including yours truly) testifying before Congress in 2009–10 to the tragic suicide of Junior Seau to the 2015 release of *Concussion*. From there, we've seen Jeff Miller, the NFL's senior vice president for health and safety, answer a question from US Representative Jan Schakowsky about whether a link between football and CTE had been established by saying, "The answer to that question is certainly yes." We had the suicide of Aaron Hernandez, and to top it all off, the infamous *New York Times* story about 110 out of 111 brains from former NFL players testing positive for CTE.

Underneath it all has been a steady drumbeat of scary research about football, CTE, ex-players suffering from memory loss and depression, and worst of all, youth football causing brain damage in kids. A lot of that research has been sloppy and poor, but if you've read the press coverage or seen *Concussion*, you're probably worried. When adults read endless headlines telling them that football turns you into a vegetable, they don't dig into the details. They pull their kids out of youth football, file lawsuits, and start calling football murder and child abuse.

Because of the endless press based on bad research with no context, millions of people have reached the following conclusion (and God help you if you publicly contradict it):

Playing tackle football = CTE

Nobody questions the research that continually pours out of a few facilities—mostly Boston University's Chronic Traumatic Encephalopathy Center (BU CTE Center). But they should because a lot of that science—especially the work coming from BU and some of the people associated with it—is flawed or incomplete.

If you look at all the information skeptically (as too few journalists are), the real equation becomes more like this:

*Head impacts + lots of other variables + time = Possible changes
to the brain that might not ever affect a person's quality of life*

WE'VE BEEN BRAINWASHED

LOOK AT ALL THE SCIENCE from unbiased sources and you start to see a different picture. Talk to doctors who aren't invested in the football-CTE connection, and you find a lot of doubt—and a lot of caution about speaking out, which is a problem all by itself. I know because I've looked at the science and talked to the scientists who are scared to go on the record.

I learned from people a lot smarter than me that the main culprit in CTE is a microscopic protein called *tau*. Tau is a protein that helps stabilize brain cells. When a nerve cell is injured or diseased, tau can accumulate in the cell. It does this by becoming *hyperphosphorylated*. That means it gets lots of phosphate groups attached to it, and it gets sticky. When cells filled with tau get sticky and clump together, they are called *neurofibrillary tangles*. Tau accumulations can be seen in a number of diseases and in aging.

Tau goes through a series of stages as it gets sticky and starts to accumulate. At first, the cells are normal looking, with some small amount of granular or dot-like staining. Those cells are functioning normally with only minimal tau accumulations. As things progress, *pretangles* form—tiny strings of tau inside the cell. As the process continues, you see the classic neurofibrillary tangles, the mature form of tau accumulations. At the end of the process, the brain cell dies, and you're left with *ghost tangles* outside the cells, where the cell used to be.

Tau deposits can build up in the brain and, over time, can interfere with neurological function. Voilà! Cognitive decline. Tau accumulation is part of what causes diseases like Alzheimer's. But you know what else can cause tau to form in the brain? Drug use, anabolic steroid use, obesity, chronic inflammation, and chronic stress. Mike Webster was rumored to be a steroid user. Yes, he absorbed incredible punishment on the line of scrimmage, but claiming that impacts to the head *caused* his problems is like standing in a downpour and blaming one particular cloud.

The researchers at BU, led by Dr. Ann McKee (and aided by the Concussion Legacy Foundation), have built their notoriety and reputations on the idea that impact to the head leads to tau buildup and then to CTE. They seem to be suggesting it's simple cause and effect, case closed. But did you know that other labs have looked at the brains of athletes who had dozens of concussions and found little or no tau? I'll bet you also didn't know that thousands of ex-football players—who've taken millions of hits to the head—have no symptoms of cognitive decline and are doing great into their seventies and older. They're not falling apart or having suicidal thoughts.

Nobody's talking about that because there's no fame or money in good news. And the news coverage is a part of this story. The press has used parental fear to sell papers and online ads and turn a few people into press darlings. At the same time, it has most Americans convinced that football causes CTE without them ever seeing the evidence. In these pages, I'll turn the spotlight on the press, too.

Here's something else you might not know. For years, BU has also selected research cases that would support its theories, suppressed information that contradicts those theories, and published science that's just plain terrible. That's not just me saying that; it's trained neuropathologists, neuropsychologists, and neurologists. In these pages, they'll tell you what they think and what they know.

I'm not glossing over reality. Taking hits to the head can cause damage, especially if the resulting brain trauma isn't managed the right way. Some ex-players do have problems. There are some risks to playing football. But we're acting as though the science is sewn up and we have all the answers when the truth is far from that.

DR. PETER CUMMINGS

RIGHT NOW, YOU MIGHT BE saying to yourself, "Merril, you're not a doctor or a scientist. How did you figure all this out on your own?" Great question, and I have a simple answer: *I didn't.* I had help from a guy who's a neuropathologist, a football dad, a coach, and an absolute warrior for the truth: Dr. Peter Cummings. This book would not have been possible without him.

Dr. Cummings is a skilled, careful scientist who's not afraid to ask questions. But the most important thing you need to know is that he holds three board certifications in pathology and spends his time investigating injuries—particularly brain injuries. He's performed more autopsies and cut more brains than my stomach would care to count. He's also an associate professor at the Boston University School of Medicine (yes, the same BU that's home to the CTE Center), where he not only teaches forensic sciences and anatomy but also runs a graduate-level course in experimental design. To me, that means two things: this guy knows about brain trauma, and he knows statistics.

It was Dr. Cummings's September 19, 2017, editorial on *Yahoo! Sports* that first made me aware of his interest in digging deeper into the evidence and hysteria surrounding CTE and let me know I wasn't alone in my concerns. It was called "I'm a Brain Scientist and I Let My Son Play Football," and this is part of what it said:

Before I began this journey, football was banned in my house. I wouldn't even watch it on TV because I didn't want my son to see it and develop a desire to play. Despite my efforts, he discovered football via a video game. He immediately fell in love with the sport and I was forced to do some serious soul searching: Should I allow him to pursue his interest and play?

Honestly, I was scared of CTE.

CTE stands for "chronic traumatic encephalopathy"; in real words it means damage to the brain caused by repetitive injury. The hallmark of CTE is the deposition of a protein called "tau" in the brain. Tau has a number of functions, including stabilizing the structure of nerve cells. When nerves are injured, tau builds up and can cause problems.

You may have a [*sic*] read about a recently published paper reporting the presence of CTE in the brains of 99 percent of former National Football League players examined. The findings of this study sent the media into a frenzy and produced a lot of negative press toward football. As a result of the media attention, people are now saying there should be no more youth football; there are even people who are insinuating I am abusing my son by allowing him to play football.

People are coming away from the constant media barrage with the belief that concussions are the sole and direct cause of CTE, most or all football players have CTE, and

> CTE has led football players to become violent, commit suicide or develop dementia.
>
> I had the same impression before I decided to look a little deeper. But when I dove into the published literature regarding CTE, I discovered the scientific evidence to support the media's narrative was lacking; in fact, I found bodies of evidence to the contrary and a whole other side to the science that is largely ignored.[1]

When I saw that editorial, I thought three things. First, *holy cow, this Cummings guy has a ton of guts.* To speak out against the overwhelming consensus of your profession—even when that consensus is wrong and based on bad information—is tough, especially when you're part of the faculty at BU, the organization spreading most of the bad information.

Second, brain science is this guy's profession, and if it took him three years of investigating to figure out that the science behind football and CTE was mostly garbage, what chance does the average person have? That's why most readers, especially parents, stop reading at the scary headlines, pull their kids out of sports, and start signing petitions to ban tackle football in their city, county, or state.

Third, I knew he and I had to work together to get the truth out. This book is the result.

WHY I WROTE THIS BOOK

I WROTE *BRAINWASHED* BECAUSE, while our knowledge of sports and CTE is at about a 2 on a 1–10 scale, we're acting like it's a 9. That's having some dire consequences. For one, when I started this book, five states were talking about restricting or banning youth tackle football based on this sketchy, biased information. (California's and Illinois's bills are dead for now, but they will be back.) I've been involved with USA Football for years, and I love the sport, but I also know how valuable it is for kids. Football is one of the biggest sports in families with lower incomes. Take it away from those kids and what will they do?

Our kids spend more time indoors today than ever, but football gives them a chance to get outside, exercise, learn skills and teamwork, and discover who they are. Pop Warner and other major programs have adopted stringent safety policies and equipment that make youth tackle football safer than ever. And some kids want to play tackle football.

Is youth football safe? It's a lot safer than sitting on the couch playing video games, eating sugar, and developing type 2 diabetes. If we're going to restrict youth football, it had better be based on solid science, not biased BS.

It also sickens me to see how CTE anxiety has spread among former athletes. Dr. Shannon Bauman, medical director of the clinic Concussion North in Barrie, Ontario, Canada, has said that she regularly sees athletes coming to her clinic months after getting concussed, terrified that they have CTE and are on a one-way trip to cognitive decline. Some pro athletes have even killed themselves because they were sure they had CTE; the terrible irony is that after autopsies, their families have found out that they didn't have the disease.

I wrote this book to set the record straight—to tell the whole story, not the half-truths you've been reading. *Brainwashed* fights back against the narrative that says football causes CTE, all ex-athletes have brain damage, and youth football should be banned. The truth is that much of the science is shoddy and misleading, and multiple parties have been getting on the bandwagon to make money, rationalize the deaths of loved ones, or get famous. The book attacks the pervasive myths about football and brain trauma in three sections:

- **Myth #1: All NFL Players Are Falling Apart.** This section looks at the reality of what's happened to NFL players as related to brain trauma, including my journey from running back to media personality to CTE truther, the story of how ex-players are doing and how the ones with legitimate cognitive problems might be helped, and the important truth about ex-players and suicide. In this section, I'm not going to completely exonerate the NFL, but I'm not going to demonize it, either.

- **Myth #2: CTE Is Settled Science, and Football Causes It.** This section digs into the influence of BU and the fawning media coverage of its research, takes a closer look at the biased and poor science behind today's "football = CTE" consensus, and presents a theory of CTE that better fits the evidence.

- **Myth #3: Youth Football Is Child Abuse.** This final section goes into the attacks on youth football based on CTE fears as well as the truth about the safety of the sport. We'll talk to experts treating brain injury with therapies that actually reverse and prevent damage and look at cutting-edge safety and treatment methods that get players back on the field safely. We'll rip to shreds once and for all the sloppy arguments behind both the assault on youth football and the irresponsible media coverage of it. And we'll examine the real benefits of youth football—and the real threats to our kids' health—and make an argument for why it should be protected.

I wrote this book because I want people to have good information so they can make informed decisions. I want everyone—athletes, parents, kids, everybody—to be as healthy as they can be. I've been through head trauma, cancer, and open-heart surgery, and the one major advantage I had over people my age in all those situations was my health. In all three situations, my doctors told me that being in great health helped me recover. Health can also prevent problems, even with the brain, and science backs that up, as you'll see.

WHAT IS CTE?

I'M AWARE THAT PEOPLE WILL label me a "CTE denier." That's what happens to anyone who questions the existing narrative, contradicts the so-called experts who dominate the news cycle, and tells the truth. I expect it. But I'm not a CTE denier. I'm a bad science denier. A lies denier. A hysteria denier. As I will repeat, I'm not saying it's good to take repeated impacts to the head. It's not. I'm not saying there aren't former pro athletes who have psychological and neurological problems. There are. But science done right is a slow process. Because we favor information that confirms our biases, millions of doctors, athletes, parents, coaches, and journalists are making up their minds based on an incomplete picture painted by headlines that are far ahead of the science. That's leading to conclusions that are harmful and wrong. It's time we stopped calling people "deniers" and had an open, candid conversation about what's true.

So before we get rolling, let's address the question I've heard from so many people: is CTE a real thing, and if it is, what is it? We know a lot less than the coverage would lead you to believe, so let's talk about what we know and what we don't:

- We know that mild traumatic brain injury—sometimes repeated injuries, sometimes just a single injury—can sometimes cause a pattern of tau proteins to accumulate in the brain. We call those tau patterns CTE.

- We also know that other factors, such drug abuse, smoking, obesity, and chronic inflammation, can also cause tau to accumulate in the brain. We don't know yet how these other factors may play a role in the pattern of tau called CTE.

- We don't know all the factors or conditions that lead to tau deposits in critical areas of the brain or why some people appear to be more or less susceptible.

- We also don't know how tau deposits in the brain lead to clinical symptoms, such as mood, behavioral or cognitive disorders—or if CTE is involved at all—since those same symptoms are also associated with many other neurodegenerative diseases, including Alzheimer's.

So yes, CTE is real, but that is all good evidence can tell us right now. In other words, at present, all that sound, conservative research can tell us is that CTE is an accumulation of tau in certain areas of the brain. *Full stop.* We're not clear on what causes those accumulations, and we're not clear on what effect, if any, they have on a person's short-term or long-term neuropsychiatric health.

This book is about setting the record straight and countering misinformation with facts. Laying all that out is a tall order for an ex-running back with no background in science. However, I have an MD in common sense, a PhD in football experience as a player, coach, and parent, and the professional judgment of Dr. Cummings and others. This is the mission of my life. It's time to fight the misinformation, get to the truth, and take action. No more acting out of fear. No more brainwashing.

Merril Hoge

MYTH #1

ALL NFL PLAYERS ARE FALLING APART

A CONCUSSION BECOMES A MISSION

Football is a part-time profession...it gets you ready for your life's work.

—CHUCK NOLL, FORMER HEAD COACH OF THE PITTSBURGH STEELERS

CHAPTER I PLAYBOOK

- How concussions and improper care ended my NFL career
- My lifesaving move to ESPN
- Making youth football safer
- The emerging CTE crisis

How DOES A RUNNING BACK, broadcaster, coach, and dad wind up on a mission to save the great game of football from the hidden agendas of people who want to destroy it? Well, I guess it happens in the same way for pretty much everybody: you see something you can't turn away from, and have to do something about it. For me, that something was and is youth football. But before I can tell that story, I have to take you back to what happened to me before and after that last fateful hit to the head.

It was 1991—when I was with the Steelers—and it was the off-season, about two years after my only documented concussion at that time. Dr. Joe Maroon, the Steelers' neurosurgeon, and Dr. Mark Lovell, then-director of neuropsychology at Allegheny General Hospital (and later, chief scientific officer at ImPACT Applications Inc.), had developed the pencil-and-paper version of the ImPACT (Immediate Post-Concussion Assessment and Cognitive Testing) test. That came about after Bubby Brister, our quarterback, sustained a serious concussion during the 1990 season.

Dr. Maroon evaluated Bubby at the time, and then before the next game, he went in to talk to Coach Noll. He said, "Coach, I didn't like some of the responses I got from him. I don't know if he should play." Coach Noll wasn't happy at the idea of losing his starting quarterback, so he said, "Time out. I've watched him all week. He looked great. There was nothing that told me he can't play, Joe. I can't have you come in here subjectively, after talking to him, telling me he can't play."

Chuck Noll wasn't just a great football coach. He was the Leonardo da Vinci of football, one of the most brilliant men I ever knew. He was a wine connoisseur and a pilot, would talk to me about jazz, and was completely willing to think outside the box. Coach was telling Dr. Maroon that if he was going to sit a starter he needed objective data, not subjective opinion. So Dr. Maroon and Dr. Lovell went off and created ImPACT, a series of questions that tested a player's reaction time and the brain's ability to process information. The idea was that you would take the test when you were healthy to establish a baseline, and then if you sustained head trauma in a game, you could take the test again. The team doc could compare your baseline to your more recent test and determine if you needed to take some time off to recover.

That day in 1991, I was in the locker room at Three Rivers Stadium, and John Norwig (a terrific athletic trainer for the Steelers, who is still there today) approached me. It was his job to convince players to take ImPACT to set their baseline. He asked me to do it, but I had just finished my workout, and I was getting ready to leave. Because I'd had a concussion a couple of years before, I was on the team's priority list to take the test, and John followed me out to my car, pestering me the whole way.

I didn't want to take it. I had pool work to do and then martial arts class, and I didn't want to waste the time. Just as we got to the car, I said, "John, I wear a helmet. Why do I have to take this?" That was my thought process at the time. That was everybody's thought process. People today ask why the NFL and doctors didn't handle concussion differently in 1991 or 1994, but the answer is simple: *we didn't know then what we know now*. We thought about a concussion as getting dazed, even knocked out, but then you rested and went back in the game, period. Nobody talked about things like brain damage or long-term cognitive problems.

But John knew the right buttons to push. He said, "The test is also to assess your knowledge, Merril," he said. "Let's see if you can be the smartest player on this team." Clever guy. So I said, "All right, let's get it on." As an aside, that's how great John Norwig is. He knew just what to say to get me to do what was in my own best interest. There are thousands across the country just like him, and we need more. Athletic trainers are vital to keeping players safe, regardless of age. They're like a nurse, doctor, and mother hen all rolled into one, just standing on the sidelines until they're needed.

I took the test, thinking I would never need it again. John said, "If something happens to you again, then we can do this test again, and we'll have a better assessment of when you should return to play." But I was right, sort of. I didn't need that test again for the rest of the time I was in Pittsburgh.

"I CAN NEVER CLEAR YOU"

IN 1994, I SIGNED with the Chicago Bears as a free agent. During an August 22 preseason game in Kansas City against the Chiefs, I caught a ball on a passing play in scoring territory. As I spun around, I saw the safety between me and the end zone, but I also knew that Hall of Famer Derrick Thomas, the best pass rusher in the game at the time, was nearby. Boy, was he!

Derrick slammed into me from the side, and all of a sudden, I was lying on my back and couldn't move. It was like being in an earthquake; everything was shaking. Tim Worley, my teammate, came running over to me and said, "Aw, man!" and waved for the trainer to come out. I don't remember doing it, but I got up and got back to the huddle and actually ran the next play. Days later, I watched the tape, and I ran the right pass route, but I ran it like I was drunk, wobbling all over the place.

I don't remember any of this, but I'm told that I stumbled to the sideline and told one of the trainers that I'd been hit in the head. They started asking if I knew where I was, and I said, "Tampa." The trainer said, "How do you know that?" I answered, "Because I can hear the ocean."

At that, I came out of the game. But at the time, there wasn't much more the team could do, cognitively speaking, to test what kind of shape I was in, so during the second half, they took me to a nearby hospital for an MRI. Their concern was bleeding on the brain; you don't want someone with that getting in a plane and flying because of the changes in pressure. By the way, I don't remember going to the hospital. I just remember people asking, over and over, "What's your name? Where are you? Hey, buddy, how you feeling? What's your birthday? What's today's date?"

Anyway, I did my time in the MRI machine, and they gave me an envelope with my scans in it and sat me in a waiting room. I was thinking, *Great. I have these scans so that when the doctors come back, I'll be able to show them that I'm fine.* After what felt like forty-five minutes, I saw a doctor running past the door like he was looking for somebody and then stop and jump back. "There you are!" he said, looking a little frantic, like he'd been looking all over for me. I was thinking, *I've been here the whole time waiting for you*, and I reached for the scans so I could show him that I was fine. There was no envelope.

The doc said, "Oh, we have the scans. They're down in the other room." Turns out they had left me in a different waiting room on a different floor downstairs; I had wandered upstairs to another room without remembering it. Now I got scared. The good news was that I didn't have bleeding on the brain, so I was able to fly home with the team, but I don't remember the flight or arriving home, either.

The next morning, quarterback Eric Kramer picked me up to take me to the Bears' facility. When I walked into the locker room, Fred Caito, the Bears' athletic trainer, saw me and said, "How you feeling?"

I felt terrible, but I wasn't going to tell him that. "I feel great."

"Yeah?" Fred said. "Go look in the mirror." I walked over and looked, and I stopped dead. I could barely recognize myself: glossy and pale, with weird coloring. I wasn't going to fool anybody into thinking I belonged on that field. Man, after seeing myself, even I didn't think I belonged on the field.

Our last preseason game was that Friday, and I wouldn't be playing in it anyway because starters don't play in the final preseason game. Instead, I assumed I would get ready to play the Tampa Bay Buccaneers in our season opener, five days after that. That's when Dr. John Munsell, the Bears' team doctor, called me.

Dr. Munsell should have examined me in person, but instead he asked me a few questions, like how was I feeling—things like that. And then he cleared me to play, just like that, over the phone. I had no face-to-face exam. No tests. Nobody looked at me to make sure I didn't have gray matter leaking out of my ears. I got cleared over the phone by a general practitioner, not a neurologist or neurosurgeon. We didn't know back then what we know now, but you don't need board certification to know that you shouldn't okay someone to play after a brain injury without at least seeing him in person.

When Dr. Munsell asked me how I was doing, I said, "Fine." Of course I did; I wanted to be there for my teammates because that's what you do. But in reality, I had a splitting headache and I didn't say anything about it. Nobody told me that was a symptom of a problem, so I didn't worry about it. I just wanted to play.

It's important to remember that at the time, the Steelers were the only NFL team doing cognitive testing of players who'd had a concussion. Nobody else was as forward thinking. That's not a criticism of the Bears; it's just reality. Even team doctors didn't know much about concussions or brain trauma. You're limited by the knowledge you have, and we didn't know very much.

Anyway, after taking the last preseason game off, I thought I was ready for the season opener against the Buccaneers in Chicago. I'd done some conditioning, but I still had a bad headache. I didn't say anything because you just didn't. A blown-out knee? Sure. But a headache? No way. If I had told my head coach, Dave Wannstedt, that I couldn't play because of a headache, he would've laughed in my face. It just wasn't done.

I practiced for the opener, but I was a mess. During an NFL season, you add a few specific plays each week to use against your opponent, but the majority of your offense is made up of staples you run every week, no matter who you play. As we got ready for our first game, I had no issues with the plays we had been running for weeks, but I struggled with the new plays we had put in for the Bucs. On Tuesday, we did a walk-through, and I was just fine until one of the new plays was called. I couldn't remember what my assignment was. I figured I could walk in what I thought was the right direction and figure it out as the play unfolded.

Boy, was I wrong. I was completely out of position, and our running back coach, Joe Pendry, finally said, "Merril, what are you doing?" I hadn't heard a coach say that in a long time. The last time I'd made such a mental error was in 1987, my rookie year with the Steelers. One of my strengths was that I always knew what everybody on the field was supposed to be doing. Now I was struggling to remember what I was supposed to do.

Obviously, something wasn't right. But I didn't say anything, and nobody asked me if I was okay. That's how ignorant we were back then. Nobody went over signs or symptoms or things I should be aware of, and there wasn't any post-concussion protocol. So I played the first game against the Bucs. In the fourth game against the New York Jets, I broke my hand, but I improvised a cast that let me grip the ball, so I was able to play our fifth game against the Buffalo Bills. That was the last game I would ever play.

If you saw the play that gave me my second concussion, ended my career, and almost ended my life, you would say, "That's nothing." But my face mask looked like I'd been in a car wreck. I took a blow on the side of the head, rolled over, and grabbed my head but then got right up. I wasn't wobbly. I went back to the huddle. I executed our next play on third down, but we didn't get the first down, so we came off the field. The trainer started to take off my helmet because my face mask had cut my chin and I was bleeding like crazy.

I don't remember any of this. They were talking to me, but I wasn't responding. Then the trainer looked at my eyes, and that's when they took me to the locker room, just before halftime. I don't remember going to the locker room, but I do remember sitting on a training table. Vinson Smith, one of our linebackers, had hurt his ankle, and he was sitting on the other table across from me, facing me. I remember him saying, "Are you all right?" and I remember thinking, *No, I'm not.* My eyes started to flutter, and everything went black.

I'm told that I fell off the table and went into cardiac arrest. The medical staff started to get into position to resuscitate me, but I eventually started breathing again on my own. I woke up that night in the hospital not knowing where I was. There were machines beeping, tubes in me, sensors attached to me, you name it. I went to scratch my forehead, and I nearly gave myself another concussion because they had put a cast on my broken hand.

Later, one of the Bears' doctors, Dr. Schafer, came in and said, "You scared me to death. I've never lost a player, but I thought we were going to." But I still didn't understand the gravity of the situation. It turned out that my brother and my daughter, Kori, who was only two at the time, had come to see me, but I didn't remember. I remember nothing other than what I've told you here.

I spent a couple of days in intensive care, and then the Bears sent me to see Dr. James P. Kelly of the Rehabilitation Institute, which was affiliated with Northwestern University. It was a week out from the Bills game, and let me tell you, I was a lost soul. I went on my own to downtown Chicago to see Dr. Kelly, and I was standing in the lobby of the building where I was supposed to meet him when I realized I didn't know where I was going or where I was. I was looking hopelessly at the information board when I heard a voice say, "Merril?" It was Dr. Kelly.

Thank the Lord.

He took me up to his office and did a bunch of tests, and I re-member him asking me who the president of the United States was. I couldn't remember. Then he asked who the vice president was. Talk about throwing me a curve ball. Finally, Dr. Kelly told me, "I think you need to sit out the rest of the year, but you can play next year."

Okay, not the worst news. I was feeling a little better when I got home, and that's when I remembered my ImPACT baseline test. I was two weeks out from the second concussion when I talked to Fred Caito and said, "I'd like to go back and retake that test." I took it, and then I went to Pittsburgh to see Dr. Maroon and discuss my results. I stayed at what was then called the downtown Hilton, but the next morning, as I was getting ready, I couldn't find my car keys. I looked everywhere, turning the room upside down. I had my mattress against the wall, every drawer pulled out, and nothing. It was one of the most surreal moments of my life, and as I sat down in despair I remembered.

I had valeted my car.

Clearly, I was still not quite right. The signs had been there: memory problems, not knowing Bill Clinton was president, and now forgetting that I'd handed my keys to the valet the night before. But I didn't really know how bad it was until I saw Dr. Joe Maroon, a neurosurgeon and the Steelers' physician.

I sat down in his office, and he said, "Merril, the tests we got back put you at about 50 or 60 percent of your baseline." I shouldn't have been surprised. A few days before, Dr. Lovell had said, "I've seen people in car accidents in better shape than you. I've never seen anybody two weeks out be this cognitively dysfunctional."

Dr. Maroon continued. "Merril, the way you're testing, I cannot put my head down on a pillow at night if I let you return to play," he said. "I just can't risk it. I don't know where you are contract-wise or insurance-wise, but I can't do it. I'm sorry. I can *never* clear you."

It was like an out-of-body experience. It was like I had the good and evil angels on my shoulders, and the evil one whispered in my ear, "You've been playing this game for twenty years, and you're just going to say, 'Okay, it's over?' You're going to accept that?" Then the good angel said, "Yeah. It happens." And just like that, I was an ex-NFL player. I was the first player in NFL history to be retired because of the results of a post-concussion cognitive test.

ESPN SAVED MY LIFE

MY CAREER WAS OVER. What was I supposed to do? What I did for a while was go through a scary period of depression, headaches, and cognitive problems. Everything was still hazy and fuzzy. There were a few months when I kept having out-of-body experiences. My career had ended during the season, like having a limb severed, and it was brutal to watch from the sidelines. There was no off-season to help me adjust.

I had just moved to Chicago, so I wasn't part of the community and didn't have a lot of support. I spent a lot of time on the couch watching television. At one point I was watching Barney with my daughter,

Kori…and enjoying it! I remember sitting there, looking at that purple dinosaur, thinking, *I like this*. Yeah, I wasn't quite right. The Bears sent me to counseling.

There was another terrifying incident when I went to a charity wine tasting event. I don't like wine and don't normally drink it. But at this event, I took one sip and suddenly…I was blind! I mean, *I could not see*. After about ten seconds, my vision came back, but that was the most terrifying ten seconds of my life.

When I told Dr. Maroon about it, he said, "Because you don't drink, you are very sensitive to the effects of alcohol. Losing your vision is a clear sign that the area of your brain that has been traumatized is not healed yet. That's why you need eighteen or nineteen months to repair and recover, and that is why I won't let you play again. What if you took a hit in that area again before you're completely healed and lose your vision permanently? Would that be worth it?" Obviously, I said no. I've never forgotten those ten seconds when I lost my vision. I had been starting to feel better, and I had been calling Dr. Maroon to see if he would reconsider. That experience ended my delusions about playing again forever.

It turned out that Dr. Maroon knew what he was talking about. In 1996, I was in Chicago, driving around a bend on the Kennedy Expressway, and when I looked up at a billboard, the image suddenly cleared up. I said, "Whoa, all of a sudden, I feel good." I'll be darned if it wasn't eighteen or nineteen months after I had retired.

But during that ugly year and a half, it was getting into the broadcast booth and later joining ESPN that saved my sanity and my life. I was really struggling cognitively; I could pay attention to what I needed to say on the air, but I couldn't listen to what other people were saying at the same time. So I would block everybody out—and I mean everybody. In 1995 and part of 1996, you could've stood right in front of me and called my mother every name in the book, and I would've said, "Thanks. Here's what I think about the three-four defense." But I had to break out of my depression, which means I had to look for my life's work and deal with my cognitive issues along the way.

I cast out a bunch of lines, including into coaching and broadcasting, and Lynn Swann, the NFL Hall of Famer and great Steelers receiver, was kind enough to grab one of them. He was on ABC, and he let me come watch him, Keith Jackson, and Bob Griese do their thing on TV. That was great because I was interested in broadcasting and had been doing a lot of it in the off-season.

Thanks to Mr. Rooney, in 1995 I joined Bill Hillgrove, the Steelers' play-by-play broadcaster, and Myron Cope, the team's color analyst, in the broadcast booth on WTAE radio. Then in 1996, I got a job at ESPN covering college football, and later I got to team up with Jaws (my buddy Ron Jaworski) on the *NFL Matchup* show. It's not an exaggeration to say that ESPN saved my life, and here's why.

When you look at the concussion rehab that we do now—the kind that was done with my son, Beau—it's not about resting in a dark room anymore. Now we're challenging the brain and trying new exercises. Well, when I joined ESPN, it was like doing the same thing in real life. I went into an arena where I had to learn a lot of new things quickly. I had to do things live on air that were cognitively challenging for me, especially in those months before things cleared up in Chicago. I had to remember facts and names and translate it all into a thirty-second segment. That was the best therapy I could have done.

That does *not* mean it went smoothly, at least not in the beginning. I had to watch lots of tape, call coaches, and find out information that I didn't know, but that was easy. Putting it together and condensing it into a TV segment? That was hard, especially doing it day after day, week after week.

As a result, I made a lot of on-air mistakes, and here's the problem with that. We acted like *NFL Matchup* was a live show, but it was actually taped. If you make a mistake in television when you're taping, you can't just reshoot that one mistake; you have to tape the entire segment again.

With all my trouble with attention and memory, I had to shut everyone else out so that I could say what I had scripted in my head. Because I didn't use a teleprompter, I had to remember what I was going to say, and the only way I could do that was by *not* listening to anyone else on set. So I made a ton of mistakes, and each time I did, we had to shoot the whole segment again. And again. And again. After a while, the entire crew was ready to kill me.

Finally, our producer, Greg Cosell, suggested that we tape notes on the bottom of the screen of the camera to help jog my memory. We called it "redneck teleprompting." Because I had that crutch, I got more comfortable. Then, after my symptoms finally cleared, I didn't need the notes because I could focus on what I needed to say and listen to my colleagues. That's when our chemistry really started to take off and I started to really have fun as a broadcaster.

BEGINNING TO TRANSFORM YOUTH FOOTBALL

AFTER THAT, LIFE WENT ON. I raised my kids, got involved in youth football as a coach, grew my broadcasting career, and, as I said earlier, appeared before Congress. Over the years, I also joined the boards of the Chuck Noll Foundation for Brain Injury Research and IntelliCell Biosciences, joined the NFL's Return-to-Play Subcommittee, and, as you know, overcame my own personal health challenges.

Still, how did all that lead me to the mission I'm on today? To answer that, I have to go back to when I got hurt. I looked at the way I'd been treated after my first concussion—cleared to play again over the phone, without a physical exam—and said, "That wasn't right." Then in 2003, when he was seven years old, Beau decided he wanted to play youth football. The minimum age was eight, but league officials said that if I would coach, they would let him play. So I signed on with the Fort Thomas (Kentucky) Junior Football League. Beau and I were put on the Red team (our league went by colors depending on where you lived in the community), and the head coach asked me to be the offensive coordinator.

I'd run football camps starting back in 1991, so there were lots of ways I figured I could help the kids. One area I have always felt needed work was the passing game. I established some drills to help our quarterback, wide receivers, tight ends, and running backs learn about running routes, throwing the ball, and catching the ball. We were a couple of days into these drills (and were doing about as well as kids can at ages seven, eight, and nine) when the head coach came over to me and asked, "What are you doing?"

"Working on our passing game," I replied.

"We will never complete any of those passes."

"I didn't say we would, but if we don't start somewhere, we will never complete a pass," I said. And he fired me. He told me that he'd been an all-state football player and that in this league, they just ran the ball. Fine. I became just a coach who helped out, but I vowed this would never happen to me again. If Beau wanted to continue playing football, I would be his head coach so he'd learn the game the right way.

Then I said to myself, *All the things that I didn't learn until I got to the NFL—how awesome would it be if kids started learning them at age eight?* I wanted to change how we coached and practiced, and I was determined that we would have a head-trauma protocol. No one had ever talked about a concussion protocol for youth sports because everyone assumed the kids didn't hit hard enough to cause real injuries.

I wanted to take charge of our league because our drills were terrible; nobody was teaching the kids how to play football the safe way. But one of the biggest problems we faced was the same one I had seen in the NFL: the idea that being tough meant keeping quiet about an injury, even when that injury was severe. That was even a problem in the military, which is why the Pentagon honored me in 2011 with an invitation to speak to the army about bridging the gap between the culture of silent toughness and the seriousness of head trauma.

My message to the kids was the same as my message to the military brass: you can be tough and smart at the same time. Toughness in the old days of the NFL meant that you ignored injuries and just played. That's why a few of the guys who played in the sixties and seventies have had such a rough time with their health; they played through trauma that would bench a guy today. Tough doesn't mean stubborn or stupid. Because of that, I had an ironclad rule: if a kid suffered any kind of head trauma, he would be removed from the game and he wouldn't play the next week. It was nonnegotiable.

The kids never argued. They understood. I never had problem with a kid about that rule, ever. I had talked to Dr. Maroon and other experts in the field of concussion and asked them the most critical part of recovering from head trauma, and they all said it was the first two weeks. You remove kids, get them out of that dangerous environment, and take care of them. So that's what my team did. No child would be at risk on my watch.

But guess who was always begging me to play a kid the week after a head injury? The parents. That's how much ignorance there was in 2004–05. The parent would come to me and say, "Johnny feels so good—he's been running around at school, and he really wants to play." And I'd say, "That's beautiful. That's exactly what I wanted to hear. But he's not playing. I know it's tough, but we have these rules for a reason, and I'm doing the best thing for him."

Some of the parents didn't like it, but I didn't care. When I ran my team, I also fired a few coaches for putting kids at risk with improper instruction. One day at one of my camps, teams were running drills when I heard this coach shout, "We're gonna take our head and run it right through you!"

Whoa. I walked over. "Coach, come here," I said. "Where'd you learn that?"

He said, "That's how I was taught."

I said, "Coach, that's not how we teach it here, okay?"

"That's how I teach."

"Well, you're done." Just like that, fired. I don't tolerate anything that puts kids at risk. There was a lot of weeding out of those old dogs who think if you drink water in the hundred-degree heat, you're soft. I'd been part of that "rub some dirt on it and keep playing" mindset, and I wasn't about to let a young player return to a game right after getting a concussion, or in the following week's game.

So we had our rules, and we followed them. We had one practice that included fifteen minutes of full contact drills every two weeks, and that was it. We practiced twice a week and played on Saturday. That might not seem like a lot, but we were always prepared and we got better each week. I saw concussion screenings improve steadily. Still, I never dreamed we would be where we are today with treatments, therapies, and protocols. Having been part of the pro game and the youth game for so long, I've watched both become safer, giving kids a great way to get in shape, learn teamwork, and develop mentally and physically.

Things are changing, to be sure. During one of my later speeches at the Pentagon, I was with former Raiders, 49ers, and Redskins linebacker Matt Millen—who represented one era—and Atlanta Falcons linebacker Deion Jones—who's from a more modern era. We all talked about our understanding of head trauma. Matt was talking about how they shoved smelling salts up your nose when he was playing and said, "You're good to go." But Deion said he had started learning about concussion protocols in youth football, which was encouraging. It's like the seatbelt law, which took a few generations to become the norm.

Deion talked about a game where he removed himself after getting hit in the head, which never would have happened in my day. Now, players are watching out for each other. We're all gatekeepers: players, coaches, and trainers in college and the pros; coaches and parents in the youth game. We're learning to play the game better and safer and be smart about head trauma. You can still be tough, but you're actually being smart and tough now because you're doing the right thing for yourself, short-term and long-term.

THE FIRST WHISPERS OF CTE

So WHEN THE SUBTLE ATTACKS on football started, I paid attention. First, it was Bennet Omalu and Mike Webster. Then it was the death of former Eagles and Cardinals safety Andre Waters. Then the congressional hearings on the NFL. Then the *Head Games* documentary. Then the *League of Denial* book. Then Jeff Miller admitting a link between football and CTE just to avoid a public backlash. In between, story after story in the *New York Times* and elsewhere about football and CTE, ex-players and suicide.

It was obvious: the blame game had started. Hidden agendas were playing out, and the public had no idea. The thing that really struck me was Mike Webster's story. He'd been my friend, a fantastic guy, and losing him tore my heart out. But he was one guy. How does one man's death turn into an epidemic?

I've been around thousands of retired NFL players. We have millions who played youth football and even more who played in high school or college. We don't have enough hospitals to house all the guys who should have permanent, progressive neurodegenerative diseases from playing football, at least according to the doomsayers. Yet those guys are all around us, some in their seventies and eighties, mostly doing fine. It didn't make sense then, and it doesn't now. I talked with Dr. Maroon and Dr. Julian Bailes, chairman of Pop Warner Football's medical advisory committee, and said, "Help me understand this." It smelled bad back then, and in the years since, that smell has only gotten worse.

But what finally made me realize how ridiculous and irrational the talk about CTE and football had become was a few years ago when I jokingly asked my players in the Fort Thomas league to stop going to recess and lunch at school. I was taking roll before practice and asking, "Where is so-and-so?" He'd slipped off the monkey bars and broken his wrist. "What about Andy?" He'd hurt his ankle playing kickball. After a few more injury reports, I said, jokingly, "Here's what we're going to do: nobody go to recess. Just eat lunch, go back to the room, and sit down, at least until the end of the season. Because I need you guys to play football, all right?"

I was messing around, of course, but it struck me then that no one was talking about banning recess, kickball, riding bikes, or climbing monkey bars. Today, nobody is talking about banning hockey, soccer, equestrian sports, or, hell, even boxing. They were and still are attacking football. But why? We had already improved the entire game, from practice rules to coaching to equipment, to make it safer than ever before. The game was obviously under attack because, unlike the NFL or NCAA, youth football doesn't have big money sponsors or a central organizing body to defend it. Somebody was building his or her reputation by building a climate of fear around the game I loved and knew was great for kids.

No. Not while I had something to say about it. I started researching and making contacts, and that's how we are where we are now. Ironically, I probably wouldn't be tilting at this windmill if I hadn't experienced the effects of brain trauma back in the bad, old days before the NFL knew how to manage head trauma properly. I don't blame the league, although some of the anger that came its way was deserved because it did try to ignore and even deny what was going on for a long time. However, in recent years, the league has stepped up and tried to make it right. More important, the guys who played in the league are not, for the most part, extras from *The Walking Dead*. That's another myth that needs busting. So let's start there, with a deep dive into what's really happening with current and former NFL players, why it's happening, and what it all means.

THE BIG PICTURE

We've had over 650 former NFL players in our center over the past fifteen years. When we take their intake over the phone, we have this supposition that they're going to come in looking really bad. We're thinking, This is going to be a tough visit. We'll have to give him some bad news. *And oftentimes, they look better than the person who had one concussion and only played for four seasons. I hope I look that good whenever I'm sixty or sixty-five. Four out of every five of them who come in, they're doing just fine.*

—KEVIN GUSKIEWICZ, PHD, DIRECTOR OF THE MATTHEW GFELLER SPORT-RELATED TRAUMATIC BRAIN INJURY RESEARCH CENTER, UNIVERSITY OF NORTH CAROLINA

CHAPTER 2 PLAYBOOK

- My teammate and friend, Mike Webster
- How I sued the Bears' team doctor to make a point
- What the facts really say about how former NFL players are doing
- Why ex-players who watch their weight and diet are doing great

MIKE WEBSTER WAS MORE THAN my teammate; he was my roommate on the road, and like roomies do, he was constantly giving me a hard time. We'd all be in the weight room, lifting together, and Webby would be saying, "Merril, you're going to play a long time until they find somebody bigger, stronger, and faster. And they're looking for him right now." He was always busting my chops, and he was always a character. I ran into him one time shortly before he passed away, and he said, "Man, you fooled them so good that you're on ESPN now? Now you're a star. How does that happen?" That was just Webby. I went to a couple of events, and I had heard that he was struggling, but he always looked like the same guy to me.

On the other hand, I remember the first time I stepped into a huddle and saw Mike's helmet. I looked over, and there was number 52. Wow. I'd been watching him for a decade, since I was a kid, and I was in the huddle with him now. But what really struck me was his helmet. It had had the crap beaten out of it, like a grizzly bear had attacked it. It had all these divots in the front, and the plastic and rubber were coming off the metal. Mind you, this was minicamp! I thought, *You don't see that on TV. They look all brand new and shiny.* After he and I became buddies (which was right away), I asked him, "Webby, why don't you get a new helmet?" But he wouldn't even consider it. A lot of guys were that way with their helmets, and many still are. A trashed helmet is a badge of honor.

Knowing Webby like I did made it hard to learn about his terrible decline and severe mental problems. It was the ugly real-life drama of his decline and premature death that jump-started the whole CTE machine—before Andre Waters, before Al Toon, before Dave Duerson.

The Webster case was the launching pad for many of the public figures and press narratives that have come to define the football-CTE connection in the minds of lawmakers, journalists, and the general public. People like Dr. Omalu, practically canonized as the discoverer of CTE in athletes, and Dr. Ann McKee, the BU researcher and CTE celebrity who's given us shockingly irresponsible statements like, "I'm really wondering where this stops. I'm really wondering if every single football player doesn't have this."[1]

The narratives? They're familiar, too. Many ex-NFL players are falling apart, losing their marbles, and killing themselves because of brain injuries received while playing. Playing football absolutely, positively causes CTE. And my favorite, youth football is child abuse. That one was courtesy of Omalu, who lost whatever credibility he still had when he made such a ridiculous statement.[2]

The players' life-and-death stories combined to create a sense of real-life drama, and we love drama. But dramatic stories aren't necessarily true stories. Even if they have a grain of truth to them, they tend to oversimplify things until the truth disappears behind everybody's desire to believe what they want to believe. That's why we're here. If we're going to make change happen, we shouldn't be looking at grains but at the whole field of wheat.

Let's bake some truth.

REASONABLE STANDARD OF CARE

IT WAS WITH THAT INTENTION that in 1996, advised by my attorney, Bob Fogel, I filed a medical malpractice lawsuit against Dr. John Munsell, the team doctor for the Chicago Bears.

After all, my career had ended prematurely—and my life put at risk—because there was no set standard of care at the time in the league. The only team treating brain trauma as a serious issue, instead of something to be joked about when a guy ran to the wrong huddle, were the Steelers. If I hadn't been with the Steelers for most of my career, I would never have known that there was a better standard NFL teams should be following.

You might not believe me when I say this, but I honestly didn't care about getting any money from the suit. I wanted to file my lawsuit on principle alone. My thought was that if the Bears had been doing cognitive testing in 1994 like the Steelers had been doing for several years, I would've had a baseline and been given the same cognitive test again after my first concussion. I would have seen a neurologist and not been cleared over the phone to play. I would have taken a lot more time off to recover and possibly played for several more years. How could one team be so advanced and everyone else be so far behind? That's what ate at me. I thought that no team in the NFL should be allowed to maintain a standard of care any less stringent than that of the Steelers. If I could, I would bring every other team up to the Steelers' level, even if I had to drag them kicking and screaming.

But Bob said no dice. The law said that I had to seek monetary damages. I didn't like it, but I had no choice. We filed a claim for lost earnings, pain, suffering, and disability in Lake County, Illinois, and went to trial.

In the trial, Bob made a strong case for my claim that I had not received a reasonable standard of post-concussion care after my first concussion in Kansas City. On the surface, the reason I didn't receive reasonable care was that Dr. Munsell was a primary care physician with no background in neurology, but the actual reason was because there was no league standard for care. NFL policy was that each team could set its own standard, and outside of the Steelers, nobody had one. That was unacceptable.

Bob laid out my story step by step: getting lost in the lobby of Dr. Kelly's office, my visits to Dr. Lovell and Dr. Maroon, my retrograde (no memory of events that occurred before a brain injury) and antero-grade (inability to create new memories after the injury) amnesia, the fact that nobody from the Bears told me or my family what we should watch for, and the fact that I was cleared to return to play on the phone without a subsequent physical exam or cognitive test.

There was nothing in my medical records about post-concussion syndrome. In testimony, Bears assistant trainer Tim Bream said that he had told Fred Caito about my symptoms, but there was no way to know if Fred had written anything down. But that was normal for the NFL. Nobody wanted to come out of the game because there was always somebody else waiting to play in your place. We were all on one-year, non-guaranteed contracts, and we all feared that coming out of a game might mean losing our jobs.

One of Bob's most convincing moments was when he called neu-rosurgeon Dr. George Cybulski as a witness. Dr. Cybulski testified that he treated a lot of plumbers for concussions because they often hit their heads during their work. When Bob asked the doctor if he set follow-up appointments for plumbers, he said he always did because they could easily hit their heads again. Bob made his point in his closing argument:

clearly, proper treatment of anyone with a concussion was to diagnose them and then see them again in follow-up. Why was a football player, whose job practically guaranteed that he would take another hit to the head, not held to the same standard as a plumber?

But the pivotal episode of the trial came from someone who never said a word. The defense tried to call Dr. Elliot Pellman, the team physician for the New York Jets and the league's chief medical officer and director of its Mild Traumatic Brain Injury (MTBI) Committee, as a last-minute witness. Pellman, who came to be known as "Doctor Yes" for clearing pretty much any player to go back onto the field after a concussion, was a rheumatologist—a specialist in diseases of the joints, muscles, and ligaments.[3] How does a doctor with that background get put in charge of a committee on brain injury?

Anyway, I suspect that Dr. Pellman was going to testify that, in his opinion, Dr. Munsell had provided me with a reasonable standard of care. It seemed clear that the NFL was helping the defense, trying to avoid a win by me that might open them to future liability. But it didn't matter because he never got to testify. The rules specify that both sides in a trial have to disclose in advance who their witnesses will be so the other side has time to prepare. Bob objected to Pellman because the time for witness disclosure had passed, and the judge agreed. Pellman was barred from testifying.

Bob did a masterful job, and the jury awarded me $1.55 million. But the verdict was overturned on a post-trial motion because of a minor discovery violation, and we settled for $500,000. It was a lot less money, but as I said, it was never about the money. What mattered to me was that the decision was public and that my case could serve as a catalyst for change.

DR. JOSEPH MAROON

BEFORE WE MOVE ON, I want to take a moment to set the record straight on Dr. Joe Maroon. To be clear, neither this book nor anything related to it would be happening without Joe's pioneering work and his courage. Unlike so many of the scientists weighing in on what should be done to change football, Joe played the game. He was a scholastic all-American at Indiana University in football. Together with his background as a gifted neurosurgeon, he understands the intersection between the game and the science better than anyone.

I bring this up now because in the movie *Concussion*, Joe was vilified as a shill for the NFL. But that's not the real story, and you don't have to take my word for it. Attorney Bob Fitzsimmons, who represented Mike Webster in his disability claim against the NFL, went to bat for Joe in an editorial in the *Pittsburgh Post-Gazette*:

> One scene depicted a critical time in this still-unfolding timeline. A meeting was held between two world-renowned neurosurgeons, Julian Bailes and Joe Maroon, together with Dr. Omalu. From this scene, it is not clear whether Dr. Maroon is one of the "good guys."

> I was present at a meeting in Morgantown, W.Va., with these doctors and I can tell you that Dr. Maroon is one of the "good guys." During this meeting Dr. Maroon and another doctor viewed and discussed the stained brain-tissue slides of the Hall-of-Fame Pittsburgh Steeler Mike Webster, among others. Dr. Maroon then took what he saw in those slides and conveyed the doctors' findings to the NFL in such a convincing fashion that the league soon took steps to make the game safer. Without Dr. Maroon's participation and stature as one of the premier

neurosurgeons in the world, such changes probably would
have been delayed.

Dr. Maroon has devoted his entire career to helping
people and has been an advocate of player safety on all
levels. He should be commended for his influential efforts
to make football and all contact sports safer.[4]

Couldn't have said it better myself, Bob. Despite the unfair picture
painted in movies or books about the NFL and the concussion issue,
Joe Maroon isn't one of the bad guys. He's an ethical physician, a pioneer for the health of players, and in my opinion, a genuine hero. I'm
proud to be working with him. Now, let's move on.

SLOW PROGRESS IN THE NFL

THE POINT OF MY CASE had been to force the league's hand and improve
the standard of care. Remember, the NFL didn't take meaningful
action to address head trauma until after 1994, labeled as the "Year
of the Concussion" because star quarterbacks like Steve Young, Troy
Aikman, and Vinny Testaverde suffered major concussions. They
tried to do something right when then-commissioner Paul Tagliabue
established the league's MTBI Committee that same year, and the
Bears and Philadelphia Eagles built on the Steelers' work when they
became the first teams to make cognitive testing mandatory in 1995.
But at the time of my trial, there was still no standard for cognitive
testing or post-concussion care.

Dr. Maroon shares his perspective on the state of the art at the
time. "We started ImPACT with a pencil-and-paper evaluation, but
until about 1996 or so even I didn't fully appreciate the significance

and power of the test," he says. "Other teams picked it up not because of our proselytizing but because it was the only thing available. I really can't fault the NFL for not immediately picking it up and insisting that it should be initiated with all clubs. The NFL was slow to mandate it until 2007, but in the early years we really weren't sure how powerful of a tool it would be.

"Not only the Chicago Bears, but many teams were slow to embrace neurocognitive testing because there wasn't that much data at the time showing how much it helped," Dr. Maroon concludes. "The science had to evolve. A famous physician once said, 'Be neither the first to accept change or something new, nor the last.'"

In other words, good science progresses slowly. It's supposed to. It's not reckless and doesn't jump to premature conclusions. We didn't go from zipper-like knee surgeries with casts to arthroscopes and next-day rehab overnight, so how could anyone expect teams to be ahead of the curve with something as complicated as brain trauma? But for a long time the league didn't seem to be making any progress, and that was unacceptable.

After my case was over, the MTBI started questioning the league's guidelines for letting players return after a concussion, which was a good sign. Meanwhile, my passion for the cause led me to get involved in the league's Return-to-Play Subcommittee, become a youth coach, speak to Congress and the armed forces, develop Heads Up Football, actually dissect brains myself, learn about CTE, and seek the truth.

All that work has begun to pay off because the game has made some real strides. Heads Up Football, made possible by the league's charter of USA Football, is making a big difference in youth safety. In 2010, the league created a new committee to address concussion and head trauma—the Head, Neck and Spine Medical Committee—headed by a new team of doctors.[5] That panel continues to suggest safety-oriented rule changes that the league has implemented, including rules to prohibit hits with the helmet[6] and to reduce the risk of concussion during kickoffs.[7] Those are just two examples; I'll talk about more later.

Dr. Micky Collins, director of the University of Pittsburgh Medical Center (UPMC) Sports Medicine Concussion Program, agrees that while there was some foot-dragging, the league has stepped up to make the game safer. "I believe there's a real commitment to get this better for everyone," he says. "Allen Sills is now the chief medical officer of the NFL, and I have incredible respect for Allen. I think he's a really good leader. I think there will be really significant advances down the road in terms of this issue, and I do believe there's a lot of real commitment to improving the science. I'm confident right now in the process."[8]

For Mike Golic, the issue is more double-edged. An eight-year defensive tackle for the Oilers, Eagles, and Dolphins, Mike is now cohost of the ESPN radio show *Golic and Wingo* and gained some attention in 2017 for saying on the air that if a test for CTE had existed when he played, he wouldn't have taken it.

"I'll say this, and I think I can say this with about as much authority as anyone can, 80 to 90 percent of players, including me, would try and hide a concussion or hide an injury to get out on the field and play," Mike says. "I got stung a couple times in the head, but I wanted to play. And if I had to hide it to play, that was my decision. Most pro athletes want to be out on the field playing. So I think this is a combination of, yeah, the NFL hid some information, and that's bad, and they're going to pay a price for that. But like anything else, now we have more information going forward, and we need to use that information as best we can."[9]

Mike's partially right. Most of us didn't say anything about symptoms we might have had, but that wasn't just because we wanted to keep our jobs. It was also because nobody told players what concussion symptoms were. How can you report a symptom if you don't know it's a symptom?

I don't want to make this a book about the NFL, so I'll conclude by saying this: I get what outsiders say about the way the league treats players. Football is a business, and it can be cutthroat. But the clubs really do care about these guys. They aren't just cogs in a machine. Nobody had more to lose than the National Football League if they got the concussion issue wrong—from a player perspective, a fan perspective, and a brand perspective. The black hat–white hat picture painted by books, movies, and a million newspaper stories doesn't do justice to what is a more complex and nuanced story than a lot of people realize.

WHERE ARE ALL THE PLAYERS WHO ARE FALLING APART?

THE BIG QUESTION IS THIS: what about all those suffering players? Aren't tens of thousands of retired NFL players—not to mention retired NHL players and soccer players—all falling apart and losing our marbles? Aren't we supposed to be developing Alzheimer's disease at an increased rate, suffering from dementia, and killing ourselves at a rate much greater than the general population? If every football player has CTE, as some have suggested, where are all the guys shambling along, unable to remember their loved ones, with one foot in the grave?

That's certainly what you'd expect if you listened to or read the news. As Daniel J. Flynn writes in his book, *The War on Football*, the pseudo-fact that the average NFL player's life span is only fifty-five has been passed around for years, primarily during 2011–12, by media outlets and journalists as respected as *ABC News*, *CBS Sports*, the *Seattle Post-Intelligencer*, and columnist George Will.[10] The general idea was that ex-NFL players could expect, on average, to live twenty years less than the average American, and how dare we continue to support such a barbaric spectacle? Or something to that effect.

There's one problem with that widely cited fact: *it's false*. In fact, there's never been any peer-reviewed research that shows former NFL players suffer from common health problems to a greater degree than the general public, according to material provided by the plaintiff's attorneys in one of the NFL's concussion lawsuits.[11] As for that specific claim that ex-players drop dead at an average age of fifty-five, it comes from actuarial estimates by two former players: the late Len Teeuws, a former Chicago Cardinals lineman who worked as an insurance actuary in Indianapolis (who died at seventy-nine, FYI), and Ron Mix, a Hall of Fame San Diego Chargers tackle who became an attorney handling workers' comp and disability claims and is still going strong at the age of eighty.[12]

What *do* we know? We know that in 1994, at the request of the NFL Players Association, the National Institute for Occupational Safety and Health (NIOSH) studied the health of more than 3,439 former players who had played at least five seasons between 1959 and 1988.[13] What they found:

- Based on actuarial tables for men in those age groups, the NIOSH researchers expected to find that 625 of the men had died. Instead, only 334 had died.

- Thirty-two percent fewer players had died of cardiovascular disease than the general population.*

- The players were 42 percent less likely to develop cancer and 20 percent less likely to die of respiratory disease.

- Overall, former players had a 46 percent lower overall mortality rate than the general US male population.

---

* One caveat from the study: players in the largest body-size category, which included 64 percent of offensive and defensive linemen, had a six times greater risk of dying from heart disease than those of normal body mass. I've included that fact because it ties in directly to a discussion of obesity and brain inflammation in a later chapter.

Even a more recent study from 2018, which found that career NFL players were 38 percent more likely to die younger than men who played in only a handful of games, was packed with waffling language. You had qualifiers about the small sample size, the relatively young average age of the players—fifty-two—at the end of the study, and then this quote from an editorial published with the study: "Although the life expectancy of professional football players was not significantly reduced based on the current evidence, the health of professional athletes should remain a focus of future research."[14]

Well, then what's all the fuss about? We'll see as we go along that this is the recurring pattern in the press when it comes to football players, health, and the brain: sensationalize first; ask questions later.

Speaking of brains, what about neurodegenerative diseases and their effects on mood, behavior, and thinking? Well, a follow-up study found that cases of neurodegenerative diseases in general—and ALS, Alzheimer's, and Parkinson's in particular—were more frequent among ex-players than the general population.[15] Case closed, right? Not so fast. As Flynn points out, the numbers were very small—ten total deaths among more than 3,400 men. Take away a case here or there, and suddenly you're below the incidence for the general population.

Dr. Cummings has more to say about this particular study. "There were only two deaths directly related to Alzheimer's," he says. "There were six deaths directly related to ALS, but these include a cluster of three ALS cases from the 1964 San Francisco 49ers. No cause for this cluster was ever found, and these three cases represent outliers that shouldn't have been included in the study. There were also seven deaths where Alzheimer's disease was a contributing factor, but the immediate causes of death in these individuals included heart failure, cancer, and suicide, all of which are unrelated to Alzheimer's and shouldn't be counted as 'neurological causes of death.' We also don't know how many of these cases were autopsy-confirmed diagnoses, and without autopsy, the death certificate is the 'best guess' of the physicians. That's my way of saying that this study is far from conclusive."

Here are some other handy facts about the mental state of ex-NFLers:

- A 2009 study from the University of Michigan of more than one thousand randomly chosen former players found that they were no more likely to suffer from symptoms of depression than the general population.[16] A 2013 study got a lot of attention when it said that players who had a history of concussion suffered from depression at a rate three times greater than the general public, but that study's results were much weaker because it only looked at thirty players.[17]

- The 2009 study found that 29 percent of retired NFL players over age fifty reported episodes of anger and losing control, compared with 47 percent of men over age fifty in the general population.

- NFL players have a reputation for being prone to violence, particularly domestic violence. But a study by Dr. Cummings that was accepted into the journal *Academic Forensic Pathology* while I was writing this book found that NFL players were less likely than the general population to be investigated for homicide.[18]

In general, former NFL players are more likely than the general population to live longer; are less likely to develop heart disease, cancer, and high blood pressure; are more apt to enjoy a life free of violence; are more likely to be religious or spiritual; and are more likely to have fewer outbursts and loss of control.

GUYS WHO TAKE CARE OF THEMSELVES ARE DOING FINE

BUT THE BOTTOM LINE, for me, is the eye test. I see former teammates and guys I played against all the time, a lot of them in their fifties, sixties, and seventies. How are they doing? Does the idea that a majority of retired NFL players are suffering from imminent dementia pass the eye test? No, I don't think it does. Yes, plenty of ex-players my age and older have knee, ankle, and hip problems from years of wear and tear. Lots of guys have had knee and hip replacements. And every one of us, from time to time, forgets where we put our keys. But in general, despite the horror stories you might have heard, the majority of former players are probably healthier and happier than the average guy on the street.

When I go to NFL alumni events or other gatherings, I just see healthy, educated, and successful men. I was on a cruise with Mean Joe Greene not long ago; Joe is seventy-one years old, and he played back in the bad, old, head-slapping days when guys would grab your face mask and wrestle you to the ground like a steer. Joe's doing great. Franco Harris, same thing.

One of my very first experiences with a retired player was with a legend, Mel Blount. I went out to his ranch, where he works with youths, and at seventy he hadn't slowed down at all. I know there are a few guys out there who are suffering and doing badly, but this brutal life that people live because of football? I've never seen it. And to blame problems on CTE without knowing anything about a guy's family background, other health conditions, drug use…it's irresponsible.

"I see a number of [guys I used to play with] during the year, whether it's at golf tournaments or at the Super Bowl," Mike Golic says. "And they seem fine. Look at Bill Curry. He played for Vince Lombardi. Snapped the ball to Bart Starr; snapped the ball to Johnny Unitas when he played for Don Shula with the Colts. Back when this guy played, if he had a concussion or was diagnosed with a head injury during a game, you know how they determined if he was ready to play? Lombardi brought him out on the field before practice and had Ray Nitschke forearm him in the head to see if he was okay. That's what this guy went through, and he's as cerebral and smart a person as you're ever going to meet, and he's seventy-five years old. I know that's just one person, but I see a lot of people who are fine."[19]

Mike's right. But let's be fair. We can't talk about a handful of guys who are healthy and sharp at seventy-five and decide that all players are that way, can we? No. Then why on earth can BU and the press take a few cases of CTE and conclude that everyone has it? There are thousands of guys like Bill Curry. There are only about three hundred documented cases of CTE in the entire world.

But Mike has another point to make. "I also see people, while some are fine, some are fine and paranoid," he says. "They think they have CTE. It is a fear right now, and it's amazing. But it's only in football. Football gets the headlines; football gets the lion's share of the articles when you have so many other sports where you have hitting constantly."

The always eloquent Solomon Wilcots, who played safety for the Bengals, Vikings, and Steelers from 1987 to 1992, now works for a life sciences company, so he was another great person to ask about the condition of ex-players. "There's no doubt that football takes a toll on your body, right?" he says. "We know that. I just don't know that we can attribute whatever malady that may befall us and say, 'Hey, it's just this one thing.' There are a lot of determining factors. I just saw Kevin Mack, who was a 240-pound bruising back. He's now at about 190 pounds. He looks great, but he's taking care of himself. Is he dealing with some knee stuff? Yeah. But he's taking care of his body.

"I focus on the population of high-achieving former players," he continues. "Guys who are old, who should be breaking down and should have neurodegenerative diseases, aren't and don't. Why doesn't Roger Staubach have [CTE]? Why doesn't Jack Lambert have this problem? He played for the Steelers the same years that Mike Webster did. But he worked in the Department of Forestry. He's healthy. He played at 215, and I think he's at about 190 pounds now. These are the guys who are taking care of themselves.

"Now, I'll share with you two really important factors that I don't think a lot of people are talking about or looking at," Solomon concludes. "One, did you have any drug addiction, alcohol addiction, or drug usage during your career? In other words, did you spend your twenties in an alcohol-induced haze? Did you experiment with cocaine? Steroids? Our neurocognitive ability equates to the electrical impulses running through our bodies, and when we start to abuse drugs and alcohol, it affects the central nervous system. No one is talking about that."

The second factor, Solomon tells me, is lifestyle choices after retirement. "Look at a guy like Alan Page," he says. "Supreme court justice for the state of Minnesota. This guy played defensive line his entire career. But in the off-season, what is he reading? He's working out his brain. You can train the brain when you're feeding it and you're reading and you're writing and you're active. What if we told players that they had to make better life choices and not abuse their bodies? What if we told them that after your career, you'll have to take care of your body? You consumed a lot of calories when you were playing, but in your post-career you're going to have to consume fewer calories because you've got to get the weight off."

Solomon is a brilliant guy, and talking to him reminds me that in the fraternity of ex-NFL players, there are plenty of other high achievers. Chris Carr got his law degree from Georgetown. Myron Rolle started his neurosurgery residency at Harvard Medical School and Mass General in 2017. Former lineman Ross Tucker writes for *Sports Illustrated*. Tim Green is a practicing attorney in New York. Steve Largent was elected four times to the US House of Representatives. Oh yeah, and *active* Kansas City Chiefs lineman Laurent Duvernay-

Tardif got his medical degree in 2018. Not bad for a bunch of guys who are supposed to be drooling into their laps, right?

FOOTBALL'S TOUGH GUY CULTURE HAS EVOLVED

BUT THE MOST IMPORTANT PART of all this might be the fact that the culture of the game has finally changed. We know more. We pay attention to the warning signs of concussion. We've made rule changes. All that has come about because of efforts by players, doctors, and the NFL.

Just think about the techniques of the game and how they've changed. Back in the day, guys would still have their hands together and block with their shoulders and head. Now, if you get your head down into somebody, defenders are so good, they'll destroy you. If you put your head down, you're going to get exposed. You have to keep your head up, and your hands and feet have to work together. Feet, hips, hands. We're back to what Chuck Noll used to talk about. Same foot; same shoulder. Get yourself into a crouching position. Use those feet and those hands to defend, not your head.

Go back to the sixties, seventies, and eighties, and you used your head a lot. You used your head to get in front of ball carriers. The helmet was a weapon, and you didn't get a new one. They just refurbished them when they got dented, and the technology wasn't even close to where it is today. But back in the day, that's all we knew. That's what was available. There was no head trauma protocol, but it wasn't because a bunch of neurologists weren't doing their jobs. Nobody had a protocol because even the experts didn't have enough information.

Today, everything is different. The league is testing everything to make sure it's as safe as possible. They've instituted a rule, put in place in the 2018 season, that forbids players from lowering their heads and deliberately hitting other players with their helmets anywhere on the body. Not everybody is happy about that because it's misunderstood.[20] The intention is the right one: keep players safer.

So if the guys from that era—when it was "three yards and a cloud of dust," a head slap, a crappy helmet, and a "rub some dirt on it and get back in there" culture, can be doing pretty well—don't you think the guys playing today, with better equipment and safety rules and lots of good information, will generally be doing fine when they retire? I think they will.

That change in the culture—in the willingness of players to tell the team when they're having concussion symptoms—has been critical. The first guy to do that was Steelers star quarterback Ben Roethlisberger, who became the first star player to take himself out of a game under the NFL's new concussion rules when he removed himself from a game against the Seahawks in December 2015.[21] Ben always had a reputation as a guy who would never stop playing, but he demonstrated the new ethos of today's NFL player: be tough, but be smart.

I asked Ben about the decision. "I was always one of those tough guys that played through anything," he says, "that never complained about things. Got dinged up and got dizzy, fuzzy, and went back out there. That's just what you did. But I think some of the CTE stuff definitely played a role in it. More important is my family. I said to my wife, 'You know, I want my kids to remember me playing the game,' and my wife made a comment that really struck a chord. She goes, 'Yeah, but don't you want to remember your kids?'"

Yeah, that would make an impact. But what really stands out about Ben's comments is the need for information, not fear. "I think the education that people are getting helps," he says. "You don't want to sound terrible when someone says you're soft for talking about concussions or you're soft for coming out of a game. But say what you want about me; I don't really care. I've got a family involved. I already know that my body's going to be beat up, and that's one thing. You can get knee replacements. There's no brain replacement.

"I didn't know at the time; I just assumed that when you got a concussion, your brain was damaged forever," Ben concludes. "Now, in educating myself and learning, talking to other doctors and stuff, there's so much you can do for your brain to strengthen it. No one ever thought about doing brain exercises and activities that can strengthen your brain and get it back to some normalcy. People need to understand. They just need to be educated about it."[22]

So how are former NFL players really doing in their lives after football? Just fine, thank you, just fine.

ALL EYES ON SUICIDE

There's something about this game, about the camaraderie, about the competition, all those sorts of things, that when you're the elite of the elite, these guys love to compete. And there's also when you're young, I think you also feel that you're indestructible.

—JIM TROTTER, FOOTBALL ANALYST

CHAPTER 3 PLAYBOOK

- Why we falsely believe so many NFL players are committing suicide

- The role that retirement plays in depression and suicidal thinking

- Ex-NFL players are less likely to kill themselves than the general population

- What science says: there is no evidence that CTE causes suicide

---

TERRY LONG WAS A TEAMMATE of mine on the Steelers from 1987 to 1991, and I loved the guy. So when the story appeared in 2006 that he'd committed suicide by drinking antifreeze, I was heartbroken. But in 2007, the talk started that he had killed himself because of CTE. Bennet Omalu, who examined his brain, made it sound like a scientific certainty: "People with chronic encephalopathy suffer from depression. The major depressive disorder may manifest as suicide attempts. Terry Long committed suicide due to the chronic traumatic encephalopathy due to his long-term play."[1]

That's ridiculous. We have some theories about the areas like the amygdala, the thalamus, and the hippocampus, but science is still mostly in the dark about the specific areas of the brain involved in clinical depression. To imply that CTE causes depression is completely irresponsible. Dr. Maroon pushed back in the same article. "I think it's fallacious reasoning, and I don't think it's plausible at all," he wrote. "To go back and say that he was depressed from playing in the NFL and that led to his death fourteen years later, I think is purely speculative." But it was too little, too late. Nobody was listening.

They should have been, because the story was more complicated. Terry tried to kill himself with an overdose of sleeping pills back in 1991 after he failed the NFL's performance-enhancing drug test. At the time, his job was also in jeopardy. That is one of the most stressful things a player can go through—fearing you will be beaten out by someone else.

After that first attempt, Terry later checked himself into a Pittsburgh hospital for a psych evaluation.[2] What nobody also talked about after Terry's suicide was the fact that people who attempt suicide once are more likely to attempt it again.[3] Everybody just blamed CTE, caused by football.

Suicide has been a part of the story of CTE almost as long as we've been talking about the disease. But Terry's death didn't ring the bell; it was more like the undercard. Andre Waters was the main event. After forty-four-year-old Waters shot himself in the head at his Tampa, Florida, home on November 20, 2006, the Waters family was convinced to sign a release and allow four pieces of his brain to be sent to Bennet Omalu's office in Pittsburgh. After his examination, Omalu announced that Waters's brain looked like that of an eighty-five-year-old man and showed signs of early Alzheimer's disease. He concluded that its condition was because of repeated hits from football, including the estimated fifteen concussions Waters had suffered during his career.[4]

So began the public perception of a link between a pro football career, neurodegenerative disease, and suicide. In the ten-plus years since, it's become an article of faith: *football players are killing themselves all over the place*. The public's morbid fascination with the subject isn't surprising when you think about it. Take the inherent drama of someone taking their life and dying too soon, combine it with the spectacle of a supposedly indestructible superman brought low and the specter of an invisible brain disease, and it's hard to look away.

Part of our belief that NFL suicides are common has to do with a part of the brain stem called the *reticular formation*. In addition to controlling our sleep-wake cycle, one of the other things this bundle of neurons controls is what's called *habituation*—the way your brain learns to ignore repetitive and familiar things while being attentive to new stimuli, especially things that are of interest to you.[5] I call it the "new Harley effect." I have always had motorcycles, but it wasn't until I bought my Harley that I started to notice all the Harleys on the road. If you find suicides of NFL players compelling (as many people seem to), you're going to notice those stories and think they're more common than they are.

But while any suicide is a tragedy, and the suicides of guys I knew and played with are especially hard to take, it's important to separate truth from fiction and to bring some perspective to the issue. In the last chapter, I said "not so fast" to the alleged fact that retired football players are all falling apart and dying young. In this chapter, I'm going to bring the same healthy skepticism to the idea that NFL players are committing suicide left and right and that CTE is behind it all.

Junior Seau (1969–2012)

A beloved linebacker for the San Diego Chargers, a ten-time All Pro, and a member of the Pro Football Hall of Fame, Junior retired in 2009 and started several businesses around the San Diego area. He committed suicide by shooting himself in the chest in 2012 at the age of forty-three and was found by the NIH to have CTE.

PRESS COVERAGE

PART OF THE PROBLEM, as with other parts of the CTE debate, is the media coverage. The press loves dramatic, heart-wrenching stories of suicide, and the coverage fuels misconceptions either by spreading misinformation or, more often, by pandering to public biases. That's how we got a somber February 3, 2016, piece in the *New York Times* called "The N.F.L.'s Tragic C.T.E. Roll Call." The story was a quasi–war memorial of deceased NFL players who were supposedly casualties of CTE: Webby, Junior Seau, Frank Gifford, Kenny Stabler, Tom McHale, and more.

Since the most notable deaths in that group were the four players who definitely took their own lives, the average reader is likely to conclude that all those players committed suicide. It's part of the "football is killing its participants" narrative that the media is happy to play to. Where are the articles about happy, healthy sixty-five-year-old former players running companies and practicing law—the guys we talked about in the last chapter?

For a more recent example, there's this: on June 26, 2018, the Mayo Clinic announced that Washington State University quarterback Tyler Hilinski, who committed suicide in January of 2018 at age twenty-one, had been found to have CTE. According to the Mayo Clinic statement, he had "the brain of a sixty-five-year-old."[6]

The press went crazy. Here was more confirmation that football is killing our kids. Stories on Tyler and the Hilinski family were everywhere. For example, *USA Today* ran a story with the headline "Why College Football Player's Death Should Terrify Parents" where the first line of the piece read, "Football killed Tyler Hilinski."[7] The story was everywhere, always featuring the same basic elements: football is dangerous; we know CTE did this; be afraid.

There was one voice of scientific common sense in all this, and it belonged to Dr. Dirk Keene, chief of the Division of Neuropathology at the University of Washington. He said in an interview that we don't know nearly as much about CTE as we think we do, especially in how the physical symptoms translate into behavior. "We need biomarkers. We need a way to diagnose the disease during life. And then we need to be able to follow people at risk. I think we're years away. Potentially, maybe less, for the biomarker that we need. And then it's just gonna take studies that are following people over time to really understand the impact of the disease on behavior and how to intervene."[8]

Now, contrast that with a more recent piece of widespread news. In June 2018, the CDC announced that the suicide rate in the United States increased by nearly 30 percent between 1999 and 2016 and that a large portion of that increase was not due to mental illness but abuse of controlled substances like opioids.[9] Now, let's factor in three other pieces of information.

First, in 2016 nearly as many people died from opioid overdose as from suicide.[10] Second, retired NFL players were found to use prescription opioids for pain at *three times* the rate of the general population.[11] Third, opioid use is known to cause deposits of tau in the brain.[12] Do you think it's possible that some of the players who've killed themselves over the years did so because of opioid abuse, not CTE? Or that some of the guys found to have CTE might have had all that tau in their brains not because of hits to the head but because they took excessive quantities of oxycodone?

Those are questions worth asking, but no one is asking them. Instead, we're getting newspaper stories that just make more readers think they already know what's going on.

ARE PLAYERS REALLY MORE LIKELY TO KILL THEMSELVES?

LET'S CONTINUE OUR DISCUSSION about football players and suicide. Again, I turn to Dr. Cummings, who has a strong opinion about his fellow BU faculty member's research on the subject.

"One of the refrains from Dr. Ann McKee's 2013 paper proposing CTE staging was that there were seven suicides among forty-three people with stage I, II, or III CTE—a terrifyingly high suicide rate of 16 percent," he says.[13] "But look closer. There were also thirty-five people in this 2013 study who had no CTE. Seventeen of them had exposure to repetitive head trauma but did not develop CTE. Eighteen others were controls with no exposure to repetitive head injury at all. How many suicides were there among those thirty-five people? Seven—the same number of suicides as in the population with CTE. There is no difference. So how does suicide then become a feature of CTE?"

Even more revealing, Dr. Cummings points out, is recent independent research into NFL players and suicide. "In a 2016 paper by Dr. EJ Lehman," he says, "out of 537 NFL player deaths, there were only 12 suicides.[14] You would expect 25.6 based on the numbers seen in the general population. Based on that, the belief that NFL players are ticking suicide bombs is just false."

But let's not stop there. A 2016 paper by Grant Iverson, PhD, director of the Sports Concussion Program at Mass General Hospital for Children, found no conclusive connection between neurotrauma, CTE, depression, and suicide and concluded that NFL players were at a lower suicide risk than the general population. Iverson, who searched multiple online resources, found only 26 suicides out of 26,702 individuals who have played in the NFL since its inception. In the paper, he writes, "Conceptualizing suicide as being the result of small focal epicenters of tau, or a progressive degenerative tauopathy, is currently scientifically premature, overly simplistic, and potentially fatalistic."[15]

A paper by Gary Solomon, MS, PhD, professor of neurological surgery and associate professor of psychiatry at the Village at Vanderbilt University's Neurosurgery Clinic, offers even more support for this fact. Taking into account the four comprehensive studies done on the subject, he concludes, "Overall, the empirical data do not support a direct, causal relationship between concussions/CTE and suicidal behaviors."[16]

Dave Duerson (1960–2011)

A safety for the Bears, Giants, and Cardinals from 1983 to 1993, Dave was a four-time Pro Bowl selection and a Super Bowl champion. He died of a self-inflicted gunshot wound to the chest; his suicide note read, "Please, See That My Brain Is Given To The NFL's Brain Bank." The Boston University CTE Center determined that he had CTE.

THE CRUSHING IMPACT OF LIFE AFTER FOOTBALL

As YOU KNOW, I RETIRED suddenly and unwillingly in 1994. I'm fortunate that, thanks to Mr. Rooney, Lynn Swann, and other great people, I was able to make the transition to working at ESPN, where I would stay until 2017. Before my broadcasting career, I was having cognitive trouble, spending too much time sitting on the couch watching television, and generally having no idea what to do with my life. It's impossible to know, of course, but if that had gone on like that for years, would I have ended up attempting suicide?

Fortunately, we'll never know, but my point is that while everyone is jumping up and down to point the finger at football-induced

CTE to explain suicide and even drug use in retired players, maybe we should be looking at something else, like *retirement*.

Think about it. You're twenty-five and playing in the NFL. Football has been your entire life since you were eight years old. You're making great money, fans are cheering you, you're healthy because you're always exercising, and for most of the year you're around your best buddies, your brothers in arms whom you go to war with. Life is good.

All of a sudden, while you still feel great and think you have a lot to offer, you're cut. Or an injury ends your career. Still, you think, you're walking away with an NFL pension and you're still young, so maybe you can open a restaurant, buy some car dealerships like John Elway, and transition into a new life. But then the new reality sets in. Nobody's cheering you. You miss the camaraderie of the guys in the locker room so much you can barely stand it.

There are practical considerations, too. You're not taking home that big paycheck every two weeks. You got used to eating whatever you wanted because you were burning nine thousand calories a day, so you're still eating that way but no longer getting that kind of exercise, so you've put on a lot of weight. You might be in chronic pain from injuries. On top of all that, you have no idea what you're supposed to do next. For years, you had a purpose in your life, but now that purpose is gone.

That's what retirement looks like for a lot of pro athletes, and not just NFL players. It's tough. I'm not saying that most retired players will become suicidal, because most don't. But what if you're a guy with a family history of depression, a substance abuse problem, or a terrible support network? It might be easy for you to slide into depression. (And before you ask, the same paper by Dr. Solomon that I mentioned earlier also concludes that the rate of depression in retired NFL players is no higher than it is in the general population.)

There hasn't been a great deal of research into the connection between retirement, depression, and suicide in professional athletes, but there has been a lot of research into the effects of retirement on mood and behavior. Some of it suggests that retired athletes often have a hard time coping with the monumental life changes that accompany the end of their careers, not to mention identities and lifestyles that revolved around sports.[17] Other research shows that retired athletes experience feelings of emptiness.[18] For some reason, the most work on this topic has taken place in Australia, where researchers have found that elite athletes often reported feeling depressed and anxious while making the transition away from life in sports.[19]

Australian athletes have been very open about their struggles after retirement. In 2017, several retired pros appeared on Aussie television to talk about the problems they faced. One, a retired Australian Rules football player named Barry Hall, candidly stated that he fell into depression after his career ended.

"I chose to retire, I wanted to retire. I got the feeling that when I went to training every day that I didn't want to train anymore," he said in an interview in the *Huffington Post*. "I didn't want to prepare to the best of my ability to perform on the weekend. I think at that stage that's the time to give up the game. Did I struggle after the sport finished? Absolutely. I had two or three months…that I really struggled. I didn't get out of bed. I didn't answer mates' phone calls, I was eating terribly, drinking heavily. A tough time. And look, I didn't know at that stage it was a form of depression."[20] Other athletes shared similar sentiments.

The irony is, the greater the athlete's career, the harder it can be to transition away from that life to a life that feels ordinary. Boxing superstar Sugar Ray Leonard once said, "Nothing could satisfy me outside the ring…there is nothing in life that can compare to becoming a world champion, having your hand raised in that moment of glory, with thousands, millions of people cheering you on." Leonard wrote about his own depression, which led to multiple unsuccessful comeback attempts even after it was clear he couldn't fight at an elite level anymore.[21]

Is it possible that a disruptive life change like retirement, not CTE, could cause an athlete to feel suicidal, especially if he fears he might have CTE? Not surprisingly, Mike Golic has something to say about this. "[Retirement] puts the fear of God into these guys because when you play sports for a living, you control the narrative," he says. "With me, I know how hard I worked. I could go out on the field, and it was me against another guy. If I was good enough, I'd beat him. If I wasn't, he'd beat me. And then we lined up and we did it again.

"These [retired] guys are not used to not being in control of the narrative," Mike concludes. "Now, guys are like, 'Well, I don't know. I read all these articles about CTE. Do I have it? Do I not know about it because there's no tests for it?' Then the first time they forget something or something isn't right with them, they think they have CTE."

JUNIOR SEAU AND AARON HERNANDEZ

IF YOU'RE LOOKING AT FOOTBALL player suicides, you'd be hard pressed to come up with two cases more unlike each other than Junior Seau and Aaron Hernandez. Seau was loved, a happy-go-lucky surfing Samoan who was a San Diego institution. Hernandez had a reputation as a troublemaker, and he ended up convicted of murder. But the two cases have one other thing in common (besides the NFL): their suicides were both immediately blamed on CTE.

The reality, however, wasn't quite that black and white. As Flynn wrote in *The War on Football*, there was a darker side to Junior Seau that a lot of people knew nothing about. He drank heavily, had a gambling habit, took a lot of prescription drugs, and had serious financial problems—including the closure of his restaurant, Seau's the Restaurant, just two weeks prior to his death.[22] Could those factors have contributed to his suicide? Certainly, people have killed themselves in despair over financial losses in the past. There's no way to know, but what I do know is that instead of asking questions, people say the magical letters "CTE" and assume that explains everything. It doesn't.

When the autopsy reports on twenty-seven-year-old Aaron Hernandez's brain became public, it was announced that he had stage III CTE—or, as the coverage described it, "the most severe CTE ever found in a person his age."[23] Everyone jumped right to the usual conclusion: CTE had made him kill his victim, Odin Lloyd, and then hang himself in his prison cell. But blaming his actions on CTE is dubious at best.

Remember, while I'm claiming that the football-CTE connection is nowhere near as ironclad or scientifically proven as BU and the press would have you believe, I'm not saying there's no such thing as CTE. We know that many factors can cause deposits of tau to accumulate in the brain, and we know that Aaron Hernandez had severe neurodegenerative disease (although to have that at such a young age, he might have had a genetic predisposition for it, something Dr. McKee even states in the *Washington Post* article I cited above). But remember, there's no good evidence that repeated impacts to the head cause CTE, or that tau deposits lead to the kind of symptoms Hernandez exhibited. Blaming football and CTE for impulsive, violent, or suicidal acts, while tempting, is not scientific.

First of all, it's possible there were bigger reasons that made Hernandez want to kill himself. He'd just had his first child and signed a $40 million contract, and now he was facing life in an eight-foot-by-eight-foot cell. He was also a heavy drug user and was part of an age group in which suicide is the second-most-common cause of death.[24] It wouldn't be uncommon. After all, a 2017 study about suicide among the incarcerated found that nearly one-fourth of prisoners interviewed had considered suicide during the past year.[25] It's not unreasonable to think that Hernandez had such thoughts and acted on them.

When we clear away all the fear and hysteria and sloppy science, we're left with this:

There is no evidence that CTE causes suicide.

"We have to be careful how we throw around the diagnosis of CTE after a suicide," says Dr. Cummings. "Just because someone dies with a CTE-like lesion in their brain doesn't mean that's what led to their death. It doesn't mean they had symptoms at all. In the literature there are close to one hundred other CTE cases featuring older individuals who supposedly had stage I or stage II CTE, and out of those cases, there were no suicides. If suicidality is a feature of stages I and II, why no suicides in these cases? We cannot correlate *any* stage of CTE with clinical symptoms at this point, and to portray it any other way is disingenuous."

Ray Easterling (1949–2012)

A safety for the Atlanta Falcons for eight years, Ray took his own life when he shot himself at his home in Richmond, Virginia. The Richmond medical examiner determined that he had moderate CTE. His death helped push the NFL into launching a free mental health hotline for players.

CONFIRMATION BIAS

DR. RUDY CASTELLANI, ONE OF the most qualified, experienced, respected neuropathologists in the country, is concerned that the constant, unfounded doom-and-gloom chatter about CTE and neurodegenerative disease could exert a dangerous influence on athletes. "You've got to be careful because there are a lot of people out there with serious psychiatric issues who either were in the military or played a sport at some high level," he says. "'CTE is a progressive degenerative brain disease'—that just rolls off the tongue. It's present in the papers. Smart people say the same thing; they repeat the same things—'progressive degenerative brain disease'—when the fact is there's no evidence for that being the case."

So why is everyone so convinced that CTE is driving a wave of suicides among former NFL players when it's not happening? Because when we see something that stirs our emotions, especially our fears, that can make us think something is more common than it really is. If you want proof, talk to parents of young kids whom you know. Ask them whether it's safer for their kids to play in the neighborhood unsupervised today or back in the 1960s or '70s. I'll bet two-thirds of them say, "Of course it was safer when I was a kid." But that's wrong. In fact, it's safer to be a kid today than at any time since the 1970s.[26] But we don't believe it. Here's a big reason why.

Back when I was a kid, if something happened outside our community—if a kid was abducted or hit by a car, say—we probably didn't know about it. All we had was the local newspaper and local and national news, so if it happened outside of our town, as far as we were concerned, it didn't happen. But today, as soon as a child is kidnapped or abused, it's all over cable news and social media. We know about all the terrible things that happen every day, so we think they're all around us. The same phenomenon is happening with NFL suicides. They're big, dramatic stories that suck up all the news oxygen, so we fool ourselves into thinking they must be happening all the time. They're not.

Don't mistake me. It's terrible that great guys have taken their own lives because they were suffering and that other ex-players suffer from cognitive problems. My heart goes out to them. But I want to get to the real reasons that some former players are hurting and others are dying. If we assume the only reason is CTE and close the books on the whole thing, we risk missing a whole lot of other factors that are more likely, from a family history of mental illness to genetics to the harsh impact of no longer being part of the game they loved. We won't make any progress like that.

THE REAL KILLER: FEAR OF CTE

BUT THERE IS AN ASPECT of CTE that actually is leading to suicide: CTE anxiety. The constant flow of stories about the horrors of CTE is convincing athletes who played contact sports that if they forget where they put the car keys, they have CTE. "When a member of the general public commits suicide, it's due to mental illness; if a football player commits suicide, it's automatically CTE," says Dr. Cummings. "Because of this misconception, athletes are thinking that every cognitive symptom they experience is inevitably progressive and fatal, when in fact many of the issues with depression and anxiety are very treatable. This is how CTE causes suicide: fear. Just look at Todd Ewen."

Todd Ewen was a retired NHL player who became convinced that his mood swings and suicidal thoughts were due to CTE. In 2015, he took his own life. The terrible irony was that examination found that he had not a single focus of the telltale tau protein in his brain; he didn't have CTE.[27] Any suicide is terrible, but this was especially sad.

But Ewen isn't the only victim of CTE hysteria. Writing for *Yahoo! Sports*, journalist Eric Adelson talks about the ironic fact that athletes who are convinced that they have CTE can experience such stress and anxiety that they begin to experience the very symptoms commonly associated with CTE, from headaches to anxiety to depression. The whole thing becomes a vicious cycle. Doctors are reporting a spike in ex-athletes who come to them convinced that whatever problem they have must be CTE—and worse, there's no hope of treatment.

"I get very worried when patients come to me and they're having an emotional problem and rather than thinking it's treatable, they think it's the beginning of CTE," says Chris Giza, a professor of pediatric neurology at UCLA, in Adelson's *Yahoo!* story. "That doesn't mean CTE doesn't exist, but when people think every football player has it, that certainly is not the case. Just because 95 percent of the brain bank has it doesn't mean 95 percent of all brains have it. The way the story is being presented to the public can cause additional fear."[28]

What an irony: the only aspect of CTE known to cause suicide is the fear of it.

That brings up the issue of mental illness. There's still a stigma attached to it in our society, and there shouldn't be. My experience tells me that stigma is even worse among athletes, who are supposed to be invulnerable. But mental illness is nothing to be ashamed of. Having depression, anxiety, or some other problem is not a sign of weakness; it's a sign of being human. The trouble starts when we blame football for problems that are more likely to be signs of a legitimate medical condition that can and often does respond to treatment. If athletes experiencing CTE anxiety or other problems think football is to blame, they're apt to think they're untreatable and become more likely to go into a downward spiral.

It's time to apply some honesty and common sense to this issue. Mental illness is a real thing, and football doesn't cause it. Anthony Bourdain committed suicide, but no one claimed that toiling in a hot New York City kitchen made him do it. Kate Spade committed suicide, but no one blamed the stresses of running a major fashion brand. Mental illness has many contributing factors, and anyone who blames one cause for an athlete's suicide—or anyone's symptoms—is being irresponsible and dishonest.

Widespread fear among athletes who think they have CTE—like HIV in the 1980s, dreaded as a death sentence—goes back at least as far as 2013. That's when Dr. Matt McCarthy wrote on *Deadspin* about encountering a distraught, suicidal NFL player in his hospital's psych ward. He speculated about all the other players and former players waking up in a cold sweat because of a tenuous scientific connection that has more holes in it than Swiss cheese. He understood what I understood as someone who's been on the other end of those concussive blows: fear is powerful, and when unscrupulous people stoke that fear, it gets out of control fast. In his *Deadspin* piece, Dr. McCarthy wrote:

> How many other ex-jocks similarly believe that a set of possibly transient cognitive difficulties unrelated to their football careers is in fact the first expression of an unrelenting, progressive physical condition that will ultimately ruin their lives? How many saw the headline, "Doctors: Junior Seau's brain had CTE," and started connecting dots between concussions and suicide that scientists aren't even close to connecting? How many know that the study of head injuries is a lot more confusing and murky than once suspected—that some very good researchers are now suggesting CTE might not even be a unique disease? How many former NFLers think they're walking around right now with a death sentence over their heads?[29]

In 2017 on the *Huffington Post*, Brooke de Lench—author, filmmaker, journalist, cofounder of the MomsTEAM Youth Sports Safety Institute, and director of the PBS documentary *The Smartest Team: Making High School Football Safer*—wrote about talking to a mother whose son had sustained a concussion while playing lacrosse. The son was still having symptoms months later and had started saying that he might be better off dead. That's terrible. It's more fallout from the headline grabbing that has everyone thinking that a concussion equals CTE and CTE equals death. But this "open-and-shut" message is spreading, and clinicians are seeing more and more young people fearful that their brains are already permanently damaged.

In her piece, Brooke wrote:

> Every clinician who routinely treat [*sic*] athletes with
> post-concussion syndrome (i.e., patients whose symp-
> toms after suffering a sports-related concussion persist
> for months or years), [*sic*] with whom I spoke for this
> article expressed variations of the same concern: that their
> patients, hearing media reports about athletes suffering
> symptoms associated with CTE (such as depression),
> were losing hope of a full recovery, to the point of consid-
> ering suicide.[30]

Children should not have to wonder if they would be better off dead so they won't be a burden to their family. No child should be considering ending his or her life. Remember, I've been there. After my second concussion, the one that forced me into retirement, it was two years before the fog finally lifted and I felt like myself again. I went to counseling because there was no other treatment for me. Granted, that was before we knew some of what we know now about treating concussion, but the brain is complex, concussions are still not well understood, and everyone responds differently to head injury and treatment.

Is the media's coverage of CTE scaring young and old athletes to death? It might be. And furthermore, misinformation and scary headlines are also convincing young NFL players to end their careers prematurely because they're convinced if they stay they'll turn their brains to mush. For every guy like Eagles safety Malcolm Jenkins, who says he doesn't fear CTE and won't stop his kids from playing ball, there are guys like Ravens lineman John Urschel, who—two days after the publication of the *New York Times* story about 110 out of 111 NFL brains testing positive for CTE—retired at twenty-six.[31]

Of course, there are plenty of worthwhile pursuits besides playing football, and John, who's a brilliant guy, is going for his doctorate in mathematics at MIT, so I have no doubt he'll do great things.[32] But if you're going to make that decision, you should be able to make it based on good, balanced information, not sensationalized garbage. Calvin Johnson, Chris Borland...the list of guys who've walked away from their dreams of playing in the NFL because of fear stoked by bad information keeps growing, and it makes me sick. Guys shouldn't be making life-changing decisions based on incomplete data sold to them as fact. Guys shouldn't be living in fear. We need to empower people with truth and balanced information so that they can make educated choices about their futures.

CTE IS SETTLED SCIENCE, AND FOOTBALL CAUSES IT

CHAPTER 4

HEADLINES

This season, puddles of ink will be spilled linking head trauma to chronic traumatic encephalopathy, or CTE, explaining how cognitive and behavioral changes continue to occur in current and former NFL players, destroying their once remarkable lives and the lives of those around them. You will see these stories on the front pages of the most prominent newspapers and magazines in the country, written by sportswriters who, frankly, don't understand the science and have long overstated what is actually known about the condition.

—DR. MATT MCCARTHY, DEADSPIN

CHAPTER 4 PLAYBOOK

- There are more *New York Times* stories about CTE than there are documented cases of CTE

- Biased, ignorant press coverage is driving the public belief that football is "child abuse"

- There are some conscientious reporters writing on this topic, and they need to be listened to

IF YOU WERE CONSCIOUS ON July 25, 2017, you saw it. Heck, you would've had to be living off the grid in a Wyoming survival bunker to have missed it: the giant story in the *New York Times* with the headline "110 NFL Brains."[1] The subhead below finished the story: "A neuropathologist has examined the brains of 111 NFL players—and 110 were found to have CTE, the degenerative disease linked to repeated blows to the head." The research was done by a team led by Dr. Ann McKee of the BU CTE Center.

Let me repeat that: out of 111 brains of former NFL players examined by McKee and her team, 110 were found to have CTE. That's 99.099 percent—a staggering, damning number.

Immediately, the story was as impossible to avoid as mosquitoes in July. CNN, *Sports Illustrated*, National Public Radio, NBC News, *Fast Company*—everybody picked it up. Finally, here was ironclad scientific confirmation of what Boston University's CTE Center and others had been claiming for years: playing pro football gives you permanent, progressive brain damage.

Seemingly overnight, press coverage of CTE, the risks of playing football, Boston University, and Dr. McKee exploded. The press had already been covering the issue for several years (and getting a lot of the facts wrong), but now CTE stories were everywhere, a lot of them either bracketed with scare quotes or fawning over BU researchers like Dr. McKee, Robert Stern, and Dr. Robert Cantu. *Forbes* ran a feature by Bob Cook entitled "The CTE Study That Could Kill Football." The *Boston Globe* named Dr. McKee its Bostonian of the Year for 2017. The *New York Times* published a piece about Hall of Fame Miami Dolphins linebacker Nick Buoniconti, painting a sad picture of his mental decline and his plans to donate his brain for study after his death.

That's a very, very tiny sample. If I listed just the ominous, eye-catching headlines of all the stories about football and CTE that have run in the last year and a half, I could fill half of this book.

The inflammatory coverage hasn't slowed down, either. On May 3, 2018, *Mother Jones* ran a frustrating feature called "Scientists Were Already Concerned about Kids Playing Tackle Football. It's Worse Than They Thought." In fact, according to Kevin Guskiewicz, codirector of the Matthew Gfeller Sport-Related Traumatic Brain Injury Research Center at the University of North Carolina and one of the country's leading authorities on concussions, the press frenzy has grown to preposterous proportions.

In an interview, Kevin said, "I gave a talk few weeks ago down at the Neurosurgical Society meeting in Florida called 'The State of Sports Concussion: Legitimate Concern versus Paranoia.' I walked through all of the [information]: here is what we know, here's what we think we know, and here's what's unknown but yet the media would lead you to believe that we have this crisis. I have this slide with two numbers on it: three hundred thirty-three on the left, and then to the right of it three hundred. Three hundred thirty-three is the number of *New York Times* articles on CTE. Three hundred represents the total number of cases of CTE in the world's literature."

Three hundred thirty-three to three hundred. That's a stark picture of hype versus facts. Hype is winning.

SLOPPY REPORTING, LIMITED SOURCES

THE PROBLEM ISN'T JUST THE AMOUNT of the press coverage of CTE but how hysterical and uncritical it is. For example, did the *Times* piece mention that Nick Buoniconti was nearly seventy-seven at the time of the article? Or that, according to a 2017 study, about 10 percent of Americans ages seventy-five to eighty-five have some type of dementia?[2] Of course not, even though that's important information that puts the story in context. The *Times* coasted right into the CTE angle without pumping its skepticism brakes even once.

There's a lot of that when it comes to football and brain injury. "Impacts to the head cause CTE; what about the children?" seems to be the narrative that sells newspapers and gets clicks, so that's where the story goes. Nobody wants to be the one reporter or paper questioning the official line and getting bombarded with angry letters and comments. But that also means that a lot of questions that need to be asked aren't being asked.

Another big problem with the coverage of this topic is that it's almost always dark and foreboding. I'm not naive; I get the "If it bleeds, it leads" thing. I understand that the public likes to read dramatic stories. But in recent years, the coverage of football and brain injury has been overwhelmingly negative. Since the July 2017 research from BU went global, you don't have to look too hard to find a gloomy "Is football doomed?" article from a major news outlet. And if they're not writing about the extinction of the NFL and Pop Warner, writers are spinning tragic tales of ex-players who are having terrible health problems, like the sad account of Gale Sayers and Tony Dorsett in the *New York Daily News*[3] or the gut-wrenching piece about Larry Johnson's struggles in the *Washington Post*.[4]

My heart goes out to those guys, especially since I've been there—no memory, brain fog, the whole catastrophe. Their problems are real, and they deserve to have their stories told. But why are those the only stories the public is reading? Where are the stories about the thousands of ex-NFL players who are doing great? Where are the stories about how flimsy so many of the conclusions being drawn about CTE actually are? The only answer, I guess, is that those stories don't sell papers or get ratings. But the stories that do are creating a frightening, false impression in the public's mind.

But the most dangerous piece of this is that it looks like the primary source reporters are using for their CTE stories is BU, Dr. McKee, and the Concussion Legacy Foundation. I did a Google search for "CTE and football" and out of the first twenty results that were mainstream news articles (not academic papers or informational content from concussion websites), fifteen quoted Boston University researchers or cited BU research as their main source—frequently, their only source. Granted, that's not the most precise tool, but it gives you a rough idea of the problem.

A ONE-SIDED VIEW OF WHAT "SELLS"

So what's wrong with coverage, you might ask? Doesn't the public need to know the risks? Yes, it does. But it needs to know the real risks based on solid, conservative science done by researchers with appropriate credentials, and that's not what it's getting. It's getting a one-sided view of things without any context that's easy for laypeople to understand. For example, the piece on Larry Johnson says that he assumes he's suffering from CTE. There's no proof of that because for now CTE can only be diagnosed after death. He *might* have CTE, but it's also possible he doesn't. The point is that we just don't know. But the average reader reads his story, sees the letters "CTE," makes the connection with all the other reporting on the topic, and as John Madden would say—*boom!* In his or her mind, Larry Johnson's another victim of the CTE plague.

What makes BU's monopoly on the press coverage of CTE dangerous is that a lot of BU's science is just not very good, which makes it easy for journalists to draw conclusions that are misleading or flat-out wrong. That's not me saying that, either; it's expert after expert in the field, from Dr. Bailes to Dr. Castellani to Dr. Cummings to Dr. Maroon. For example, the media's interpretation of the infamous "110 out of 111" brains study ignored some serious flaws in the research and its widely publicized results.

I'll go into those flaws in the next chapter, but even the *Journal of the American Medical Association* paper in which the results were published admits that the study has serious limitations: "The VA-BU-CLF Brain Bank is not representative of the overall population of former players of American football; most players of American football have played only on youth or high school teams, but the majority of the brain bank donors in this study played at the college or professional level."[5] But just like the print and online stories in the mainstream media, that information is buried at the end, where the authors know most people won't read. All they see is "110 out of 111 brains" and it's case closed.

No wonder a September 2017 poll from UMass Lowell found that 53 percent of one thousand adults surveyed felt that tackle football isn't safe for kids younger than high school age—and 83 percent believed that the science indicating that playing football causes brain injuries is settled.[6] Fear and the mainstream media are powerful things.

But if you know what to look for, you can find the same flaws and biases in a lot of the research on CTE, concussion, and football published in the last three or four years. Some people argue that the potential for serious impacts on the health of adults and children justifies the story getting so far out in front of the science. I disagree. Without sound science, we don't know what's real and what's not. If we don't know the prevalence of symptoms, the true risk factors, and people's susceptibility, how can we prevent and treat brain damage and neurodegenerative disease?

One of the problems is that experts who receive extensive media attention, like Dr. McKee, sometimes make statements that stoke the fear surrounding CTE and football. For example, Dr. McKee is on record as saying that she now finds football too painful to watch. To her credit, she does seem to be aware that the hype surrounding her work, and the CTE Center's work in general, has gotten carried away. In a piece published by the NCAA in 2015 that questioned much of the CTE science being done at that time, she said, "There's a certain level of, I don't know, it's just sensationalism or it's what sells. I think there are times when it's overblown. I do think we need to be concerned... sometimes it goes a little far."[7]

"It's what sells" certainly describes the spirit of the reporting on the subject, which has leaned toward melodramatic headlines and ominous-sounding factoids without much context or perspective. Case in point: that statistic about there being more stories about CTE in the *New York Times* than actual diagnosed cases. The press, and the select group of experts who benefit from their stories, has turned concern over CTE into a booming cottage business.

THERE ARE SANE VOICES IN THE PRESS

TO BE SURE, SOME JOURNALISTS have held on to their professional skepticism. Eric Adelson from *Yahoo!* has written some of the smartest commentary around on the questionable quality of the evidence for CTE, citing experts who call the conclusions being reported in the media simplistic, fueling hysteria among people who get one concussion and begin to panic that they have CTE. Other writers such as *Slate's* Daniel Engber, Jeff Wheelwright at *Discover*, and A.J. Russo of the *Baltimore Sun* have produced strong, inquisitive reporting on the subject.

I spoke with several reporters about how the press covers CTE and the science behind it, and they expressed concerns that there is simply not enough skepticism or hard questions being asked about the issue—by journalists or doctors—and too many prominent scientists who fear speaking out publicly because of the potential blowback. The consensus was that while it's important to be skeptical about the people who say CTE doesn't exist and that football has no risks associated with it at all, it's just as important to be skeptical of the people who claim that the science is all sewn up, because that's simply not the case.

One of the running themes of my conversations with journalists was that the public should always question the motives and interests of the reporters who are building their careers around reporting on the CTE-football controversy, as well as the motives and interests of the media outlets that making money from the coverage, including stalwarts like the *New York Times*. Are the writers talking to multiple sources from all sides of the issue, or do they tend to quote the same people again and again? Are they asking hard questions about the quality of studies or accepting them at face value? Are they being objective or letting the drama of a suicide or an ex-athlete with dementia turn factual reporting into something intended to manipulate readers' emotions?

I've looked into the issue for years myself, and I've never spoken to a reputable physician or scientist who knows the body of research around CTE who feels like the scientific community is anywhere close to a conclusion about what causes it, or even what it is. But we don't see that uncertainty in the press, because "We're not sure" doesn't sell papers. That's why I think it's so important to support journalists who are asking tough questions and demanding better science. To do otherwise does a disservice to everyone from professional athletes to kids.

One of the journalists asking sharp questions and not drawing premature conclusions is Lindsey Barton Straus, an attorney who is Brooke de Lench's cofounder at MomsTEAM.

Her article "CTE: Is Media Narrative Ahead of the Science?" is one of the best and most comprehensive looks at the conflicting opinions and narratives within the neurology and concussion community over the quality of the evidence and what should be done about it. From that piece (which I recommend you read), it's extremely clear that there's nothing *close* to a consensus about the quality of the evidence for football and CTE, much less what should be done about it.

Still, those voices are in the minority. Even now, too much of the coverage of CTE and football simply accepts the surface results of poorly designed studies at face value, slaps scary headlines at the top of the page, and features only opinions from Boston University. Bottom line, the scope and drama of the story of football and CTE have attracted eyeballs and made people famous, and when that happens, money and conflicts of interest won't be far behind. It's in the best interest of everyone who cares about health, football, kids, and the truth to be skeptical when we read sensationalistic headlines and to demand that the journalists and bloggers who write and talk about CTE, concussion, youth football, and pro football do so with an eye on the facts and solid science, not just ad rates and click-through.

Now, let's take a closer look at the real force driving the coverage machine: Boston University's CTE Center.

CHERRY PICKING DATA

It is part of the human condition to have implicit biases—and remain blissfully ignorant of them. Academic researchers, scientists, and clinicians are no exception; they are as marvelously flawed as everyone else. But it is not the cognitive bias that's the problem. Rather, the denial that there is a problem is where the issues arise.[1]

—*LISA COSGROVE*, THE SCIENTIST

CHAPTER 5 PLAYBOOK

- How Boston University research is skewed and shielded from scrutiny

- Attacking freedom of speech

- Using lawyers to suppress the sharing of information

- Todd Ewen, Zarley Zalapski, and the death of the "dose-response" theory

---

I'M NOT A SCIENTIST, but I hang out with them. Really. Since I took an interest in the science behind CTE and its impact on the game I love, I've spent time with some of the best and brightest in neuropathology, neurosurgery, neuropsychology, neurology—pretty much anything with *neuro* in the name. And while sometimes I've had no idea what they were talking about, I have picked up on one central, repeated theme:

Good science is hard.

Good science is about teasing *causality* out of a whole bunch of data points—which, in the case of brain injury and CTE, are either living people or people who used to be alive and experienced a whole lot of stuff: tackles on the football field, drug and steroid use, mental illness, childhood trauma, and so on. If you're doing research, your job is to figure out if A causes B, and that's a lot harder than it seems because data is messy. All kinds of factors can affect your final outcome, and since the idea is to get to that clear causal relationship, you've got to account for and explain all those other factors.

If you don't, then you end up not with causality but *correlation*, which means that something might be associated with another thing but doesn't actually cause it. It's kind of like looking at the fact that lots of teenagers drink alcohol on prom night and concluding that formal wear actually *causes* underage drinking.

This is important because there are a lot of ways to bias the conclusions of scientific research to support what you want them to, and for lots of reasons: to sell something, avoid liability, or pump up your professional reputation. That's shady, it hurts the credibility of science, and sometimes it damages the careers of scientists who want to work the right way. Like everything else, science is run by human beings with egos and agendas. So there's peer pressure, pressure to conform, and professional rivalry.

When all that becomes more important than the quest to get to the truth, you get what I believe is going on with Boston University's CTE Center. In working on this book, I've noticed a pattern of cherry-picking data, trying to suppress information that contradicts their narrative, and standing in the way of open inquiry. That's not the way science is supposed to advance.

So in this chapter, I'm going to lay out the various ways that I believe BU is affecting the conversation around CTE through suppression, cherry-picked data, or bias. In some cases, I had trouble getting researchers to talk to me on the record because they feared that speaking out would hurt their ability to publish and get grant money. But that makes telling these stories even more important. Here's what I know, what I was told, and what I suspect.

PRESSURE ON ACADEMIC FREE SPEECH

OF COURSE, MOST OF the widely publicized work on CTE is coming out of Boston University. Universities are supposed to be bastions of free speech, where people can disagree openly and respectfully. Ironically, that doesn't appear to be the case, at least not with my collaborator, Dr. Cummings.

He's told me on several occasions about encountering hostility and efforts to discourage him from sharing his views about CTE, which contradict those of Dr. McKee and the media stars of the CTE Center. But he was extremely specific about the pressure he received from BU regarding the piece he wanted to write for *Yahoo!*, and he shared that story with me in a written statement:

> I have been an assistant professor at Boston University since October of 2015. Before that, I began teaching as an affiliated faculty member in 2010. In order to engage in any media, I thought I needed to obtain the permission of the Boston University Public Relations Office. On August 10th I corresponded via email and spoke on the phone with Gina DiGravio-Wilczewski [a spokeswoman for Boston University] regarding the *Yahoo!* article. I advised them I was going to describe my decision-making process, which involved analysis of the science and new football rules.
>
> Gina advised me that as a parent, it was okay for me to share my feelings as to why I chose to allow my son to play football. She asked if I was going to discuss the CTE research. I said that I would and that I had some concerns, but that I did fully support the work of the BU CTE · research center. I told her that I had directed families of

deceased athletes to the CTE center and I had recruited
a friend of mine, who was a female rugby player, to the
CTE studies.

Gina voiced support for my article and advised me that BU
encouraged collegiate dialogue. She just wanted to make sure
I wasn't affiliated with the CTE labs to avoid the impression
there was "in-fighting." I assured her I had no affiliation.
I told her that I was writing it and if it made her more
comfortable, I might be able to get her a draft. It was not
my intention to damage BU or the CTE research, only to
tell my story.

On September 6th Gina emailed me and copied some
questions sent to her by Eric Adelson, who was requesting
a comment from Dr. Ann McKee in regards to issues I
raised in my article. Gina asked to see my draft. I advised
her I would check with *Yahoo!* After discussions with
Yahoo!, we felt it best if the draft was not supplied to BU.

On September 7, 2017, I received an email from Gina requesting that I call her ASAP. I phoned her as soon as I was
free. In the conversation Gina requested to see the article
and told me she felt a little upset that I first told her I might
share it with her and then was refusing to. I told her that my
comments about the CTE research were simply pointing out
the facts the work has not been replicated or independently
verified and that there were weaknesses in our current understanding. I told her that I ended the piece by stating that
I wholeheartedly support the CTE research and that I have
recruited patients to the studies.

Gina understood why *Yahoo!* wouldn't want me to let her see the copy. She advised me this was a very sensitive issue for BU. She stated that she had been placed in a difficult position with her boss. She asked that I send her the article without telling Eric Adelson or *Yahoo!* I told her that made me uncomfortable and would feel dishonest to me. At that point, she threatened to tell the dean of the medical school what I was doing, a move that was clearly meant to intimidate me.

Gina was pleasant, but her tone through the conversation was stressed. Near the end of the phone call she told me without question she needed to see the piece. If she didn't, I would face the consequences, and BU would say that I proceeded without their permission, and the school would not be able to protect me. I decided to end the conversation at that point and told Gina I would talk to Eric and get back to her.

I felt as though my job and standing at BU were at risk if I wrote the article and I certainly felt as though my academic freedom of speech was being compromised.

Dr. Cummings's *Yahoo!* piece questions the state of the science without undercutting BU. But the point is that the possibility of the op-ed running made BU very nervous and led it to make Dr. Cummings feel that his academic free speech—and possibly his position—was at stake. That is not okay and makes you ask, "What is BU so afraid of?"

But Dr. Cummings's experience with suppression didn't end there. He told me that every time he had a letter come out in the *New York Times*, every time he spoke publicly, every time he expressed his thoughts about the state of CTE science, someone at the BU Communications Office would call the chair of his department to complain. That doesn't sound like academic free speech to me.

A PRO-CTE PROPAGANDA TOOL

BUT WHILE BOSTON UNIVERSITY got hinky about letting Dr. Cummings even question the CTE Center's findings in his *Yahoo!* piece, it seems to have no problem trotting Dr. McKee out before every media outlet from here to the Sudan to promote her view of the data. The medical school's Twitter feed alone has become a pro-McKee, anti-football propaganda tool that's ignored Dr. Cummings's expert views contradicting the accepted science.

In fact, since his *Yahoo!* op-ed dropped on September 19, 2017, the Boston University Medical School Twitter account hasn't posted a single tweet about that piece, Dr. Cummings's editorial with twenty-six other medical experts, or radio interviews he did from California to Texas to Canada. BU tweeted once about Dr. Cummings's paper on CTE in the brains of woodpeckers that received international coverage and even made it into *Discover* magazine, but that tweet didn't even mention him by name.[2] However, since that date, the account has run more than ninety anti-football tweets (and counting), including:

- June 27, 2018: Parents of former Washington State QB Tyler Hilinski say he had CTE when he committed suicide.[3]

- May 1, 2018: New study shows playing tackle football before age 12 could result in earlier CTE symptoms. "It makes common sense that children, whose brains are rapidly developing, shouldn't be hitting their heads hundreds of times per season," says BUSM's Dr. McKee.[4]

- February 2, 2018: When Brett Favre sees little kids playing football, 'I cringe.'[5]

- January 29, 2018: Some parents saying 'no' to tackle football over CTE fears.[6]

- January 25, 2018: Bob Costas will skip the Super Bowl because of the NFL's connection to brain trauma.[7]

- November 13, 2017: Column: Harvard and Yale should stop playing football.[8]

- October 23, 2017: From @chronicle: Professors are complicit in football players' brain damage.[9]

There are also endless tweets about the Concussion Legacy Foundation and its "Flag Football Under 14" program and Dr. McKee's being honored in *Time*. But how many papers, studies, or op-eds did the BU School of Medicine tweet about that contradicted the narrative. None that I could find.

Again, you might think, so what? Dr. McKee is a leading researcher in the field, and her winning honors is something that her parent organization might be expected to promote. But the BU School of Medicine is a scientific institution, and science is supposed to be neutral and agenda-free. We all know it isn't, but it's supposed to at least strive for that. By aggressively pumping up a figure like Dr. McKee and by ignoring Dr. Cummings's opinion as a faculty member, it bolsters her credibility while harming his. BU is taking a side in this debate. By ignoring other opinions, the school is concealing the fact that the debate even exists and discouraging people from looking for other opinions.

LEGAL BLOCKADES

WHEN THEY CAN'T SELECTIVELY PROMOTE INFORMATION, BU's policy seems to be to use legal means to block access to it. Dr. Cummings told me that he has tried to get records relating to a legal case he was asked to review. The client wanted to get copies of the BU CTE Center's research data on the legal case—completely understandable since the conclusion of the neuropathologist was that the subject of the case had CTE.

But when Dr. Cummings delivered a release form signed by the decedent's family, what he got back was a mess of legal barbed wire that Dr. Cummings (who's been working with lawyers for more than a decade) called "a way to keep control and not allow people to independently review the material." He told me, "In the twenty-five-plus states and seven countries I've been involved with, you send the medical examiner's office or the university a release letter, and they get the stuff to you."

In this case, the associate general counsel of Boston University informed the opposing parties in the case that his first signed release had been misplaced (how convenient). Then he wrote that despite receipt of a signed medical authorization, the CTE Center wouldn't comply with the family's request without a subpoena because of the time and expense involved in pulling one athlete's records.

That's "go pound sand" in legal terms. According to my understanding of medical privacy laws (and I'm not a lawyer), medical records have to be turned over when an institution is presented with a signed release from the patient or family members. But it didn't stop there. Later, the clients produced a subpoena, as BU insisted. Fine, said the university. They would provide the records. However, it would take six weeks and cost $7,000, and the client would have to withdraw the subpoena.

That's outrageous. I asked Dr. Cummings about it, and he said, "One of the reasons it's going to cost $7,000 is that Dr. McKee charges

$800 an hour to review the case, according to BU's legal office. That is double the going rate for consultation fees in my world. The hourly rate will be charged for McKee to review the copies of the slides to make sure they match the original slides, a very common practice as part of quality control. I think it's 'double-dipping' and totally unethical to charge to review work you've already done to make sure slides match. We were not asking for an opinion, and therefore charging the consulting fee is inappropriate. I would never charge for that, and I have never charged for that—that's unusual in the pathology world."

Dr. Cummings asked several other pathologists what they charged under these circumstances. All replied that they would never charge a "consulting fee" for looking at slides before sending them out. One pathologist said they charge only the direct cost of producing each slide. Another pathologist was more direct and said that the BU request could be seen as obstructionist.

The saga didn't end there. When Dr. Cummings finally obtained the records, a vital piece of documentation was missing: a consensus panel diagnostic sheet completed by individuals at the BU CTE Center confirming the clinical diagnosis of CTE. He got pushback when he asked for the sheet; after all, it's part of the clinical record and should have been released with the other material. After a lot of back and forth, he finally received the paperwork, but guess what? The names of the individuals who reached the clinical diagnosis of CTE were blacked out!

"I have never seen the name of a clinician blacked out of a medical record," Dr. Cummings told me. "It is vital to the defense of the case to see who was involved—not just in this case but in every case. Who was involved is part of the permanent record, and if they reached a medical diagnosis, we are entitled to see the names." As of the writing of this book, he still hasn't seen the names. If BU is so certain of its ability to diagnosis CTE, why is it hiding who is making the diagnosis? What does it have to hide?

Do you think Dr. Cummings's involvement in this case triggered a complaint to the dean of the medical school? You bet it did. It was a warning that he should be careful and disclose all his potential conflicts of interest in his BU employment paperwork or risk repercussions.

"It was laughable," he says. "But I was warned to watch my back because it was obvious the CTE Center was putting a target on it."

This obstructionist legal strategy goes beyond single cases. Since 2015, the National Hockey League has been trying to get BU to release information gathered from players and families of deceased players about everything from the frequency of concussions to their moods and behaviors—including the results of postmortem neuropathological exams—as part of a lawsuit filed by more than 150 former NHL players against the NHL. The players contend that the league wants the information so it can attack BU's science, especially since the CTE Center has formally diagnosed six players with CTE so far, most recently former Buffalo Sabres and Hartford Whalers skater Jeff Parker.[10] So the university has refused to comply with the league's request.

In 2017, the NHL served BU with a subpoena in which it demanded correspondence with players, agents, and players' families as well as conversations with peer reviewers, media, and university officials, in addition to all its laboratory findings. That's a lot of material, and since it has to be made anonymous to protect the privacy of the deceased (a process that the CTE Center says would take thirteen years), BU—including Dr. McKee, who claims that the NHL demands would "threaten the foundation on which science thrives"—is claiming that what the league is asking for is such a burden that it will effectively shut down the CTE Center's research.[11]

Don't defendants in a lawsuit have a legal right to review the body of evidence that's being assembled against them? It seems to me that BU's objection is more about the fact that the NHL's medical expert is Dr. Rudy Castellani, who has publicly expressed skepticism about the state of CTE science. I asked Dr. Castellani about all this, and this is what he had to say.

"These are my opinions only. I don't really make any representations of fact as the law understands it. I just want to make that clear because it's a very toxic environment. There are lawyers everywhere," he says. "Some years ago, attorneys for the National Hockey League contacted me, and they asked if I would discuss with them the whole issue of CTE. I assumed it was because they were being sued. I visited with them, and we discussed the issues. I have to say, the attorneys for the NHL have been very professional, and they are not interested in anything other than the honest truth of the matter.

"So, they retained me, and over the course of time, they wanted to obtain some material from Boston University, so they filed [an affidavit]," Castellani continues. "Part of the rationale for obtaining the Boston University material was to point out that CTE interpretations are just that. They're interpretations, and if they're going to be sued as an adversary in a civil proceeding, they should have the ability to review the material themselves to see the basis for the diagnosis and to have other individuals, perhaps less biased than them, review the material."

Dr. Castellani said that the Mike Webster CTE case and the 2005 paper on that case, coauthored by Dr. Bennet Omalu, was used as an example of how alleged experts could misinterpret neuropathology and find CTE when it wasn't really there.

"It was a case report, so at the outset, it is scientifically meaningless. It also had no objective data from a neurological or psychiatric examination by a physician, so the report has little value otherwise. But the main problem is that it depicted a normal brain, with scant changes that can be found in any fifty-year-old, regardless of occupation. Yet this case has since been interpreted as an exotic new disease in football players. Some language to that effect, I believe, was included in an affidavit. It said, 'Here's a case where professionals interpreted it as CTE when, if you really look carefully, there's nothing there.' That was part of the rationale as I understood it. [The argument was that the NHL] should have the ability to see the primary data coming out of Boston University if that's going to be used against their interests."

After the subpoena landed and became a news story, Dr. Castellani found out how BU operates. "Some friends came up to me and said, 'Hey, I see that Boston University lawyers are trashing you in the media,'" he says. "I said, 'Oh, really? What did they do? What did they say?'" It didn't take long to find a *Washington Post* story that read, in part: "A lawyer for Boston University, Lawrence Elswit, argued in a written response that Castellani's contention was 'inconsistent with accepted scientific methodology.' If Castellani wanted to argue with McKee's findings, Elswit argued, the methodology was already public through peer review."

Elswit finished with a snarky little dig: "Perhaps the NHL's expert distrusts the scientific method." But the attack dogs weren't done. This is the last paragraph in the story: "At a motions hearing in February, Charles Zimmerman, a lawyer representing the former NHL players, said the NHL's subpoena request 'will harm all ongoing CTE-related research at BU and at all…institutions that collaborate with BU and/or rely on their research. This may be exactly what deniers want, deniers like Dr. Castellani and deniers like the NHL, but we shouldn't allow that to happen.'"[12]

Castellani was not happy about the jabs. "I thought that was highly unprofessional because that does real harm," he says. "When university lawyers make comments about individuals in the public domain or in the media, that comes back to the private individual. I've had friends ridicule me. I've met colleagues at other institutions who have accused me, incorrectly, of being sponsored by a sporting organization, of playing the part of a lackey for 'the man'—all this kind of nonsense. Unfortunately, the news media is monolithic on this issue and seems to be driving the issue ideologically and not scientifically, and that influences the perception of anyone who dares to say the conclusions are outstripping the scientific evidence.

"I thought that making comments, an ad hominem attack against an individual like me, who—all I've done is study neurodegenerative diseases for the last twenty-five years—and who made a very legitimate point, was pretty outrageous," he concludes. "I suppose they don't like the cause of the [NHL], so they thought it necessary to make these remarks about me in the public domain."

The plainspoken Castellani had a lot more to say that I'll get to later. But his disgust at the comments of the BU and NHL lawyers makes an important point. That's not law.

Don't believe it's bad science? Fine. Give Castellani and the NHL access to the work and have a public debate about it. Let the best scientific argument win. But that's not what's happening. Instead, the credibility of a dissenting voice is being attacked.

By the way, in April of 2017, US district court judge Susan Nelson ruled against the NHL, saying that its request was excessively broad and represented a "significant, overwhelming burden."[13] So for now, the vast majority of the CTE Center's research remains inaccessible to anyone, even if he or she has a subpoena.

ISSUES WITH PEER REVIEW

BY THE WAY, I EXPECT that one of BU's defenses for all this will be that its work has passed peer review. That's true, but anyone working in a field where he or she is expected to publish in scientific journals knows the peer review system is often meaningless. The NFL's former chief medical officer, Dr. Elliot Pellman, was able to publish a series of questionable papers in the peer-reviewed journal *Neurosurgery*—papers that outraged the independent scientific community.[14]

Peer review works like this: when you write an academic paper, you submit it to a peer-reviewed journal, like the *Journal of the American Medical Association*. A group of experts knowledgeable about your field "referee" the work to assess its quality and scientific rigor. If it passes peer review, it's published; if it needs changes, the referees will specify those changes and send it back to you, and you can resubmit it. That's the process all good science is built on.

The problem is, opinions about the sorry state of peer review are everywhere. A common complaint is that the process is biased in favor of authors who are already renowned.[15] There's also pressure to protect other peers who could end up reviewing your work—sort of a "you scratch my back, I'll scratch yours" ethic. Guess what the most prestigious names in the world of CTE are? Ann McKee and BU. Because of that, BU scientists are called as peer reviewers constantly, and that gives them a lot of power to promote work that supports their theories and bury work that doesn't.

I'll bet you didn't know this (I sure didn't): if you're trying to get a paper published, you can often suggest the names of people to review your paper, and you can also ask that certain people not review your paper. Seriously? That's like allowing the head coach of a football team to choose refs who were his fraternity brothers in college! Here's another tip: go to www.retractionwatch.com so you can see for yourself how often bad science makes it to press. Dr. Cummings makes all the students in his experimental-design course monitor the website to see how flawed a lot of research really is.

Peer review as evidence that your work is sound? Sorry, not necessarily.

TODD EWEN AND THE END OF DOSE-RESPONSE

FINALLY, WE COME BACK TO the case of Todd Ewen. What I want to talk about here involves some speculation, but it's also something that needs to be talked about. And, because BU has a pattern of managing to find CTE in just about every brain it studies, it's also worth me getting out my crystal ball so if the prediction I'm going to make comes true, you'll be prepared to call BS.

As I wrote about a few chapters back, Ewen was a retired NHL enforcer nicknamed "the Animal" who, terrified that he was developing CTE, shot himself in the head on September 19, 2015. He was just forty-nine years old. After Ewen's death, his widow, Kelli, sent his brain to the Canadian Concussion Centre for examination. In February 2016, neuropathologist Dr. Lili-Naz Hazrati came back with the findings that I've already mentioned: *Todd Ewen did not have CTE.*

Dr. Cummings knows Dr. Hazrati, and he described her as a cautious, meticulous scientist who also approaches the subject of CTE with a healthy skepticism. That's why, in the story about her Todd Ewen findings, she said, "These results indicate that in some athletes, multiple concussions do not lead to the development of C.T.E. Our findings continue to show that concussions can affect the brain in different ways. This underlines the need to not only continue this research, but also be cautious about drawing any definitive conclusions about C.T.E until we have more data."[16]

This view is important because it highlights a critical flaw in BU's commentary: its theory that head impacts lead to CTE is a lot weaker than anyone realizes. My conversation with Kyla Zalapski helped me realize that. Her brother, Zarley, played in the NHL for eleven years and in European pro hockey for another ten years and even played against Todd Ewen. In fact, Zarley and I had been part of a Pittsburgh safety-helmet campaign back in the 1980s, and Kyla reached out to me a while back about helping him and other transitioning pro athletes. She was good enough to speak with me for this book.

Zarley died in December 2017 from a hemorrhagic stroke resulting from a damaged heart, and after his death everybody asked Kyla if he had committed suicide—presumably because he had CTE. Doesn't everybody? But Kyla's whip-smart, a CTE skeptic, and someone who cares deeply about the mental health of athletes, and she hated the idea that legitimate mental health concerns that needed medical treatment might be blamed on CTE. Eager to get answers, she also sent her brother's brain to Dr. Hazrati in Canada for examination.

The result? While Zarley had some tau in his brain that fit the pattern that BU identifies as stage II CTE, Dr. Hazrati couldn't definitively diagnose CTE. She also told Kyla that to be as thorough as possible, she sends samples of all the brains she examines to three independent neuropathology labs as a matter of course. That way, they can either confirm her findings or flag any problems that might invalidate her results. That's what a good scientist does.

But the big story here is the difference between Todd Ewen's brain and Zarley Zalapski's brain. Part of BU's theory of CTE is the idea of *dose-response*. The more hits to the head you take and the earlier you start taking them, the more tau you're supposed to have in your brain. So if Zarley had some tau in his brain and Todd had none, Zarley must have taken a lot more hits to the head than Todd, right?

Not according to Kyla. When I asked her if Zarley had suffered a lot of concussions during his career, she told me that her brother almost never got in fights. He had won sportsmanlike conduct awards all his career and always said, "You don't win hockey games in the penalty box." She told me that while Zarley did sustain a few concussions, he was exposed to a fraction of the brain trauma that an NHL enforcer like Todd Ewen would experience.

Ewen's job was to slam opposing players into the boards, and he got into more than 150 fights during his career.[17] So Zarley Zalapski, the guy who rarely fought, had some tau in his brain. Todd "the Animal" Ewen, the enforcer whose job was to get his brains knocked out, had none. How is that possible?

Time for some speculating and prognosticating. Since, according to Kyla, Dr. Hazrati always sends samples of the brains she examines to three independent labs, and since she examined Todd Ewen's brain, we can assume that three other labs have looked at his brain. There are only so many neuropathology labs in North America with experience in looking for CTE, and one of them is at BU. So it's possible that BU has examined Todd Ewen's brain. Heck, given their love of the spotlight and interest in proving that pro athletes are all destined to develop CTE, the people at BU were probably dying to look at his brain under a microscope and announce to the world that he had CTE.

I suspect we'll hear from BU about Ewen one way or the other, because the difference between his brain and Zarley's puts its core theory in serious jeopardy. Add to that the fact that there have already been cases where CTE has been found in people with no history of head trauma, and the theoretical foundation for BU's claims—dose-response and the idea that head trauma inevitably leads to CTE—looks about as sturdy as a house of cards.[18]

I don't know if BU has seen Todd Ewen's brain or if it ever will. But if it releases a statement about it one day, you can look at it with the same skepticism that a lot of scientists have expressed to us privately but won't talk about on the record.

THE TRIUMPH OF JUNK SCIENCE

Extraordinary claims require extraordinary evidence.

—CARL SAGAN, ASTRONOMER

CHAPTER 6 PLAYBOOK

- The selection bias that makes the infamous "110 out of 111 brains" finding worthless

- The incomplete, BU-influenced diagnostic and staging guidelines for CTE

- Why the "subconcussive impact" isn't scientific

- How failure to control for other factors invalidates much of CTE research

- There is no such thing as stage I CTE

Author's Note: I'm not a scientist, so my understanding of this material, such as it is, has only been possible because of the help of some brilliant people, including Dr. Peter Cummings, Dr. Joseph Maroon, Dr. Micky Collins, Dr. Mark Lovell, Dr. Rudy Castellani, Dr. Kristen Willeumier, Dr. Kevin Guskiewicz, Dr. Julian Bailes, and others I've probably forgotten. Thank you for your service.

LONG BEFORE I HAD THE IDEA to write this book, I had my doubts about the conventional wisdom about head injury and CTE. It all seemed designed to play on people's fears about their kids and brain injury and built on distrust of the NFL. But plenty of revolutions fail to get started because everybody thinks he or she is the only one who sees what he or she sees. When we think we're alone, we don't speak up. I thought I was the only one who saw what was really going on, and then I read Dr. Cummings's *Yahoo!* piece.

Suddenly, I had an ally, or a possible ally, at least. Then I saw this down near the end of the op-ed: "Editor's Note: *Yahoo! Sports* reached out to Boston University to offer Dr. Ann McKee, director of the Boston University CTE Center, a platform to reply to the points specifically raised in this op-ed. Boston University did not provide an answer."

Of course it didn't! As I think I've shown in the first two chapters of this section, BU has a vested interest in blocking inquiry and keeping a monopoly on as much of the data on CTE as possible. Responding to Dr. Cummings's editorial would have validated it and forced BU to answer questions that it can't answer. When I saw that, I thought someone needed to get the word out about all this in a way that nonscientists can understand. That became this book.

At the heart of the debate over CTE is the quality of the science. Science is everything here because that's the only way we know if there's really a connection between contact sports and neurodegenerative disease. And despite everything you might have read and everything that BU, the Concussion Legacy Foundation, and the *New York Times* have been trying to jam down your throat, the reality is this:

*The science saying that playing football
causes CTE is very, very shaky.*

I know some people are going to say that I'm shilling for the National Football League. Not true. I'm not an NFL employee. I don't work for ESPN anymore, either. I'm saying this because I believe it, and I believe it because I've lived it as a player, a coach, and a parent. I've been walked through the science by some of the best minds in the field, and the current story doesn't pass the smell test.

According to the current theory, repeated less violent hits to the head—*subconcussive impacts*—are what really cause dangerous changes to the brain over years. And maybe if you're talking about professional soccer players heading away corner kicks hundreds of times in a single season, I could buy the idea that there's some risk. But since there's no g-force threshold for subconcussive impacts; in theory *any* impact could qualify as one. The average g-force delivered to the brain by a vigorous pillow fight is about 20 g's.[1] Does that mean there are millions of middle school kids who had pillow fights with their siblings every night during summer vacation walking around with neurocognitive damage? Should we ban pillow fights? And what about jumping on trampolines? Should we ban trampolines?

You can see how quickly this becomes silly. It's time to shed a light on the junk science that's fueling the sensationalism, the fear, the bad policy proposals, and the suppression of opinions that don't agree with the stereotype. But before I begin, a few things. First of all, I'm going to run the claims I make through the filter of good science: avoiding bias; using controls; making claims based on causation, not correlation; and having work replicated by independent researchers before treating it as definitive.

Second, I'm not saying that every bit of science in this area is bad or that it can't teach us something. I'm also not saying that it's great to keep taking hits to the head or that we should ignore the problems some athletes are having. But let's do good work and figure out what's really going on. Why do some guys play football for thirty years and live to ninety in pretty good shape while other guys aren't as fortunate? Are there genetic and lifestyle factors involved? We don't know, and that's the point.

The more data we collect, the better we'll understand CTE, head injuries, neurodegenerative disease, and how to keep adult and youth athletes safe. But when someone does sloppy, biased science, slaps a vague disclaimer where he or she knows it won't be read, releases it to the world through the news media, and then puts the conclusion in a vault and says, "This is fact," important questions don't get asked. Money goes to people serving their own agendas, not to quality research. Laws get passed based on hysteria, political pressure, and bad data. We and our kids deserve better.

Third, I'm not alone in this. An op-ed published in the *Minneapolis Star Tribune* in February of 2018 contained the names of twenty-six of the top names in the fields of neuroscience, neuropathology, neuropsychology, and more specialties than I can shake a stick at.[2] All were calling for more careful, conclusive science before we start talking about banning youth football. This is a hot topic that generates strong reactions. But it's time to stop retreating from those reactions and look at this head-on.

I'm going to talk about each of the major weak points behind the current science surrounding CTE. In some cases I'll talk about an important piece of research that either falls apart on closer inspection or contradicts the widely known conclusions. Again, I'm not a scientist, so I'll rely heavily on the words of the real scientists who've guided me. And if you want a more definitive analysis of the science written by experts, visit www.brainwashedbook.com.

SKEWED DIAGNOSTIC GUIDELINES

BEFORE YOU CAN SAY THAT you've found something, you have to know what you're looking for. In medicine, diagnostic criteria are what tell scientists what they're looking at. But those criteria don't just happen; people decide what they are based, in theory, on research. But if you can control the diagnostic criteria, you can control the conversation.

The criteria for diagnosing CTE were determined by a consensus panel of experts that convened in 2015, but the results were cherry-picked by BU. I'll let Dr. Cummings have the floor for this topic. "The 'consensus panel diagnostic criteria'—which sounds very formidable and set in stone but is neither—established in 2015 were supposed to be preliminary, with the idea that additional meetings would be scheduled to refine the concept," he says. "To date, one subsequent meeting has been held, but the results have not been published in two years since.

"The lesion said to be 'diagnostic' of CTE was the collection of tau in neurons and astrocytes around blood vessels located at the depth of the *cortical sulcus* in the brain—the folds of the brain," he goes on. "However, this criterion was developed using ten handpicked stage III and stage IV cases from BU's files. No stage I or stage II cases were examined, which boggles my mind. If you are trying to develop a diagnostic criteria for a disease, wouldn't you want to see the full spectrum of the disease from the least severe to the most severe cases?

"What's also troubling is that none of the historical boxing cases or any of the Omalu cases—both of which differ in their diagnostic criteria from BU's cases, though all are labeled as CTE—were included in the process," Dr. Cummings concludes. "To really establish a consensus diagnosis, cases should be from a wide range of exposures and span the full spectrum of the disease. Cases should also be from multiple centers in multiple countries. I'd like to see experts from Europe, Australia, and Canada bring their cases to one neutral institution so we really start the process of figuring this out. Right now, CTE is CTE because BU says it is."

If that seems sketchy, Dr. Cummings agrees with you. "The only thing accomplished at this meeting in 2015 was the determination that these perivascular tau accumulations could be used as a preliminary finding to diagnose CTE as a unique tau disease," he says. "The consensus panel did not evaluate the concept of staging or the relationship between the pathology in the brain and clinical symptoms. This is important because the concept of staging has not been validated by the independent scientific community.

"This makes it hard to replicate work, and without accepted staging criteria, correlation between pathological findings and clinical symptoms is not possible," he continues. "The staging of CTE should be used with extreme caution because the concept is only based on one center's interpretation of the data, not the opinion of a multidisciplinary group that has evaluated all phases of the disease from least to most severe.

"This process of validating staging has been performed many times in all other common neurodegenerative diseases such as Alzheimer's and Parkinson's," Dr. Cummings concludes. "In one of the most recent Alzheimer's consensus meetings, the findings of the various expert panels were distributed to the scientific community on a website so other experts could comment on the proposed findings. In the end, these comments were taken into consideration in developing the various Alzheimer's staging criteria. That's transparency. There is no transparency in the BU work."

Dr. Cummings also told me that one of the problems with CTE is that the reported symptoms overlap with every other neuropsychological and neurodegenerative disease known to man. There is nothing unique about it, he said—no unique clinical feature separating CTE from any other disorder. If you're depressed or have anxiety, and you ever played football, voilà! CTE must be the cause. But all of these CTE-related symptoms are associated with disorders common to the general male population:

- 30.6 percent of men will report an episode of depression in their lifetimes, and men eighty-five and older have the highest rate of suicide among men.[3]

- One in eight men is diagnosed with a mental illness. Depressive disorders are the second-leading cause of living with disability in the United States and Canada. Suicidal ideation is also very common among males.[4]

- Suicide is the second-leading cause of death among males ages ten to twenty-four; 8.8 percent of males eighteen to twenty-four have had suicidal ideation; and by age twenty-nine, 57.3 percent of men had self-reported suicidal ideation at least once.[5]

As Dr. Cummings tells me, with these numbers and the abundance of other risk factors, it's very difficult to attribute these symptoms to CTE alone. But according to BU, if you have ever played football and are depressed or anxious, football outweighs all other factors. Dr. Cummings says, "The careless way the CTE cases where there is a coinciding neurodegenerative disease are reported in the literature can easily lead readers to believe that CTE is the sole cause of the disease. In the consensus paper orchestrated by BU, the recommendations state that there are to be exclusions to the sole diagnosis of CTE. In other words, if there are changes consistent with other neurodegenerative diseases, the guidelines *exclude* CTE as a single diagnosis.

"But this isn't the way these cases are reported," he continues. "The papers indicate which CTE cases have other diseases like Alzheimer's, but the results are written to make a reader believe that CTE is the sole cause of the underlying cognitive symptoms. The role these other diseases may play is neglected. Some people interpret this as suggesting that football *causes* the coinciding neurodegenerative disease. The possible presence of CTE is trumping all other findings."

I don't think there's much else to say.

NO REPLICATION

As FAR AS I OR any of the scientists consulted for this book know, none of the research published by Dr. McKee, the Concussion Legacy Foundation, or the BU CTE Center has been replicated by other researchers—meaning that, using the same samples, controls, and methods, no independent researchers have been able to duplicate their results. That's damning.

In fact, there are plenty of researchers who would argue that science without replication is *not* science. Writing in *Wired*, Megan Meyer nails it: "Too often, exploratory studies are designed and reported to the public as cutting-edge and novel, yet in the same breath positioned as fact. When this happens, fewer scientists (and journalists) consider whether the results are clinically relevant, how the results align with similar research, or whether the methods were even appropriate. In other words, context gets cut from the conversation."[6]

That casts a lot of doubt on BU-related work all by itself. What casts even more is that when independent researchers have done work that's similar to Dr. McKee's research—sort of *quasi*-replications—their results have been very different. Remember the study everyone went crazy over, where 110 out of 111 football player brains were found to have CTE? Well, in 2016 some Canadian neuropathologists led by Dr. Shawna Noy examined 111 brains, collected over eighteen months from people ages eighteen to sixty, for signs of the telltale tau pattern. According to McKee's own staging system, they found signs of CTE in just 4.5 percent of the brains. But the researchers realized that there is no floor to stage I CTE. In theory, you can have it if you have a single focus of tau in your brain that never causes any symptoms. When they expanded their criteria, suddenly 35.1 percent of the brains showed some level of CTE.

But here's the rub. "The major predictor of CTE pathology in these cases was either a previous head injury, like a bicycle crash, fall, motor vehicle accident, or assault in conjunction with substance abuse," Dr. Cummings says. "Only two individuals with CTE-like lesions had exposure to contact sports—a wrestler and an amateur boxer. A single high school football player in the study had no CTE changes. With this many nonathletes showing CTE changes, it proves that repetitive hits are not the sole cause of CTE."

In other words, the researchers showed that tau in the brain could occur in people who were not taking constant hits to the head. They wrote, "We conclude that CTE-like findings are not confined to professional athletes; the risk factors of head injury and substance abuse are similar in the routine population."[7]

That research undermines the idea that if you have tau in your brain, you've either had to have played contact sports or been in the military. In fact, it suggests that people like you, who probably haven't played in the NFL, could get CTE from a bike accident or a fight. You don't need to be a football player to get it. In that context, the 2017 "110 out of 111 football players have CTE" paper is embarrassing for BU. So let's talk about that paper right now.

SELECTION BIAS

THE 2017 BOSTON UNIVERSITY STUDY caught all the headlines (and scared millions of people) by shouting that 110 out of 111 brains from former football player had symptoms of CTE.[8] It's still cited right now in stories. But the work was deeply flawed, a fact that didn't make the news. I could go on for a while about all the flaws, but let's focus on the blunder that makes this study's results worthless for proving anything: selection bias.

Good science means you select the samples you study randomly. Otherwise, you could just cherry-pick the samples you look at based on what you're trying to prove. That's selection bias. The 2017 study looked at the brains of 202 former football players, and of the 111 that came from former NFL players, they found CTE in 99 percent. But there are several big problems with this. First of all, this study only looked at brains from former players whose families had reported that they had experienced severe mood, behavior, or cognitive problems. There should have been a control group of former NFL players who had *not* experienced any of those problems. I could've helped recruit because I've known hundreds and hundreds of ex-players who are doing just fine. But there was no control group.

That's a little like walking into an Alzheimer's disease brain bank, testing the brains for Alzheimer's, and then saying, "Yes, 99 percent have Alzheimer's disease!" That tells you nothing about the cause or the risk of me or you getting Alzheimer's if we play football.

In other words, if you study people you already have reason to believe are sick, don't be surprised when you find that they're sick. But BU announced the findings with a tiny disclaimer at the end of the paper that obviously no one would pay attention to. But hardly anyone knows about the other huge selection problem.

Out of the 110 NFL players who were found to have the distinctive tau pattern in their brains, fifteen were at stage I or stage II, and those players' average age when they died was forty-four. The other 95 players had stage III or stage IV CTE, and their average age at death was seventy-one. But as the research I just talked about suggests, it may be normal for us to develop tauopathy in our brains as we age even if we don't have any cognitive problems.[9] If that's true, then of course the older guys had more tau in their brains. You probably have tau in your brain, even if you've never taken a hit to the head.

"How can we even draw a conclusion that football caused the tau deposition when we have no information regarding family history of dementia or previous head injury?" Dr. Cummings asks. "As Noy showed us, you don't need to play football to have CTE. Any of these 110 players ever crash a bike or a car? Fall down stairs? We don't know, and because of that and the selection bias, it's impossible to draw any firm conclusion from this paper."

One more example of bias in this field is that nobody seems to be studying women's brains. Why not? It's not because women don't play sports, and it's sure not because they don't suffer head trauma. A 2017 study found that women's soccer has the highest per capita rate of concussion and traumatic brain injury of any sport.[10]

It's not because girls don't play football, either. USA Football estimated that twenty-five thousand girls played youth tackle football in 2015,[11] and there are at least two all-girl leagues dedicated to tackle football today.[12] How can you claim your science is settled when you've excluded half the population? If we don't study female brains in relation to CTE, how can we draw any firm conclusions? It doesn't make sense. Maybe there's just less fame and fortune in studying female sports.

UNRELIABLE INTERVIEWS WITH LOVED ONES

ANOTHER BIG FLAW IS THAT many studies that try to associate mood, behavior, or cognitive problems with physical symptoms of CTE do so by relying on "informant reports"—surveys of next of kin about the deceased, in which people are asked about whether their son, husband, or brother ever showed neuropsychiatric symptoms like rage, depression, or suicidal thoughts.

It's easy to see the problems with this. The reliability of informant reporting is considered questionable when the family member is talking about a living person he or she might see every day. Now ask him or her to describe behavior that might have taken place ten years earlier, and it's not hard to see how a fuzzy memory or leading questions could make reports unreliable.

A more recent study with Dr. McKee's name attached to it claimed that the earlier the age at which children were exposed to youth tackle football, the more likely they were to experience mood, behavioral, and cognitive disorders as adults. It was widely reported on and guaranteed to terrify parents, and it relied on informant reports as well as an ad hoc "reliability scale" used to assess the quality of those reports.

Meanwhile, two similar studies used what Dr. Cummings calls "validated and objective, not subjective, neuropsychiatric tests," instead of family member reports, to diagnose mood, behavioral, or cognitive problems. Those studies found no association between the age of first exposure to tackle football and long-term neurocognitive problems like anger or impulsive behavior.[13] In other words, when you use objective data, not subjective reporting, the effect seems to disappear.

What a surprise. I'll come back to this study again, by the way.

MOVING THE GOALPOSTS

ON JANUARY 18, 2018, another frightening story dropped, courtesy of BU: it isn't concussions but subconcussive impacts (SCI) that are the real cause of CTE. What made this story so powerful was that it claimed that over a period of years, repeated hits to the head that didn't cause any concussion-like symptoms would still lead to changes in the brain's white matter and, eventually, to CTE. In other words, everything from heading a soccer ball to a hard slide into second base in Little League could add up to neurocognitive disease given enough time.

The idea of invisible brain injuries slowly adding up over time to produce long-term damage in children is enough to make any parent freak out. And as I've made clear, I'm not encouraging kids to go out and take repeated hard knocks to the head. We want to prevent that when we can and respond quickly and properly when it happens. I'm not saying that we should ignore this.

But this new focus on SCI looks a lot like moving the goalposts. Even though there's a lot we still don't know, concussion science is better than ever before. We now know there are six distinct kinds of concussion, and we know how to treat them so that in the vast majority of cases, kids and adults will recover fully and be back playing their sports with no long-term consequences. So, less able to spread the fear of concussions, the good folks at BU decided to go all in on SCI as their new bogeyman. (Any day now, I expect to see the Concussion Legacy Foundation change its name to the Subconcussion Legacy Foundation.)

As I alluded to earlier, the big problem with the SCI is that because there's no g-force threshold for it, it's not scientific. Science is about measuring and defining. When he was writing his paper on special relativity, Einstein didn't get to say that the speed of light was just "superfast." There's a number. Even concussion, a syndrome of symptoms that can't be measured in a lab or seen with imaging, has a definition. But an SCI is literally any hit to the head that doesn't cause a concussion!

Quick, take this book and hit yourself on the forehead with it (not too hard, please). Congratulations! You just sustained an SCI.

People are quick to point out a couple of studies that show white matter changes in the brains of football players with no concussive symptoms to support the idea that SCIs cause brain damage. But the science is very preliminary and much of it hasn't been defined yet, so jumping to conclusions—as BU and the media have done—isn't warranted. Even studies that have found neurological changes in the brain are based on small sample sizes and filled with qualifiers.

One late 2017 study that found white matter changes in the brains of nonconcussed players after a single season of high school football also included cautious statements from the authors warning that it was a pilot study, that it didn't include controls, and that the players' brains might return to normal with rest.[14] Another, which showed that visual motor function changed in NCAA football players who sustained SCIs, also said that after three weeks, the players' vision was back to normal.[15]

Even one of the most cited studies in the field, from Steven Broglio, assistant professor of kinesiology and director of the Neurotrauma
Research Laboratory at the University of Michigan, comes with qualifiers and disclaimers from Broglio himself. In an article by Lindsey
Barton Straus at MomsTEAM, Broglio makes it clear that the science
is far from settled on this:

> "The last thing we want is for people to panic. Just
> because you've had a concussion does not mean your brain
> will age more quickly or you'll get Alzheimer's," Broglio
> was quick to emphasize. "We are only proposing how
> being hit in the head may lead to these other conditions,
> but we don't know how it all goes together just yet."

> Broglio stressed that the influence of various lifestyle and
> environmental factors, such as smoking, alcohol consump-
> tion, physical exercise, family history (genetics), whether
> or not a concussed athlete "exercises" their brain, and even
> how dense the gray matter in a person's brain is, which
> gives them greater "cognitive reserve" to draw upon may
> also impact the brain's aging process, and that "concussion
> may only be one small factor."

> In addition, he said, this line of research is still in its in-
> fancy. "It's not entirely clear," Broglio told the *Kalamazoo
> News*, "if and how the brains of young athletes are affected
> by the sports they play."[16]

As Dr. Cummings tells me, the same white matter changes seen
in these football players are also seen in people with learning disabilities, obesity, diabetes, low socioeconomic status, and ADHD and also

in endurance athletes. Yes, when you run a marathon. Nothing here is settled by any means.

Other researchers are more blunt about the concept of the SCI: it's unclear and poorly defined, and the science is in its infancy. A paper from March 2018 concludes that studies on the effects of football and subconcussive trauma on the brain are filled with sources of bias, including improper control of errors and inappropriate controls.[17] Another, also from 2018, concluded that "there was insufficient to weak evidence for the relationship between repetitive hits to the head and deterioration in neurocognitive performance" and "insufficient evidence was presented to determine a minimal injury threshold for repetitive hits to the head."[18]

Plus, there's the UK study from 2016 that looked at thirty-two young professional soccer players over a five-year period to see if they had neurocognitive damage from heading the ball. The conclusion: "These longitudinal prospective data indicate no significant neurological, structural brain imaging or neuropsychological change among a sample of young elite professional footballers over the first 5 years of their professional career."[19]

Again, I'm not saying we don't need to take the possible effects of SCI seriously, especially when we're talking about kids. But we shouldn't overreact to science that's barely out of the crib, either. Dr. Micky Collins, one of the country's foremost experts on concussions, agrees: "[Subconcussion] is not a scientific concept because it hasn't been studied scientifically. So it's something that creates a lot of undue fear. It's a concept that I think would scare the hell out of anyone because of the idea of subconcussive blows to the head. Now, with that being said, absence of proof doesn't mean proof of absence. We do need to be measured in how we talk about this. We need to look at this scientifically. What we need to do is really good prospective, long-term research.

"That research just hasn't been done," Collins continues. "I take issue with creating constructs without having science to support those constructs. I do understand both sides of it. I could go on and on about the benefit of sports for kids, but we also don't want to put kids at risk for some insidious problem that's going to occur down the road. So let's look at this in a balanced way. Let's look at this in a scientific way. Let's put the right research in place to answer these questions before we make some statements that don't have any scientific merit."

NOT CONTROLLING FOR OTHER FACTORS

As I've said, Mike Webster was the first football player allegedly found with CTE. But as we know from published accounts, Webby's behavior in the years before his death was severely disturbed. He had a documented history of severe mental illness on both sides of his family and had been an alleged heavy steroid user early in his career. Both of those factors could have been responsible for the changes in his behavior, but you never read about them in any of the research.

That's typical with CTE. Researchers are quick to draw conclusions without accounting for (or at least revealing) that there are other factors that could cause or increase the likelihood of the results they claim are due to CTE. For example, there have been several studies claiming that kids did worse on cognitive tests after playing football or soccer. But in most of them, there's no mention of controlling for things like learning disabilities. I had a reading disability when I was a kid, and that definitely could have affected my performance on some of these assessments. But rarely, if ever, do you read about that.

The literature is full of this problem. One of the worst offenders was the paper I mentioned before—the one that claimed that the earlier a kid was exposed to contact football, the greater his chances of developing a mood, behavior, or cognitive disorder later in life.[20] Damning stuff, right?

Not if you look closer. According to Dr. Cummings, this study was riddled with flaws. "There was a negligible difference in reported neuropsychiatric symptoms between the CTE-negative and CTE-positive individuals," he says. "As the authors suggest, the reported symptoms might not be specific to CTE; in fact, they may not be related to playing football at all. There are several potential confounding factors left unaccounted for, each of which increases the risk of developing neuropsychiatric symptoms, including childhood psychosocial and developmental factors and illicit drug use. Furthermore, cardiovascular risk factors were significantly higher in the group that had its first exposure to youth football before age twelve. That alone could account for the neurocognitive symptoms.

"More interestingly," Dr. Cummings continues, "there was no relationship between the age of first exposure and the severity of CTE. In fact, the CTE-negative group started playing football at a younger age than the CTE-positive group. If we add up the substantial flaws in this study, the idea of 'dose-response' loses all validity."

Then there's this easy-to-miss line in the study: "Asymptomatic participants were not part of analyses examining age of symptom onset." Wait a second. You're claiming that youth football increases the risk of psychological symptoms later in life, but you're not factoring in the adults who had *no* symptoms when you calculate how common this is? Talk about skewing the results! Without looking at asymptomatic people, we have no idea how many kids exposed to youth football would develop symptoms anyway. Again, that's a sampling bias. You can't generalize this finding to the youth football population because you're only looking at people with symptoms. What percentage of players developed symptoms? We don't know. We only know the age of symptom onset of people who had symptoms, not members of youth football teams in general. As far as estimating the risks of youth football, this data is meaningless.

Also, the paper says, "In this sample of deceased tackle football players, younger age of exposure to tackle football was not associated with CTE pathological severity." Then why does a diagnosis of CTE even matter?

But the sloppiest part of this study is that the researchers did not control for the many, many other factors that could have caused these men to experience mood and behavioral disorders later in life. Dr. Cummings says, "All this paper says is this: in a small subgroup of football players, there was a weak association between playing football before the age of twelve and the age of onset of emotional and behavioral issues. However, we have no idea of the histories of these kids. Did they come from different socioeconomic backgrounds? How many were from divorced families or single-parent homes? How many experienced the divorce or death of a parent? How many had legal issues? How many had what would now be classified as learning disabilities? How many had overbearing parents pushing them too hard or putting pressure on them that the only way to get out of their environment was a football scholarship or the NFL?

"These life stressors are all strongly associated with development of psychiatric issues in adulthood, but this paper controls for none of them," he continues.[21] "Forty percent of kids who play youth tackle football are from the bottom two US income groups,[22] and kids from this disadvantaged background are known to have mood and behavioral issues,[23] especially depression.[24] Not controlling for that is an inexcusable oversight.

"Is this paper telling me that even if a kid is exposed to divorce, poverty, child-welfare services, substance abuse or any other significant risk factor for depression, if he ever played football, that's the only factor causing his symptoms as an adult? Really?" Dr. Cummings concludes. "Nothing else matters in this person's life other than exposure to football when he was a kid? So if we eliminate football, his later neurocognitive problems will disappear, and any diseases will be cured? It's ridiculous."

Between this study and the Todd Ewen–Zarley Zalapski comparison, I think we can lay the "dose-response" idea to rest as another example of sloppy science, too.

IS THERE EVEN A STAGE I CTE?

IF WE'RE GOING TO PUT dose-response six feet under, then another accepted idea needs to be put down, too, which is the idea that stage I CTE is a real disease. We've talked about the sketchy process used to come up with the diagnostic criteria and staging for CTE. Well, because BU controlled the criteria, they've created a situation where someone who has a single deposit of tau near the blood vessels in the folds of the brain automatically has stage I of the disease. Case closed.

But to me and Dr. Cummings, the whole thing looks like a rigged game—one intended to make CTE look like an epidemic.

Dr. Cummings hit back hard against the idea of diagnosing CTE based on a single microscopic tangle of tau. "I have a hard time grasping the idea that one single perivascular collection of tau can result in this vague shopping list of disorders," he says. "Especially when people can have their brains riddled with tau as part of age-related changes and have no symptoms. So, a single microscopic focus is allegedly deadly and may lead to suicide, yet late-stage CTE cases with heavier tau loads can live longer and not commit suicide? How does that happen if tau is causing all this anxiety and depression? Shouldn't suicide rates should go up as tau depositions increase?"

One response to that argument is that neuropathologists can diagnose other diseases based on a single lesion, so why not CTE? But Dr. Cummings says that's not true and uses the example of Lewy body disease, a well-known form of dementia caused by protein deposits called—you guessed it—Lewy bodies, as an example.

"Dr. McKee has argued that she can use a single focus of tau because in neuropathology 'we' can diagnosis Lewy body disease based on a single Lewy body," he says. "That's not true. I would never diagnose Lewy body disease based only on the presence of a single Lewy body. There is a well-established, internationally verified Lewy body score, and it has to be in the correct clinical setting—the neuropathology has to be associated with specific clinical symptoms unique to Lewy body disease. The current preliminary diagnosis criteria of CTE don't permit an asymptomatic, preclinical phase of the disease where we say 'possible CTE' or 'probable CTE.'"

But Dr. Cummings doesn't stop there. He makes a claim that should stop a lot of researchers and journalists in their tracks: *there may be no such thing as a stage I lesion.* "Stage I and stage II are not recognized diagnoses," he says. "None of the stages are. All we can say with even a glimmer of scientific certainty is that the preliminary diagnostic criteria describe the CTE lesion as a collection of tau around a blood vessel at the depth of the sulcus. That's it. And even that is based on ten cherry-picked cases. BU is using staging as though it's gospel, and we, as scientists, are to take their word for it? I don't think so."

The authors of the Noy paper, Dr. Cummings goes on, said that they had difficulty using the BU staging scheme and voiced a concern that tiny abnormalities might not have any clinical significance.[25] "They share my opinion that there should be a lower limit to the staging criteria," he says. "Without that, stage I has no relevance pathologically. In her research, when Noy applied BU's staging criteria with no lower limit, the number of cases with mild CTE increased by a factor of nine. That's a huge difference, and it highlights a major problem with the widespread diagnosis of CTE that we're hearing about today."

Dr. Cummings is a triple-board-certified pathologist who's seen thousands of brains, so when his "spider sense" tells him that someone in his field is up to something suspicious, I take it very seriously. The suspicious activity: is BU is effectively manufacturing a CTE diagnosis out of thin air?

"In my opinion, stage I is close to a normal brain," he says. "One single focus of tau and no neuronal loss? That's not diagnostic of anything. Trying to correlate a single focus of tau with a clinical symptom is impossible, especially when you're telling me you can correlate it with symptoms that are common in the general public, like anxiety. The most you could credibly argue is that stage I is 'clinically silent' or represents an asymptomatic phase of the disease," he goes on. "But BU hasn't given us any good evidence for dose-response or disease progression, so that early stage might remain clinically silent, and therefore clinically irrelevant, for a person's entire life."

Dr. Cummings is not alone. As we'll see in a bit, a lot of other well-qualified neuropathologists outside of BU can't seem to find CTE in some cases either.

LABORATORY ARTIFACTS

You're probably not going to read about this one anywhere else, but it's important. The research that BU conducts is done on slides containing thin slices of tissue from different sections of the brain. To be able to see the brain's neurological structures, neuropathologists have to stain these slides, just like you might remember staining slides in high school biology. Well, the process of staining and slide preparation can actually create artifacts—an alteration in tissue caused by an outside factor. That, says Dr. Castellani, can fool researchers into thinking nothing is something.

"Keep in mind that these perivascular lesions are man-made," he says. "They are produced by the reagents that the technicians add to the tissue. That's another nuance that people don't understand. The CTE with these tau stains is not independent evidence of head trauma, such as, for example, a brain contusion. Trauma has to be inferred from information provided. The tau stains are nothing more than reagents changing colors. You also have many different antibodies that react with various parts of the tau molecule; those antibodies have certain dilutions; we treat the tissues with chemical reagents to enhance the reactivity; we add polymers to amplify the signal beyond what's actually there. And you always have to consider artifacts: colors changing that look like CTE but are not real because of a problem with the procedure. You also have to look at many controls of all ages.

"Assuming that one lesion is actually there, and it's not an artifact of the procedure or manipulation of the laboratory procedure, to presume that means the person had a progressive degenerative brain disease is just the height of ridiculousness," he continues. "If you're given to that paradigm, you might look at that one focus and say that it would spread from region to region, and had the patient lived another ten years, he would have suffered behavioral problems followed by dementia. It's science fiction."

HASTY CONCLUSIONS

Do you know how scientists identified the symptoms of Alzheimer's disease and determined how to diagnose it? Many consensus panels made up of experts from different fields collaborated to find answers. In one consensus group, a total of twenty-four National Institute of Aging centers followed 1,094 patients for years and collected information regarding clinical symptoms, neuropsychological symptoms, and finally, neuropathological signs in their brains after death. Multiple groups with international representation then set out to refine the diagnostic criteria, including asymptomatic phases and preclinical phases. Their findings were posted for public comment, and comments were taken into consideration and integrated into the criteria by the committee.

Also, the diagnostic criteria for Alzheimer's use both clinical features and neuropathological findings to categorize diagnoses as "unlikely," "possible," "probable," and "definite." In other words, the entire process was painstaking, collaborative, and transparent, and it allowed for uncertainty. None of that same caution is part of the rush to declare CTE the "football plague." Instead, the work is hasty, conclusions are broad and seemingly designed to draw an emotional reaction, and the process is largely concealed from the public and independent scientists.

CORRELATION DOESN'T EQUAL CAUSATION

WHEN YOU BOIL ALL THIS DOWN, what you get is a lot of correlation but no causation. In other words, a lot of stuff that goes together but with little good evidence that A causes B. That matters because without knowing what causes a problem, we can't take steps to prevent it or repair it. For example, there is no neuropsychiatric profile for people with the physical signs of CTE, so we have no idea how a person with CTE is supposed to behave. We have traits that BU has told us are associated with CTE, like impulsive behavior, mood swings, depression, and suicidal thoughts, but not all people who have tau in their brains also had those problems. Also, some people who do have those problems have never had any brain trauma because other factors can cause those troubles, from drug use to mental illness.

Also, BU is taking small sample sizes of a few dozen brains and then extrapolating those results to the entire population of football players at every level. That's ridiculous. What we really need are *prospective* studies, long-term projects that follow hundreds or even thousands of people from different backgrounds—football players, players from other sports, and people who've never lifted a lacrosse stick in anger—over decades, monitoring their health and behavior and doing periodic cognitive screenings and MRIs. Seeing how those people's brains change over time, while taking their backgrounds, family histories, medical histories and lifestyles into account, would give us some conclusive scientific results. But those studies are very costly, and that kind of work hasn't been done yet. It needs to be.

I understand why people don't want to wait for it, though. Nobody wants to put kids in harm's way if there's any risk of them getting brain damage from playing football. I get the concern and fear. But rather than jump to conclusions and react rashly, let's do good research while we work to make all sports safer. As I'll show in the next section, it can be done and is being done.

However, I'd be remiss if I didn't give some love to a project called DIAGNOSE CTE, which stands for Diagnostics, Imaging, And Genetics Network for the Objective Study and Evaluation of Chronic Traumatic Encephalopathy. DIAGNOSE CTE is a study funded by the National Institute of Neurological Disorders and Stroke of the National Institutes of Health that proposes to follow men ages forty-five to seventy-four—including both football players and men who have never played sports or suffered a brain injury—for seven years. Among other goals, the study will look for biomarkers that could identify CTE in the living, follow the progression of CTE in men who may have it, and attempt to develop clearer criteria for clinical diagnosis of CTE— in other words, diagnosing it based on mood or cognitive problems.

BU is involved with DIAGNOSE CTE, which raises some red flags. But so are multiple other centers in Arizona, New York, and Las Vegas. And while we'll have to watch closely to make sure the work avoids the issues and traps we've talked about, it's a step in the right direction and worth acknowledging here.

But since the results of DIAGNOSE CTE are years away, let me give the last word on the state of CTE research to Dr. Gary Solomon, who wrote the incredible overview of the state of CTE research I talked about back in chapter 3. The powerful conclusion to his paper says it all:

The logic posited by the Boston Group about the etiology of CTE appears to be: 1) mTBI and/or subconcussion causes p-tau deposition at the depths of the sulci, 2) the p-tau deposition then causes neurocognitive, mood, and neurobehavioral symptoms, with age-related patterns of symptomatology reported, 3) p-tau then spreads, causing: a) additional neurocognitive, mood, and neurobehavioral symptoms, and b) a cascade of other neuropathological changes...and 4) upon autopsy, if p-tau is found in any amount at the depths of the sulci, then: a) this fulfills the necessary and sufficient criterion for a diagnosis of CTE, b) explains/ causes the presence of comorbid neuropathology and overrides their relevance, and c) is conclusive, causative proof of the etiology of the neurocognitive, mood, and neurobehavioral symptoms. I would maintain that at the present time, conclusive scientific evidence is absent for all four tenets.

Some CTE clinicians and neuroscientists seemed to have adopted Freudian-type thinking..."If you don't agree with our interpretation of our findings, then you are in denial." This position can be dangerous. It does not reflect all the evidence to date, carries significant public health risks, and does not promote the development of balanced empirical science. The current thinking among some clinicians and neuroscientists seems to be that sport-related concussions and/or subconcussive impacts directly cause suicide, psychiatric illness, cognitive disorders, and/or degenerative disease, and that the detection of postmortem p-tau is causal proof of the ante mortem cognitive, mood, impulse dyscontrol, and neurobehavioral changes seen in contact/ collision sports athletes. However, it is not certain that

p-tau causes these aberrations, nor is it clear that the
only reason for the presence of the p-tau is concussion or
subconcussive impacts. For purposes of cause and effect
it is necessary to account for genetic, medical, psychiatric,
substance abuse, and biopsychosocial variables that could
be relevant in the short- and long-term neurobehavioral
and neurocognitive outcomes.[26]

In other words, we need better science. If we're not getting it, it's
our responsibility to understand the difference between good science
and bad, and to hold researchers, research institutions, and the media
accountable.

THE INFLAMMATION THEORY OF CTE

Theories cannot claim to be indestructible. They are only the plough which the ploughman uses to draw his furrow and which he has every right to discard for another one, of improved design, after the harvest.

—PAUL SABATIER, CHEMIST

CHAPTER 7 PLAYBOOK

- Evidence suggests that chronic inflammation, not head trauma, causes tau deposits in the brain

- An inflammatory, toxic immune response may be the key mechanism behind CTE

- Treating obesity, which is a proinflammatory state, improves cognitive function and brain health in former athletes

- It may be possible to make the brain resistant to inflammation and damage and to essentially prevent CTE

WHAT'S DRIVING THE COMPETITION for brains and the hysteria over sports is the theory that taking a lot of impacts to the head over a period of years causes progressive brain damage that ends up becoming CTE. The trouble with that theory is that the facts don't back it up. Cases like Todd Ewen's blow this dose-response idea completely out of the water.

There's a genetic factor that makes some people more susceptible to the proteins associated with Alzheimer's disease, but that doesn't explain all the other inconsistencies in the research findings. It also doesn't explain the most damning indictment of the current theory on CTE: the fact that retired NFL players as a group are *healthier* and live *longer* than the general population. If SCI add up to CTE, dementia, rage, disinhibition, and eventual suicide, shouldn't we be reading and seeing stories every day about mentally unstable former NFL and CFL players all over the country? Yet some of these guys played for ten, fifteen, even twenty years and took thousands of hits! What's going on?

Figuring this stuff out, as I've said, is above my pay grade. But it's not above Dr. Joe Maroon's. For years, he's been working not only to better understand brain injury, concussion, and CTE but also to foster better brain health and healing from injury using nonpharmaceutical methods, nutrition, and lifestyle changes. And together with Dr. Cummings, and building on the work of some other visionary experts, Dr. Maroon may have hit on the *real* mechanism behind CTE.

Everybody associated with BU, the loudest voices in the world of CTE research, insist again and again that impacts to the head are directly responsible for both the tau deposits and the damage to brain tissue seen in cases like Aaron Hernandez. But what if the impact was only the first step in a process that causes runaway inflammation in the brain? Everybody wants to blame sports-related impacts for CTE because that seems like common sense, but what if it's inflammation of the brain? After all, we already know that inflammation is involved in most chronic health problems.

"There is a lot of science to support the idea that when you have a head injury, you have an acute inflammatory response," says Dr. Cummings. "If that inflammation isn't treated properly—like in the old days when guys would get concussed and sent right back into the game—it can develop into a chronic inflammatory state and eventually tau deposition in the brain. If you treat and reduce the inflammation early, allow the brain to recover completely before more impacts are sustained, and make the person systemically resistant to inflammation by measures like proper nutrition and maintaining a healthy lean body mass, you get neurorestoration and recovery."

The inflammation theory says that CTE is not the direct result of multiple head injuries but the effect of *mismanaged inflammation* potentially caused not only by impact but by obesity, stress, and alcohol abuse, among other factors. In the case of head impacts, instead of the impact itself leading directly to the characteristic patterns of tau, the impact produces them indirectly by way of runaway inflammation and impaired blood flow in the brain.

The implications of this are huge. If the cause of CTE is not repeated concussions or SCI but instead a combination of improper post-injury care, rest, and rehab that doesn't address the underlying inflammation and proinflammatory conditions like obesity, then head injuries don't have to lead inevitably to CTE. If we treat concussions properly, as Dr. Collins is doing at UPMC, we can keep guys healthy. Just as important, if we can make athletes resistant to neuroinflammation through things like stress control, dietary supplements, and nutrition, maybe we can also make them more resistant to brain trauma.

If it's correct, this theory would potentially make CTE treatable and preventable without forcing professionals to quit playing football and other sports and without forcing parents to pull their kids out of Pop Warner. And if you think this is wishful thinking intended to save football, think again. There's good science to support all of this.

WHAT HAPPENS WHEN YOU GET HIT IN THE HEAD?

A TRAUMATIC BRAIN INJURY IS a lot more complex than "get hit in the head, damage the brain." When a person sustains an impact to the head that delivers a force of more than about 50 g's (though we're not really sure how much force is needed to cause damage), a whole cascade of events occurs in the brain at the microscopic level. In very simplistic terms, the nerve cells in the brain simultaneously release a cascade of neurotransmitters, excrete lots of potassium, start taking in a massive number of calcium ions, and reduce their energy production. As a result, those cells start breaking down glucose to supply energy to the cells. All this chaotic activity damages the microscopic structures of nerve cells and also leads to cell death.

Again, there's a lot more to it than that, but I'm going to let Dr. Maroon explain what happens. "It's like what happens when you get a splinter under your finger," he says. "The finger becomes red hot, tender, and swollen, right? Why does that happen? That's the body's normal immune response to injury, and when you get a concussion, the same things happen. There's a neural inflammatory response. The same kind of cells that lead to inflammation in your finger lead to inflammation in your brain. Normally there's a reparative process, just like in your finger. But if you get hit again before the brain goes into this reparative process, the inflammatory chemicals—cytokines, chemokines—continue to pour out, and your brain becomes like a dry bush in a forest. If it catches on fire, that inflammation can continue uninterrupted and give you progressive neurological symptoms."

The idea that chronic inflammation is the underlying cause behind our worst chronic diseases isn't new. The theory, which is well supported by evidence, says that our modern lifestyle, with processed foods high in sugar and soaring levels of obesity, puts many people's bodies in a constant state of inflammation. Inflammation is a necessary part of the immune system, but your body was never meant to be in an inflammatory state 24/7. When it is, your immune system can attack everything from the good bacteria in your gut to your joints, lead to arterial plaques that cause coronary artery disease, and encourage the growth of cancer cells. Chronic inflammation is bad news.

But in the case of CTE, Dr. Maroon's research shows that a specific kind of inflammatory immune response called *immunoexcitotoxicity* might be the hidden engine behind the degenerative neurological problems we see in some athletes. In a 2011 study, he and Dr. Russell Blaylock found that people who suffer from repeated mild traumatic brain injuries like concussions (as well as people with certain neurodegenerative diseases) experience the release of compounds that can be toxic to the brain, causing progressive nerve damage if left untreated.[1] The two doctors also found that these excitotoxins also cause the tau deposits so commonly associated with CTE and blamed directly on impacts to the head.

Critically, this same immune system reaction can also cause tau deposits in people who have Alzheimer's disease, have certain infections, have been exposed to toxic chemicals, or who use some illegal drugs, especially methamphetamine. In other words, tau in the brain can (and often does) have nothing to do with any kind of hit to the head.

"Having subsequent concussions or repeated blows to the head while you're still symptomatic is one way to get to this situation," says Dr. Cummings. "Another way is to improperly treat the concussion. That sets off that acute inflammatory reaction that is not just a combination of inflammatory cells and proinflammatory chemicals but also neurotransmitters that are excitatory and also toxic to neurons. Both of those processes work together to take you from acute inflammation, which is generally treatable, down the pathway of chronic inflammation, which is like going from a small brush fire to smoldering ashes blowing through the air that catch everything else on fire.

"If you can change the way those chemical mediators affect the tissue, then you can alter that outcome," he continues. "If not, you'll go from injury to acute neuroinflammation to chronic neuroinflammation, and then you can develop tau deposits, amyloid plaques, or deposits of other bad proteins that are your brain cells basically crapping out. If we can shift the body during this period of acute inflammation to a state of neurorestoration and recovery by reducing inflammation and reducing the levels of excitatory neurotransmitters, then we have a chance to decrease recovery time and prevent chronic inflammation."

Amazing. But wait, it gets better! The compounds associated with immunoexcitotoxicity have also been linked to many of the behaviors commonly blamed on CTE, such as panic attacks, aggressive behavior, suicide, obsessive-compulsive disorder, anxiety, and depression.[2] Also, Drs. Blaylock and Maroon found that when there's no underlying disease or the athlete is resistant to this kind of inflammatory immune system overreaction because of genetics, diet, or some other factor, he or she is less likely to suffer effects that look like CTE.

To be clear, we have a theory that may explain CTE and the psychiatric symptoms associated with it but also explains why some football players and other athletes don't get it. We're proceeding carefully, since there hasn't been any research done yet to show that these ideas are correct specifically as it relates to CTE. However, as we move beyond what causes CTE to how to prevent it, the picture gets even clearer and the potential gets more exciting.

THE LINK BETWEEN OBESITY AND CTE

IT TURNS OUT THAT ONE of the major contributory factors in chronic inflammation in the entire body, including the brain, is obesity. We'll talk about the plague of obesity a little later when we look at things that are detrimental to kids' health, but for now let's examine the specific role that obesity plays in creating conditions that can lead to tau in the brain and eventually to CTE.

I spoke about this with Dr. Kristen Willeumier, a UCLA neuroscientist who does a lot of work with current and retired athletes, helping the ones who are experiencing mood or cognitive problems improve the condition of their brains and get back to living healthy, happy lives. She told me that when she and her team did functional MRIs on a group of players, looking at blood flow in the brain, they saw that the guys who were having the most problems also had impaired blood flow, also called *hypoperfusion*, to parts of their brain.

"From the first paper we published looking at one hundred professional football players, we saw severe global hypoperfusion of the brain compared to a healthy group of individuals," Dr. Willeumier says. "We had age-matched them by age and gender, so that part was alarming. It was pretty much across the whole group with the exception of a backup quarterback. The functional deficits were very strong, and the electrophysiological changes were quite severe. This was a living group of players as young as twenty-five and as old as eighty-two, and we noted that of those one hundred players, nineteen of them had dementia, which is a lot higher than the national average. Twenty-eight percent of them had clinical depression, which is three times the national average. Eighty-one percent of them scored abnormally on the Conner's Continuous Performance Test, which is a test of focus and attention that tells us about their executive function and how well they can focus."

That's alarming, but Dr. Willeumier went on. "We also found that 48 percent of them were obese, which hampers brain health because obesity increases the risk for degenerative diseases. Thirty percent of them had sleep apnea, which doubles your risk for Alzheimer's," she says. "We gave them cognitive tests as well, and they scored quite poorly on the sections for cognitive proficiency and function, information processing, speed and accuracy, attention, and memory. That really opened my eyes because I'm an athlete and I also worked in a psychiatric clinic, and I was quite surprised at the number of them that had suicidal thoughts."

That news would seem to contradict our calls for caution in how we approach the risks of football. But not so fast. Dr. Willeumier then told me about the therapeutic options she and her team brought to the table in trying to help these players, as well as a major factor she thinks might have contributed to the problems her players—and many former players—are experiencing: *obesity*.

"We compared NFL players who were overweight or obese to those who were normal weight," she says. "Then we looked at their brain function and matched them by position and age. We found the ones that were overweight or obese based on waist-to-height ratio—a better indicator for these players—had poor cerebral perfusion in the frontal and temporal lobes. Those are the areas that in CTE were found to have more of the pathology.

"What it goes to show, and illustrates so beautifully, is that having that excess weight impairs your brain function," she concludes. "So if you're a football player, and you want to know what you can do that can proactively change the trajectory of your life, get your body mass index within a healthy range."

There's plenty of research that shows that one very effective way to do that is to lower your insulin resistance, and you can do that by reducing your consumption of the number one poison of our time, sugar. Excessive sugar consumption can lead to obesity, insulin resistance, and diabetes, and diabetes is a major risk factor for cardiovascular disease. When your arteries become narrowed by plaque, what's one part of your body that suffers from reduced blood flow? Get your head out of the gutter—it's your brain. Want to protect your brain and your heart? Eat a lot less sugar.

Research published by Dr. Willeumier and her colleagues in 2011 found a strong connection between a high BMI, reduced blood flow to the brain, and negative impact on behavior,[3] and another study by the same team, specifically focused on NFL players, found that the players with body mass in the overweight category also had impaired blood flow to the areas of the brain involved in attention, reasoning, and executive function, and severe cognitive impairment.[4]

Even more compelling was a study published in 2016 that compared a group of overweight NFL players to healthy controls and found that the players had reduced blood flow in thirty-six regions of their brains in comparison to the controls.[5]

So there is a mountain of research showing that the combination of obesity and a bad diet contributes both to chronic inflammation and reduced blood flow in the brain. Now, imagine taking that already-compromised brain and adding a mild traumatic brain injury that sets off that cascade of events I described and damages small blood vessels. You're not only going to have neurological damage but compromised circulation, and as Dr. Maroon says, that can prevent the brain from repairing itself.

"What I see in the brains of people who have brain injuries are two general patterns of blood-flow-related injuries," he says. "One is that they're not getting any oxygen into the tissue. The other is that they can't get the waste material out of the cell. As a consequence, all this inflammation is building up, and all these excitatory neurotransmitters are building up, the cell is stressed, and it's altering its metabolism into a more anaerobic metabolism—it's producing lactic acid and other things that are toxic to the cell. If you can't get the waste out of the cells, it'll be toxic to the brain…and then you're set up for a smoldering, chronic inflammation state."

NEUROLOGICAL DAMAGE MAY BE REVERSIBLE

IT'S HARD TO ESCAPE the conclusion that a combination of low blood flow and chronic inflammation is responsible for so many of the problems we see with athletes, including the buildup of tau in the brain. Then, add an insult to the brain that starts things going downhill toward poor circulation, low oxygen, and inflammation. If that constellation of conditions isn't treated properly, you can wind up with progressive, permanent damage.

However, the great news is that if this theory is correct—if tau is a sort of side effect of these other factors, and not the root cause of CTE—the damage may be reversible, even in kids, as work done by Dr. Mark Lovell shows.

"I had a $3 million grant from the NIH to study functional MRI—

looking at physiological dysfunction related to blood flow in the brain," he says. "We studied three hundred kids where they got hit playing football on Friday night. We brought them in. We did brain scans. They had abnormalities of blood flow in their brain. We brought them back after their symptoms had gone away, and their MRIs were normal, and we let them go back and play. In other words, it was a temporary dysfunction."

That brings something to the CTE conversation that's been conspicuously absent: *hope*. This theory would allow us not only to treat obvious insults to the brain like concussions, but the more insidious hits, the SCIs. Remember, it's those hits that have been scaring the crap out of parents because according to that theory, practically any knock to the head can damage the brain. What can you do to protect your kids from that?

If this theory is correct, quite a lot. You can make the body of an adult or child more resistant to inflammation using a variety of natural, nonpharmaceutical strategies, from a great diet to taking certain supplements to reducing stress and getting lots of exercise. The more of those things an athlete does, the less likely his or her body is to go into immune system overdrive when he or she takes a hit to the head. In other words, it may be possible to make the brain *resistant* to the effects of head trauma.

Dr. Maroon says that the key may lie in the field of *epigenetics*, or how factors like diet and lifestyle influence how our genes function. "We have a genome that is like a blueprint to a house," he says. "Epigenetic factors tell the genome what proteins and what agents to make. So, what are the epigenetic factors that are controllable and modulate inflammation and excitotoxicity? Number one, diet. You want a Tom Brady diet: very low sugar, natural anti-inflammatories, omega-3 fatty acids, some berries, curcumin, maybe resveratrol, magnesium, vitamin D3. Those are all agents that are very important in the inflammatory problem. So that's number one.

"Number two, we now know we don't cocoon patients who have

concussions," he continues. "In the past, we were putting people in a dark room and taking their cell phones, TVs, and iPads away. That's now dramatically changed. We rehabilitate athletes relatively quickly in terms of their aerobic capabilities, as long as it doesn't induce headaches or coughing.

"Three, you don't use alcohol or drugs, except maybe cannabidiol or CBD, which can be very therapeutic as a natural anti-inflammatory, anxiolytic, and analgesic. The fourth thing is controlling stress. Those are the four epigenetic factors that really lead to healing."

That's a long, long way from the despair and fear over the image of CTE as an inevitable condition that progresses without mercy until it changes who you are. If these scientists are right, CTE is not only treatable but may be *preventable*.

UNDERSTANDING CHANGES IN THE PERSON, NOT JUST THE BRAIN

BUT ONE OF THE MOST important parts of this story to me is that it might let us finally connect the clinical symptoms associated with CTE—the problems Dr. Willeumier saw in so many of her players, like dementia, issues with attention and focus, memory failures, and mood disorders—with physiological symptoms. That's essential for giving people a better quality of life.

The trouble has been that BU researchers, who control the narrative, have the world convinced that everything is about tau in the brain, which can only be diagnosed after death. That leaves questions about the correlation between physical disease state and psychiatric symptoms impossible to answer.

How much tau in the brain causes symptoms? Tau in which part of the brain is associated with dementia? Suicidal thoughts? Rage? Poor executive function? Do we really believe that a *single* focus of perivascular tau can cause major changes in behavior? What about players who took tons of hits to the head but have no psychiatric issues? Do they have no tau in the brain, or are their brains full of it but it somehow doesn't cause problems?

Unknown. Right now, as I said before, the state of the art is to look for guys with symptoms, cut up their brains after death to look for tau, ask their loved ones if they had clinical symptoms, and then connect the dots. It's basically crude guesswork that does nothing to help the player while he's alive. We need something more…well, scientific. In fact, experts such as Grant Iverson and Dr. Castellani have been calling for a better way to separate the neurological features of CTE from the clinical so we can determine if this is always a progressive, degenerative disease or something else in some people.[6] Based on the prevailing theory, we don't have that method.

But what if that telltale buildup of tau we call CTE is the end product of a process that involves inflammation, the buildup of toxic neurotransmitters, and restricted blood flow? That changes the game. We can detect all of those in a living person today, which means we can correlate clinical symptoms with physiological symptoms. Instead of the half-baked staging criteria we have now, in which a single fragment of tau in your brain always equals stage I CTE, we could build a staging system that links certain symptoms to specific levels of inflammatory markers and neurotransmitters, along with blood flow and oxygenation, in precise areas of the brain.

Now, no two brains or head traumas are exactly alike, so it would take years of consistent and careful observation and testing under controlled conditions in multiple labs by multiple independent researchers to identify those patterns, confirm them, and develop really strong diagnostic tools that could be used to treat clinical symptoms while people are living. But the point is, we could do it. With improving imaging technology and our knowledge of nutrition, supplements, and alternative therapies like cryotherapy and hyperbaric oxygen therapy, we could make a real difference in a lot of lives—and even save some.

MONEY, MONEY, MONEY

BUT IF WE'RE GOING TO prove that this alternative theory is effective in identifying, treating, and even preventing neurodegenerative disease in athletes and nonathletes, we need to do a lot of research. That takes money, and right now BU is sucking up all the financial oxygen in this field. Even as the NFL has pulled its funding from the CTE Center, sources like the NIH are pumping millions in grant money into BU, with who knows what strings attached.[7]

Meanwhile, researchers (who won't let me use their names for fear of damaging their careers) have told me that they're afraid of publishing peer-reviewed papers or getting grants if their work contradicts the conventional wisdom about CTE. They fear the backlash if their work threatens the flow of money that CTE research brings to certain labs and universities from sources with their own financial interests. In other words, anyone who wants to speak up against the unfounded conclusions and hidden agendas in this shady corner of science and medicine is being stomped on.

The reason is simple: there's a lot of grant money out there. The National Institutes of Health alone award about $30 billion per year in grants to individuals at universities, medical schools, and other research institutions.[8] When a university gets a grant, 50 to 60 percent of the money goes to the university development office, the school's fundraising arm. The leftovers go to the research. That makes grants a huge cash cow for universities, and one of the ways you get grants is by promoting your faculty. If your faculty are publishing research and getting in the news, when they apply for grants, they're more likely to get the money.

Basically, grants turn private universities like BU into for-profit machines. The more the CTE Center can keep its work in the news and paint CTE as a scourge, the more status the center and BU have and the more grant money they can bring in. They're blatant about it, too: the 2016 BU *Annual Report* is essentially a plea for money and features an entire spread with Dr. McKee and Robert Stern driving home the same grim story about suffering football players in order to increase the school's endowment.

I don't have a problem with a school having healthy finances. But when one university gets a majority of the press coverage for its research by playing to the press, it sucks up the lion's share of the grant money as well. That means there's less for out-of-the-mainstream studies that might reveal new and unexpected findings.

That's not how good science happens. That's not academic freedom. That's not how people get help. We need more independent researchers with the resources to investigate alternative theories like this one without being afraid they'll be ignored and buried under an avalanche of fearmongering. We need people who don't care about anything but the truth. That's why I've written this book. We need to work together to fund and promote research into these alternative ideas, as well as work to break the monopoly that special interests have on the CTE narrative.

Because players, their families, and everyone else who's ever headed a soccer ball or jumped on a trampoline deserve to know the truth: *CTE is not a death sentence.*

YOUTH FOOTBALL IS CHILD ABUSE

UNDER ATTACK

I'm a big believer in the benefits of organized sports and the benefits of football. I have two children who play football, and I believe football is safer than it's ever been.

—DR. JULIAN BAILES, DIRECTOR OF NEUROSURGERY AND CODIRECTOR OF THE NORTHSHORE UNIVERSITY HEALTHSYSTEM NEUROLOGICAL INSTITUTE

CHAPTER 8 PLAYBOOK

- The hysteria-fueled attacks on youth football
- Much of the research that claims to show the dangers of youth football is fatally flawed
- The legislative bills to ban tackle football for kids and the fight against them
- The misleading agenda and flawed science behind Faces of CTE

As I DISCUSSED IN THE first section of the book, even though the NFL made some mistakes and acted in bad faith before stepping up and addressing head trauma and its aftereffects, the only organized attack against the pro game came in the form of the class action lawsuit filed against the league on behalf of players. But as big a mess as that suit was (and is), it didn't threaten the survival of the NFL. The league is too popular and wealthy for that.

But that hasn't stopped the people who either hate football or are trying to increase their own fame by claiming that the game destroys people's brains. Over the last few years, they've started going after youth football, the game played by kids typically from eight to thirteen years old (though Pop Warner has divisions for kids as young as five). Why attack youth football? Simple: it's a soft target. The NFL and NCAA are powerful and relatively unified. Years of attacks on the NFL might have hurt the league's reputation, but anti-football types know that's a losing battle.

Youth football is fragmented. Pop Warner isn't everywhere; the majority of youth football is made up of independent youth leagues around the country, especially in rural areas. And while many adhere to USA Football's recommendations, standards, and best practices, not all do. Youth football is an easy target for critics. They know that if you make parents afraid to let their kids play the sport, eventually it will suffer at the college and pro levels.

I'm going to try to prevent that from happening. Youth football is the safest it's ever been right now considering the equipment improvements, rule changes for practice and games, reduction in contacts, focus on coach education and certification that teaches better techniques, and improvements to managing injuries including concussion protocols. In my view, the attacks against it are based on bad science, ego, the desire for revenge, and ignorance. I believe that youth football might be the greatest tool for turning young boys (and girls) into disciplined, honorable, healthy young adults. That's why my main purpose behind this book isn't to expose the bad actors; it's to spread the truth about youth football and let people know how good it is for kids both body and mind.

YOUTH FOOTBALL AND FEAR-INDUCING HEADLINES

ORGANIZED YOUTH FOOTBALL STARTED IN this country in 1929, when a Philadelphia factory owner asked a friend, a New York stockbroker, to start a youth football league to keep local kids from vandalizing his property. By 1933, the new Junior Football Conference had sixteen teams, and famed Temple University coach Glenn "Pop"

Warner became its face. Pop Warner football boomed until there were more than three thousand teams by the 1960s.

The NFL Players Association and the NFL saw a need for an organization to help determine how large the youth football community is within the United States. To do this, through the NFL Youth Football Fund—a joint fund between the players union and the league—USA Football was endowed. Today, USA Football has earned credibility across all levels of the sport as well as the sports medicine community. The independent nonprofit is the only US Olympic Committee member organization dedicated solely to football. USA Football also trains more high school and youth coaches combined than any organization in the country. Other organizations like American Youth Football (AYF), Pop Warner, and the Police Athletic League operate youth leagues and play a critical role in promoting the game and delivering the necessary standards to all that play it. By 2015, there were about 3.2 million boys ages six to seventeen playing tackle football in the United States.

But that number represents a steep decline. According to the Sports and Fitness Industry Association, youth tackle football participation dropped nearly 19 percent from 2009 to 2015, and it's continued to fall. To be fair, that's part of a nationwide drop in overall youth team sports participation—something that's a bigger concern than the alleged dangers of Pop Warner.[1] But this is what's really concerning: a 2016 HBO/Marist University poll found that 44 percent of parents with a son under eighteen said they were unlikely to let him play football—8 percent more than in the same poll taken in 2013.[2] All over the country, youth programs report declining sign-ups. According to the National Federation of State High School Associations, even the high school game is hurting.[3]

Fear is winning, and it's easy to see why. The sensationalist media coverage that's brainwashed half the country into believing the science behind CTE is sound has parents feeling like they're putting their children in danger because they want to let their sons play tackle football instead of sitting on the couch playing *Minecraft*. That has a real human cost because the segment of the population that's seen the most precipitous drop-off in team sport participation—from 46.9 percent of kids in 2012 to just 34.6 percent in 2016—is the segment where the household income is less than $25,000 a year.[4] For a lot of those kids, mostly from isolated rural areas or rough urban neighborhoods, sports is all they have after school. Take that away from them and where will they end up?

Here are just a few of the manipulative headlines from the last couple of years:

- "Banning tackle football for kids? There's nothing 'nanny state' about it if the science is sound"[5]

- "Former NFLers call for end to tackle football for kids"[6]

- "It's Time To Ban Youth Tackle Football"[7]

- "Editorial: Ban California kids from playing Pop Warner football"[8]

- "'Concussion' doctor: Youth football is child abuse"[9]

- "Tackle football is not for children"[10]

- "We have no idea how dangerous football really is"[11]

- "Children should not be playing tackle football, says Packers great Brett Favre as he fears HE may have C.T.E. after suffering 'thousands' of concussions"[12]

To be fair, not every voice in the media has been alarmist on this topic. Some level heads have spoken out about the shortcomings of the science, from Eric Adelson of *Yahoo!* to a former orthopedic surgeon and former NFL head team physician writing as ProFootballDoc[13] to mom and author Christine Organ, who wrote:

> We can't put our children in a permanent protective bubble, nor would I want to; and even if we could, we all know there are no guarantees in life. Accordingly, I believe it is my job as a parent to teach my children to become aware of the risks involved in an activity and then weigh those risks against the benefits, so that they can make informed but brave decisions throughout their life.[14]

Thank you. There are people who see the fearmongering that's going on. Even the *Popular Science* piece I cited previously included some sound scientific reasoning:

> These statistics are alarming, but they shouldn't be interpreted as universal truth. The study just shows a relationship between football and disease, not that football directly causes disease. And researchers haven't found a similar link in athletes who stopped playing after high school.
>
> "It's correlation, not causation, and that's a problem," [neurologist Mayumi] Prins says. "And we're not seeing a huge number of players coming down with disease. The numbers are actually pretty small."[15]

Exactly. As I've already pointed out, the scary numbers actually represent a tiny subset of a tiny subset of the football-playing population, but they're being treated like they represent everyone who's ever played football at any level. They don't.

Even the science fueling the fear doesn't hold up. The study that a lot of the editorials and panicked articles cite was led by BU's Dr. Lee Goldstein. It was accepted as conclusively showing that even one SCI could lead to CTE in the brains of teenage athletes. But the research looked at the brains of just four athletes, and the "one hit can cause CTE" effect was demonstrated with mice, not kids. Mice don't play football, and they certainly don't wear helmets. In what's become a classic pattern, this study was also riddled with qualifiers and caveats at the end, including this one: "Clearly, not every individual who sustains a head injury, even if repeated, will develop CTE brain pathology. While clinicopathological correlation in our case series suggests that closed-head impact injury can trigger early brain pathologies associated with CTE, the causal mechanisms, temporal relationships, and contextual circumstances that link specific brain pathology to a particular antemortem insult are impossible to ascertain with certainty based solely on postmortem neuropathology."[16]

That's reasonable scientific caution. But the press that Goldstein's paper triggered was anything but reasonable or cautious. The *Boston Globe* ran a breathless piece with the headline "CTE Can Begin Soon after Head Injury, Even in Teens, BU Study Finds."[17] If you're a football parent, you're not going to look up the Goldstein paper and wade through pages of dense neuro-speak about "microglial activation." You're going to freak and yank your kid out of Pop Warner.

Then there's that terrible *Annals of Neurology* paper I debunked in the last section, the one that claimed that kids who were exposed to youth football earlier were more likely to develop mood, behavior, and cognitive problems as adults.[18] That scared the daylights out of parents, but listen to what else Dr. Cummings has to say about the findings:

"The non-CTE group in that paper started playing football younger, but they had a shorter duration of play, only eight years," he says. "Those with CTE started playing older but had longer careers. So CTE is not a problem of youth football; it's a problem for college and mostly NFL players. Only about 6 percent of high school players will play in college,[19] and only .09 percent of high school seniors will play in the NFL—the same chance of having an IQ above 150.[20] They want to prevent .09 percent of the football population from getting CTE by eliminating youth football? That's ridiculous. Even within that .09 percent, CTE is rare."

When the doc is on fire like this, I like to just let him keep going. "These neuropsychiatric diseases are common in the general population, but the authors are saying they happen earlier in the kids exposed to football before age twelve," he says. "But that's not exactly true, as there was almost no difference in the prevalence of neuropsychiatric symptoms reported by the next of kin between the CTE-negative and CTE-positive subjects.

"In the paper, the relationship between the age of first exposure to tackle football was *not* associated with the severity of CTE pathology," he goes on. "In fact, the CTE-negative group in this paper had more exposure to contact sports than the CTE-positive cases. The mean age of exposure to tackle football in the CTE-positive group was 11.8 years compared to 11.3 years in the CTE-negative group, but the people who grew up *without* CTE started playing football at a *younger* age than those who ended up with CTE. Plus, the CTE-positive cases actually lived *longer* than the CTE-negative cases!"

This fact, however, shatters the entire argument. "The average playing career of those without CTE was eight years—about what you'd expect for kids who start playing youth football and stop after high school," Dr. Cummings concludes. "That represents 99 percent of the football-playing population. That tells me that CTE is overwhelmingly a concern for professional players, not youth or high school players, and that it's due to chronic inflammation caused by untreated and misdiagnosed concussions from decades ago when we didn't know any better."

Do you think it's a coincidence that this *Annals of Neurology* paper was released the day before a California bill to ban tackle football was scheduled to meet in committee? Neither do I. So if the evidence is this flimsy and the manipulation this blatant, how are we still talking about lawsuits and bans on youth tackle football? Because some very crafty people with their own motivations have decided to target the sport. Let's take a closer look at who they are.

FACES OF CTE

ONE OF THE LOUDEST VOICES in the shouting match over youth football often belongs to the organization Faces of CTE.

To understand Faces of CTE, you'll need a bit of background, starting with its cofounder, Kimberly Archie. Archie is a former cheerleader and cheerleading coach who became an advocate for cheerleading safety after her daughter broke her arm at a practice in 2003, and then a friend of her daughter's died at cheer practice in 2005. Archie founded the National Cheer Safety Foundation and cofounded Advocates Against Athlete Abuse—both great things. She helped cheerleading become recognized as a legit sport, became a paralegal, and worked as an expert witness and consultant in court cases related to youth sports injuries.

But then came September of 2014. Her son, Paul Bright Jr., then twenty-four, was killed when a car pulled out in front of him while he was riding his motorcycle. Archie was concerned that Paul's behavior in the months leading up to his death had become strange and erratic. He had also played youth football from 1997 to 2004 and played high school ball as a freshman. So, she sent Paul's brain to Boston University to be examined. The results? Say it with me: "stage I CTE."

Together with Mary Seau (sister of Junior Seau), Cyndy Feasel (wife of the late Seahawks center Grant Feasel), and Debbie Pyka (whose son, Joseph Chernach, committed suicide at twenty-five and was later found by BU to have stage II/III CTE), Archie cofounded Faces of CTE, a nonprofit that began with the mission of "raising awareness and increasing brain donations to further science and research to prevent/treat and cure CTE."

That's commendable, but what Faces of CTE has ultimately become about is a campaign of misleading information, emotional appeals, and lawsuits intended to destroy youth tackle football.

This is where I have to tread lightly. Because while I might not agree with the organization's cause, we're still talking about families who have lost loved ones. Grief deserves to be respected. I'm a father, and if I lost one of my children, I would be beyond devastated. However, this group is leading the charge to put an end to youth football.

BRING OUT THE LAWYERS

WHAT'S DISTURBING ABOUT FACES OF CTE is how willing they are to manipulate people's emotions. The Faces of CTE website calls CTE a "mind-robbing disease," which is ridiculous since there are many retired football players who have taken numerous hits to the head and are doing just fine.

Representatives for Faces of CTE are fixtures at sports-safety events, like the Aspen Institute's Sports & Society panel on the future of football or former President Obama's 2014 Concussion Summit, and at opportunities to lobby lawmakers in Washington in an attempt to convince them to ban tackle football. They are often on the short list for interviews for any reporter writing a story about CTE (even those who don't boast medical backgrounds).

The press also often portrays Faces of CTE as a group of mothers taking on the football establishment. A few example headlines:

- "Mom on a Mission"[21]

- "Moms take on football, suing Pop Warner for their sons' head trauma, deaths"[22]

- "Can Grieving Mothers Stop the Public from Forgetting the NFL's Brain-Trauma Crisis?"[23]

- "The NFL Must Listen to Football Moms If It Wants to Survive"[24]

That last piece even cites the Goldstein study as gospel. Then there's the *San Diego Union-Tribune* article from April 26, 2018, about the proposed California ban on tackle football for kids under age twelve, in which Archie states that Assemblyman Kevin McCarty, the chief architect of the ban bill, "encouraged her and Cornell to 'play the grieving moms.'"[25]

Just visit the Twitter feeds of Faces of CTE or its proponents—"CTE Twitter," as *Deadspin* reporter Lindsey Adler has called them. You'll find commentary on science; the spread of misinformation about youth sports; shade thrown at the NFL, NCAA, and others; and attacks on anyone who questions the Faces of CTE narrative.

But in the end, Twitter is a small stick. Lawsuits are a big one, and the allies of Faces of CTE have been filing those, too. Here's a quick rundown of major legal actions, past and present, attacking football and connected to Faces of CTE:

- In 2015, Pyka—whose son, Joseph Chernach, hanged himself in her backyard shed in 2012—sued Pop Warner in federal court in Wisconsin, claiming that the youth football organization knew about the danger of football and failed to protect her son by properly training coaches, implementing rules, and using the right equipment.[26] Pop Warner settled the suit in 2016 for an undisclosed amount.[27]

- In 2016, Archie and Jo Cornell filed a lawsuit against Pop Warner. Cornell's son, Tyler, played football for ten years, but after leaving high school and suffering from years of anxiety and depression, he committed suicide at twenty-five. Cornell sent his brain to BU, where he was found to have CTE. In 2018, US district court judge Philip Gutierrez ruled the claims of negligence, fraud, fraudulent concealment, and negligent misrepresentation in the case against Pop Warner Little Scholars Inc. could move to trial.[28]

- Also in 2018, Darren Hamblin filed lawsuits in Ohio and California against the two top makers of youth football helmets, Riddell and Schutt Sports, on behalf of his late son, Cody. Cody Hamblin died on May 29, 2016, when he suffered a seizure while fishing, fell into a lake, and drowned. A neuropathology exam in Illinois determined that he had CTE. Hamblin is represented in California by Girardi Keese, the law firm that is also representing Archie and Cornell of Faces of CTE, and Archie contributed research to the case.[29]

That looks to me like a concerted effort to cripple youth and college football through the courts—especially when you consider that the Archie/Cornell and Hamblin cases feature the same plaintiff's attorneys. College football is also facing a flood of litigation related to concussion and CTE.[30] The gavel-to-gavel press coverage has hurt youth football's reputation even more and made it even tougher to get laypeople to listen to anyone not affiliated with Faces of CTE, Dr. Ann McKee, or the Concussion Legacy Foundation. But we're not done.

THE FIGHT TO BAN TACKLE FOOTBALL

On January 24, 2018, New York Assemblyman Michael Benedetto announced the "John Mackey Youth Football Protection Act," which, if passed, would ban tackle football for children under the age of twelve in the state of New York. That was the first domino. Others followed.

The next day, Illinois representative Carol Sente announced the Dave Duerson Act to Prevent CTE, which would also ban tackle football for kids under twelve in Illinois. On February 9, 2018, Maryland state delegate Terri Hill filed a bill in the general assembly to ban tackle football for kids under fourteen. New Jersey waited awhile, but on March 30, 2018, it got into the act by rolling out A-3760, which would ban children under the age of twelve from participating in youth tackle football.

But my favorite was in California, where, on February 8, 2018, Kevin McCarty and Lorena Gonzalez Fletcher of the state assembly announced AB2108, the Safe Youth Football Act, which would prohibit children under twelve from playing in organized tackle football programs.[31]

Why is the California ban bill my favorite? Because on February 22, 2018, the state legislature announced Chronic Traumatic Encephalopathy Awareness Day in recognition of the advocacy of organizations like—wait for it—Faces of CTE.[32] In other words, proponents of Faces of CTE likely lobbied and pressured California lawmakers to bow to public panic, put a youth football ban bill on the agenda, and then cover their butts with an "awareness day."

That brings up a huge problem in the fight against the people who want to destroy youth football: *If you object, you get accused of valuing the sport more than children.* The reason Faces of CTE has the power they do isn't because they're right; it's because parents are afraid for their children, and policymakers know it. Faced with a choice between putting a football ban bill on the legislative docket or seeing headlines like, "State Legislator Refuses Law to Protect Children from Brain Damage" (followed by a barrage of furious emails, calls, and letters), policymakers give in.

It's enough to frustrate anyone who knows the truth. Because of all the changes made in the game since 2012, youth football is the safest it's ever been. But when bills to ban tackle football find their way into the legislative agenda, the real story of the youth game gets lost in fear and controversy, and anyone who supports the game is labeled a denier.

Immediately, CTE awareness groups jumped on the idea of a ban. The Concussion Legacy Foundation published a white paper called "Flag Football under 14: An Education Campaign for Parents" that conflated a lot of bad information and a few quotes from pro and college coaches to convince parents that kids should not play tackle football before age fourteen.[33] Faces of CTE launched its own "Flag 'til 14" campaign. All of a sudden, everybody was talking about how wonderful flag football was, and a lot of coaches, players, and lovers of the game started worrying that the youth game was going to be changed forever.

What's wrong with having kids play flag football? I get asked that a lot, and the answer is *nothing*. Flag football is great for some kids, and I think if they want to play it or their parents want them to play it, they should. But let's not kid ourselves that it's the same as tackle football.

First, flag football isn't safer than tackle. I know that seems counterintuitive, and I'll go into it more in the next chapter, but a study has shown that kids are more likely to be injured in flag than in tackle.[34] One reason is that, typically, kids who play flag football don't wear helmets. Things like momentum and force don't get suspended because kids have no protection for their heads. Children playing flag football still run into each other and still hit the ground hard.

Another reason kids under fourteen (and even twelve) should have the option of playing tackle is that flag football does not prepare a child for playing tackle football once he gets to high school. He might learn how to line up, block, and run a pass route, but he won't learn how to properly tackle and take on a tackler the correct way. When he finally gets to ninth grade and lines up against bigger, stronger kids who've been playing tackle for years and are really starting to pop those pads, there's a good chance he'll get *annihilated*.

It's obvious that nobody promoting tackle football bans before twelve or fourteen has a clue what happens on a football field or is thinking about what happens to kids (especially boys) around those ages. Puberty hits. I coached youth football and ran camps for over a decade, and I saw boys go from 105 pounds to 145 pounds in a few months.

That means these kids are bringing a lot more force when they tackle. The brain continues to develop until a person is in his or her mid-twenties, so why is the brain at less risk during those years of development? In all my years of involvement in youth sports, concussions were more likely once kids hit puberty, not before. There is no rationale for starting tackle at twelve or fourteen. No one can guarantee that a player won't get hurt, but the earlier kids learn proper technique, get better coaching, and develop some level of physical fitness, the better their chances to be a safer player and have more fun in the process.

Doesn't it make more sense to teach kids proper tackling techniques and limit their exposure to contact like USA Football does? Three of the largest sports medical organizations in the United States endorse USA Football's practice guidelines for tackle football: the American College for Sports Medicine, the American Medical Society for Sports Medicine, and the National Athletic Trainers' Association.

Dr. Cummings continues. "Flag before fourteen or eliminating youth tackle football before twelve or fourteen years old makes no sense," he says. "It's an arbitrary cutoff with no scientific evidence to support it. Brain development continues into the twenties, which is why some brain diseases don't manifest until adolescence or early adulthood.

"The people who are at possible risk for CTE are professional football players, and even then we're talking about 110 out of almost 27,000 people," he continues. "Why are we talking about eliminating a sport because of an alleged disease that doesn't affect more than 99 percent of the people involved in it? We also know that CTE-like pathology is seen in nonathletes, or more specifically, in cases not associated with repetitive head trauma, such as cases of single head injury and in those individuals with head injury and histories of drug and alcohol abuse. More interestingly, CTE has also been found in people with no known prior head injury. And what about the girls? If this was really about safety, not anti-football hysteria, we'd be talking about girls' sports, too.

"One thing is clear: CTE is not inevitable or even a significant risk for young athletes, especially with the radical changes in youth football," Dr. Cummings concludes. "Let's keep the focus on what's important—better concussion detection, diagnosis, and treatment—and let's help parents and kids make better health-related choices. Being aware and staying healthy will go much further to prevent adverse neurological outcomes than eliminating tackle football altogether."

But the number one reason is simple: letting a kid play tackle is a choice his parents should make. Again, there's nothing wrong with flag for some kids; it can be a great way to teach them the game when they're small. But there should also be a system for introducing them to contact gradually and safely, in a controlled environment—and there is, through youth tackle football practice guidelines from USA Football, endorsed by three of the largest sports medical organizations in the country. But no one is talking about it because endless attacks have the public convinced that youth football leagues want to turn their kids' brains into scrambled eggs. Nothing could be further from the truth.

TAKING DOWN THE CALIFORNIA BAN BILL

DR. CUMMINGS IS FAR FROM the only person who opposes these arbitrary bans. Everything California does seems to get a ton of publicity, so the "flag before twelve" ban bill there became ground zero for the fight for youth tackle football. Almost as soon as AB2108 was announced, the Save California Football Coalition formed to oppose it, and a Twitter group called SaveYouthFootballCA was formed by a small group of Southern California coaches and league administrators. Both sides quickly retreated into their armed camps, with SaveYouthFootballCA and "CTE Twitter" chewing on each other on social media.

But from the beginning, it was clear that the California ban didn't have unanimous support. Within three days of the bill's announcement, an online petition opposing it had gathered more than thirty thousand signatures and as of this writing has about forty-six thousand signatories.[35] Editorials started appearing throughout the state and online making reasonable points that the pro-ban forces couldn't seem to refute. Yes, we should make sure football is as safe for our children as it can possibly be; yes, youth football has made and continues to make changes to make it safer; yes, playing football has undeniable benefits for children; and the choice should be up to informed parents, not government. Members of the Southern California Football Coaches Association correctly called it "government overreach."[36]

Then, on April 25, 2018, Assemblyman McCarty, the bill's co-sponsor, pulled the bill before it would have been voted on by the seven-member committee for Arts, Entertainment, Sports, Tourism, and Internet Media. The news media spun the failure of the bill as a lack of support, but that's not the real reason the bill died before even making it to the floor of the legislature.

I found out the real reason when I talked with Steve Famiano, one of the founders of SaveYouthFootballCA and a youth football administrator who runs the youth program in Apple Valley, California. He told me something the news media doesn't even know yet: members of his organization went to the legislative committee and found out some of the members didn't like AB2108 any more than Steve and his group did. "The vibe we got was that none of the assembly members on the committee were convinced by the science," he said.

"We worked with the committee that was going to hear the bill and rewrote the bill right out from under McCarty," Steve went on. "We took it from a ban bill to a safe youth football bill that set practice limits and everything that should be happening in the game. After we finished, McCarty was presented with a choice: take this new bill and try to get it through, or try yours and the committee was going to vote no on it. McCarty pulled [AB2108] to avoid the embarrassment. He didn't want anyone to know that he had the bill rewritten on him. He was really pissed."

Steve also told me that McCarty is expected to come back with a new ban bill, so the plan is to round up some supportive legislators and try to pass a bill that formalizes comprehensive safety rules for California youth football—improve the game, not ban it. But he also said that the grassroots opposition to the ban really made a difference, which is encouraging. "The letter and phone campaign we did just killed [the legislators'] offices," he said. "An office assistant in McCarty's office told me she was effing tired of hearing about youth football.'"

As this book goes to press, the Maryland House has rejected its ban bill, and the sponsor of the Illinois ban has withdrawn her bill pending amendments. The New York and New Jersey bills are still being debated, but I have no doubt that Faces of CTE and ban bills in these and other states will be back. This fight's not over.

THESE YOUNG MEN DID NOT HAVE CTE

BUT IT SHOULD BE. Because after looking into the rationale behind Faces of CTE, the lawsuits against Pop Warner, and the entire movement, not only is the science of poor quality in general, but the specific cases that motivated the anti-youth football crusades just don't hold up.

I'll say this plainly: Paul Bright Jr. and Tyler Cornell did not have CTE. And, while the diagnosis of CTE in Debbie Pyka's son, Joseph Chernach, met the 2015 BU consensus panel preliminary criteria, Dr. Cummings told me there are confounding factors that no one seems to want to talk about. There are also other cases where a deceased athlete was diagnosed with CTE by Boston University but another neuropathologist looked at the same brain and found no CTE. That again calls into question BU's credibility and objectivity.

Let's dig into this with the help of Dr. Cummings. First of all, Joseph Chernach. BU found him to have stage II/III CTE, and after viewing the neuropathology report (which is publicly available), Dr. Cummings said that yes, the pathology described in the BU report did match the consensus panel preliminary criteria for the diagnosis of CTE.[37] However, he wouldn't go so far as to stage it because of the unaccepted guidelines. So the question of Chernach's CTE remains murky.

However, Chernach wasn't just a football player; he was also pole vaulter on his school's track team and wrestled for twelve years. A 2015 study of college athletes found that men's wrestling had the highest rate of concussion.[38] Yes, the work was about college wrestlers, but it seems reasonable to apply that to younger wrestlers, too. And yes, there's the theory that SCIs, not concussions, cause CTE, but it's also pretty safe to assume that a sport that results in a lot of diagnosed concussions also results in a lot more hits to the head that don't produce symptoms. Chernach's death is tragic, but there's no evidence that football caused it.

That's the *least* damning of all these cases, so let's move on to Tyler Cornell's case.

"Tyler died as the result of a gunshot wound to the head in an apparent suicide," Dr. Cummings says. "He had a history of concussions playing football; it's unknown how many were diagnosed by physicians or how many he had. His brain was examined by forensic pathologist and neuropathologist Cho Lwin, MD, from the Los Angeles County coroner's office.

"The report clearly states: 'Neuropathological evidence of chronic traumatic encephalopathy is not found such as neurofibrillary tangles, astrocytic tangles, and axonal injury in the superficial cortex, depths of the sulci, subpial, and perivascular locations,'" he concludes.[39] "But when the BU CTE Center examined the brain subsequently, they found stage I CTE."

Next, Dr. Cummings looked at the case of Paul Bright Jr. We were able to see Paul's neuropathology report because I talked for a long time to his father, Paul Bright Sr., a longtime football coach. Paul granted us permission to see his son's report and write about it.

"Paul Bright Jr. died in 2014 as the result of a motorcycle accident," Dr. Cummings says. "In his neuropathology report, the BU CTE Center found the following: irregular foci of tau-positive pretangles and tau-positive grain-like dots around blood vessels. They called this stage I CTE. But according to their own diagnostic criteria, these pretangles and dot-like staining patterns in isolation are not diagnostic. Those features can be *supportive* of CTE in the right circumstances but can't be used alone to diagnose the disease. Without the mature tangles in neurons and astrocytes, you cannot establish a diagnosis of CTE. To have CTE, you have to have the fully developed neurofibrillary tangles. Paul doesn't."

THE CASE OF KOSTA KARAGEORGE

So far, that's two cases of young men diagnosed by BU as having CTE but not by outside neuropathologists looking at the same evidence, plus another questionable case. But there's more here.

Sometime around Thanksgiving 2004, Kosta Karageorge, a twenty-two-year-old Ohio State football player and wrestler, committed suicide by shooting himself in the head. In keeping with the *New York Times'* interest in turning CTE tragedies into good copy, it became a gut-wrenching feature, "A Young Athlete's World of Pain, and Where It Led." The story detailed Karageorge's wrestling and football activities, concussions, mood swings, headaches, and finally suicidal thinking.

Then I saw that Dr. McKee had been called in to do a neuropathological examination of Karageorge's brain. Based on finding a single focus of the tau protein, she declared that he had stage I CTE. Case closed, right? Yes, from the perspective of the *Times*. But not from mine.

The *Times* piece says that BU's CTE Center got back to the Karageorge family with its stage I CTE diagnosis about a year after his death, which would mean in November of 2015. But Ohio autopsy reports are public, and on March 2, 2015, approximately eight months before Dr. McKee would send her findings to the Karageorge family, Dr. Norman Lehman, a professor at The Ohio State University College of Medicine (and formerly an experimental neuropathologist and director of neuropathology at Ohio State) did his own examination of samples of Kosta Karageorge's brain. His conclusion from the surgical pathology report:

No evidence of neurofibrillary tangles or other tauopathy
(no evidence of chronic traumatic encephalopathy).[40]

Dr. Lehman didn't respond to my request for comment, so I don't know how Karageorge's brain ended up at the BU CTE Center. But I can guess. His family, grieving and desperate, sent his brain to Dr.

McKee when the OSU autopsy didn't give them closure. I understand their pain, and I don't want to disrespect them.

Is it possible that Kosta killed himself because of brain trauma that led to mental problems? Sure. But Dr. Cummings isn't buying the jump to CTE. "Kosta died as the result of a gunshot wound to the head in an apparent suicide, and his body was discovered in a trash dumpster a few days after Thanksgiving," he says. "According to family members, he had a history of concussions and began to experience disorientation and mood swings in the months leading up to his suicide. According to Franklin County, Ohio, coroner Anahi Ortiz, Kosta's brain was sent out for further testing because of his history of being involved with high-impact sports and concussions."[41]

Dr. Lehman examined the brain and found no evidence of CTE. But when the brain subsequently made its way to the BU CTE Center, the determination was stage I CTE. If you read the *New York Times* story about Kosta, there's no mention of the discrepancy in diagnoses.[42] BU gets all the headlines, and the story implies a direct connection between CTE and suicide without ever questioning its validity.

One more thing. With all the controversy surrounding CTE and youth football, it's easy to forget that these cases were also young men who were just starting their lives. Let's remember them that way. Paul Bright Sr. would like people to remember his son (who he calls PJ) as an aspiring chef with a girlfriend—someone who was just starting to find his way in life and always taking care of everyone else. "PJ wasn't a great athlete, so he was never an MVP on the field," Paul says. "But he was an MVP at life."

...AND JEFF WINANS

BEAR WITH ME; THERE'S ONE more case to talk about. Jeff Winans spent eight years in the NFL and died in 2012 at the age of sixty-one. A neuropathology report prepared by Boston University said that he also had CTE, but Dr. Cummings begs to differ.

"The neuropathology report describes some complex pathologic changes," he says. "The final diagnosis is that of a combined disease process with features of a type of dementia called argyrophilic grain disease and CTE. There are pretangles and dot-like tau staining patterns in Jeff's brain, as well as some neurofibrillary tangles. However, the perivascular tau accumulations at the depth of the sulci—the lesions that define CTE—are not described in the report. None of the described findings meet the diagnostic criteria for CTE.

"However," he continues, "all of the features described as 'supportive' in this report are also diagnostic of argyrophilic grain disease. Clinical symptoms can be a slow and progressive cognitive impairment leading sometimes to dementia, personality alterations, emotional disturbances, and memory loss—exactly what Jeff experienced. Argyrophilic grain disease is typically seen in older individuals, but it is not exclusive to elderly people.[43]

"There is nothing in the case diagnostic of CTE according to BU's diagnostic criteria," Dr. Cummings concludes. "Even if there was CTE, you can't ignore the presence of another well-established neurodegenerative disease, and that takes precedence in diagnostic reporting. CTE is being touted as the sole and only cause, and it's not even there. No one is mentioning another well-described disease which is present and can account for every symptom in this case. According to the CTE consensus panel, other primary neurodegenerative diseases must be taken in to consideration when reporting. The closest we can come to CTE in these cases is tau in the brain. This is a case of trying to jam a square peg into a round hole."

A CTE DIAGNOSIS MILL?

THERE'S A REASON THAT OTHER neuropathologists with multiple board certifications don't diagnose stage I CTE even when BU finds it: they're seeing a *normal brain*. But if the case for stage I is so weak, why are so many highly publicized stage I cases still discussed on the Concussion Legacy Foundation website and in the media, even though they no longer fit BU's own diagnostic criteria?

Paul Bright Jr. and Tyler Cornell died in 2014, so it's likely that BU looked at their brains before the new diagnostic criteria were determined. The same for Winans, who died in 2010. It's possible that all three cases were misclassified based on outdated information. But if that's true, why hasn't BU updated its diagnoses or reexamined the brains based on the new criteria? It's like they're hoping nobody will notice.

What we have here is a pattern: four cases (that we know about) where BU diagnosed CTE while another neuropathologist found no CTE. In two of the four, the brains of the deceased were sent to BU *after* the first neuropathological exam said no to CTE. The other brains belonged to Paul Bright Jr., whose mother was already convinced that her son had CTE, and Jeff Winans. It appears that people were shopping for a CTE diagnosis, and BU—it appears—was happy to oblige. So I have to ask a disturbing question:

Do people expect a CTE diagnosis when they work
with Boston University's CTE Center?

"Wait a second, Merril," you might be saying. "You're putting BU's findings up against these other neuropathologists. But haven't the folks at BU seen more brains with CTE than anybody else? Shouldn't they be able to spot CTE when no one else can?"

That's a good question, and here's one answer: Dr. McKee, the director of the BU CTE Center, doesn't have the same credentials as the neuropathologists who looked at the reports for Cornell, Bright, Karageorge, and Winans. This is what Dr. Cummings told me about the differences between how neuropathologists are trained:

"After medical school, a doctor will enter a pathology residency, where they will learn about the different fields of pathology," he says. "At the end of the residency, the doctor can and often does enter into a fellowship program, where the doctor will specialize in a certain area of pathology. At the end of training, the new pathologist will take exams in each area they wish to practice in order to become board certified."

Dr. Cho Lwin, who did the first report on Tyler Cornell, is board certified in three different areas of pathology: anatomic pathology (general pathology of the entire body), forensic pathology (a specialized area of pathology where the pathologist does autopsies to determine a cause of death and has to interpret injuries and injury patterns), and neuropathology (a specialized area of pathology focused on diseases and injuries of the brain, eyes, muscles, and nerves).

Dr. Norman Lehman, who issued the first neuropathology report on Kosta Karageorge, is a neuropathologist at the University of Louisville. He trained in anatomic pathology, clinical pathology (an area of pathology focusing on laboratory testing), and neuropathology and is board certified by the American Board of Pathology in anatomic pathology, clinical pathology, and neuropathology.

And as I told you at the beginning of the book, Dr. Cummings, who reviewed Jeff Winans's and Paul Bright Jr.'s neuropathology reports from BU, is board certified by the American Board of Pathology in anatomic pathology, neuropathology, and forensic pathology.

Ann McKee, despite her notoriety, wasn't trained as a pathologist. She is a neurologist. She's board certified in neurology—a clinical area of medicine dealing with nervous system diseases—and in neuropathology. While she spent one year in a general pathology training program, she is not board certified in anatomic pathology or forensic pathology. In other words, while Dr. McKee has medical credentials, she does not have the same training as Drs. Cummings, Lwin, and Lehman, who are reporting findings that contradict her work and the work of the BU CTE Center.

"The bulk of CTE research has been done by one research group over the span of a few years," says Dr. Cummings. "That group controls the narrative, and because they've been acting in isolation, their motives and biases are unclear. Contrast that with Alzheimer's disease research, which has been going on for more than forty years and involves a global effort of numerous international consortiums comprised of experts from different disciplines. The Alzheimer's community has always had full transparency and extensive collaboration, and despite that, we still don't know exactly what causes it. How can we expect a single institute working alone over a few years, with no collaboration or transparency, to have solved all of the mysteries of a complex condition like CTE? It defies logic. We are far from a full understanding of CTE—despite what you read."

It's clear that the rationale for the whole "Let's ban youth tackle football because it will give our kids CTE" campaign is garbage. It's based on a one-sided look at the evidence—a bias that the news media not only isn't questioning but is actively endorsing.

"The diagnostic discrepancy is alarming," Dr. Cummings says. "It's not just one case, it's almost every case I've had the opportunity to look at. And it isn't just me—several other well-qualified neuropathologists are not able to come to the same diagnostic conclusions as the BU CTE Center. This should alarm everyone. If your diagnostic criteria isn't replicated by other physicians, then what good is it? Something isn't right. Maybe this is why the CTE Center is so proactive in blocking access to the case material—for example, not letting the consensus panel look at stage I and stage II cases, not letting the NHL have access to the neuropathology files of former players, blacking out names on clinical records, or charging outrageous fees. My years of forensic experience tell me that someone has something to hide."

SPEAKING UP AGAINST THE PRESSURE TO STAY SILENT

As I've said, my intention here is not to disrespect people who have lost loved ones, but to serve the truth. And the truth is, youth football is the best it's ever been. But should we be doing more to make it safer and learn more about the risks? Of course we should, and we are.

One of the things we have to do is to get parents and coaches better information. That means getting rid of the one-sided narrative, which is going to be an uphill battle. Once, while coaching youth football, I had a parent who wanted his kid in an NFL-type helmet versus a youth helmet. I had to explain to him that the weight of the NFL helmet put his son's neck in danger and that not only were our helmets from Schutt (one of the leading helmet makers), but they were safer for his son because they were lighter and had the highest standards at that time for impact. I'm telling you, fighting misinformation is an uphill battle.

One guy fighting it is Chris Fore, a consultant, coach, athletic director, special teams coordinator, and adjunct professor in the Department of Kinesiology at Azusa Pacific University, who was also one of the founders of SaveYouthFootballCA and helped kill the California ban bill. He told me in an interview that he's been trying to get more people to take a stand and talk about the poor quality of the evidence for CTE but has found depressingly few takers.

"I reached out personally through emails and phone calls to every NCAA school in California playing Division I football, to private schools like USC playing D1 football, to Stanford, the Chargers, the Rams, and the 49ers. Only one institution got back to me, and that was USC," he says.

"The other side is using NFL guys as spokespersons: 'I'd never let my kid play football!' That is speaking very loudly to parents who are hearing just one side," Fore continues. "Part of my thought was from a PR perspective; we've got to get some players and coaches whose names are recognizable to say the opposite. But nobody here in California would help our cause. Not one of those institutions, not one of those NFL teams would respond to us in our fight here, which was discouraging."

This jibes with what Dr. Cummings has told me time and time again about the scientists in his field: everyone's reluctant to speak out against the prevailing narrative for fear of blowback that could harm their career or finances.

Dr. Cummings has been one of the more outspoken voices calling for greater transparency on this subject, and he's felt the heat from BU, his employer. "I think the lack of mention of my work is intentional, and it is part of their attempt to discredit experts who disagree with them," he says. "They can't slam me directly because then someone would ask, 'If he's so bad, why is he teaching your students?' But they can delegitimize my work by failing to acknowledge it. If they ignore it, then it has no credibility. They've even actively tried to discredit me in a piece on Boston.com about my July 2017 op-ed."

He points to this passage: "Reached for comment Thursday, BU School of Medicine Assistant Dean of Communications Maria Pantages Ober simply said Cummings made the decision in his capacity as a parent to allow his son to play football. Ober declined to respond to any of the specific points Cummings raised in his article about the limits of CTE studies. 'The Center responds with peer-reviewed scientific publications,' she said."[44]

Dr. Cummings says, "Responds only with peer-reviewed scientific publications? Not true; they are always responding in the media. Also, they say I made my point as father, not a scientist. That's an obvious attempt to denigrate my opinion. The reporter didn't even get my job right—I'm not a neurologist. He did reach out to me for comment on this story. I kicked it over to BU because it sounded like he was trying start a fight, and I didn't want that.

"I felt like they threw me under the bus. That's not academic freedom of speech, and it's sure not science. After this experience I went to my chair and the university ombudsman to protect my rights and my job."

That's not right, and we're going to change it. We're going to keep speaking up and putting pressure on people who know the truth to join us. We're going to keep designing better safety equipment and learning more about the effects of head impacts on young brains so we can institute more rules and policies that keep players healthy so they can enjoy the game without fear. The other big thing we have to do is to get more good information into the hands of parents so they can make decisions about what's right for their kids based on knowledge, not fear and propaganda.

Vinny Fazio, a California football coach and activist for protecting youth tackle football, constantly sees the need to get parents educated. "Parents need to do research," he says. "You need to look at the team in your area, the coaches, and their qualifications. There are a lot of youth football leagues out there, and we don't know who all those coaches are. As a parent I would be very cautious about making that decision. But to take that decision out of the hands of the parents, when there is no real scientific basis for that, in my opinion, is kind of silly."

Most of all, we need to come at this issue with the levelheadedness of Dr. Julian Bailes, who is not only chairman of the Pop Warner Little Scholars medical advisory committee but one of the pioneers of CTE and concussion research. "This is a personal choice by athletes, their parents, their coaches," he says. "Everybody's got to decide what's right for them and weigh the risk-benefit ratio."[45]

That's all we want: a choice.

DON'T BAN FOOTBALL, BAN SUGAR

I got a lot of the greatest values in life from playing sports, from playing football—teamwork, sportsmanship, my work ethic, resiliency, dedication—I got it all by being on a team.

—JON GRUDEN, HEAD COACH OF THE OAKLAND RAIDERS

CHAPTER 9 PLAYBOOK

- The many ways that football benefits kids
- The misleading beliefs about the risks of playing youth football compared with other activities
- How football helps kids build character
- Youth football as a cure for today's obesity and diabetes crises

THE ENDLESS ATTACKS ON YOUTH FOOTBALL are fueled by the never-ending stream of news stories coming mostly out of BU and BU-affiliated organizations and researchers. They suck up all the air in the conversation about football and CTE until it's less a conversation and more an angry uncle shouting in your face over the Thanksgiving table. Sensationalistic headlines that make people afraid get attention, and they bury research and opinions from other experts saying, "Wait a second—there's more to this story. Can we discuss it?" Caution doesn't get bold type.

So you probably missed this piece of research that came out in May 2018, but it says a lot about the conversation we should be having. The researchers looked at 181 orthopedic surgeons and neurosurgeons who were also the chairs of their departments—some seriously accomplished physicians—and how many of them played contact sports in high school or college. Then they compared the rate of play with the general population.

They found that orthopedic and neurosurgery chairs were more likely than the general population to have played contact sports in high school, a *lot* more likely to have played in college, and also more likely to have suffered at least one concussion. Their conclusion: "The high prevalence of youth contact sports play and concussion among surgical specialty chairs affirms that individuals in careers requiring high motor and cognitive function frequently played contact sports."[1]

You might be tempted to dismiss that kind of study as a novelty, but its point is important. Not only did playing youth contact sports not prevent these people from reaching the top of their profession but might have helped them get there by helping develop their work ethic, self-confidence, and persistence—all qualities you need when trying to survive medical school and build a career as a surgeon.

We don't see those kinds of stories these days because scaring the daylights out of parents and coaches sells more advertising. But that doesn't mean they're not out there. The truth is, there are many ways that playing youth tackle football benefits kids physically, mentally, emotionally, even socioeconomically. At the same time, there are threats to children's health much more dangerous than anything that goes on during a Pop Warner game.

So let's do something that should be happening but isn't: take a levelheaded look at all the ways youth football benefits kids and the things parents should really be watching out for.

MORE BAD SCIENCE, YOUTH FOOTBALL EDITION

IN THE CHAPTER ON BAD SCIENCE, I looked at the huge flaws in the work being done on SCIs, which basically comes down to, "It's not good for kids to get hit in the head, and when they do, it can cause changes in their brains. But we don't know if those changes are permanent, how they affect behavior, or if they lead to CTE. We don't even really know what a subconcussive hit is." Still, the specter of kids playing Pop Warner, taking mild hits that produce no symptoms, and then committing suicide in their thirties because of progressive neurodegeneration makes it easy to scare parents.

Here's the trouble. It's difficult to tease out the effects of playing youth football on adults because when you're trying to connect the health of men in their forties and fifties with the football they played decades earlier, many factors can skew the research, and it's impossible to control for them all.

For example, a paper came out in 2016 that became one of the go-to pieces of research for people who claimed that youth football was too dangerous. Called "Cumulative Head Impact Exposure Predicts Later-Life Depression, Apathy, Executive Dysfunction, and Cognitive Impairment in Former High School and College Football Players," it concluded with a finding that was pretty damning: adults who played youth football were more likely to have cognitive, behavioral, or mood problems later in life.[2] If you took the paper at face value, as most people would, you'd pull your kid out of Pop Warner before the ink was dry.

But when you look deeper, the research was riddled with problems. Dr. Edward Riley from Stanford pointed out that the researchers didn't take into account the baseline mood, behavioral states, and cognitive states of the subjects before they started playing football in their youth.[3] If you don't have a baseline for your subjects in a study like this, your findings are meaningless. You might as well throw the study in the trash.

There were other big flaws with this research that I could spot, even with my complete lack of a medical degree. For one thing, the average body mass index, or BMI, of the men in the study was 31.5.

That's obese, and there is a well-documented link between obesity and everything from depression and impaired memory to executive function problems.[4]

For another, these guys would have played their high school and college ball in the 1970s and 1980s, when we didn't know what we know now about head trauma, and the coaching attitude to "getting your bell rung" was to tough it out. Comparing the mental health of guys who played then with kids who play today is like looking at car accident death rates from the 1950s, when we all rolled around in the back of Mom and Dad's station wagon, and concluding that it's not safe to drive, even though today's cars have seat belts, anti-lock brakes, airbags, and crumple zones that make driving a lot safer.

The point here is that accepting the conclusion that makes the most noise doesn't always lead to the best decision. For instance, in the last chapter, I talked about the push in several states to ban tackle football for kids younger than thirteen or fourteen, forcing them to play flag football instead. Makes sense because flag football is safer, right? Wrong. A 2017 study from the University of Iowa found that kids who played flag actually suffered more injuries than kids who played with contact, and the rate of concussions between the two was the same![5]

Or how about this: a 2018 study from the University of New Mexico found that middle and high school students were 60 percent more likely to get a concussion during PE class than during sports.[6] Or you could look at a study published in August 2017 that directly contradicts the earlier study about youth football leading to cognitive problems, concluding that "cognitive and depression outcomes later in life were found to be similar for high school football players and their nonplaying counterparts from mid-1950s in Wisconsin. The risks of playing football today might be different than in the 1950s, but for current athletes, this study provides information on the risk of playing sports today that have a similar risk of head trauma as high school football played in the 1950s."[7]

Like with the BU findings that turned out not to be CTE, when you look closer, the effect vanishes. So let's move on and look at the very real ways that youth football (including high school football) benefits kids in body and mind.

THE GREAT GAME

First of all, there's an element of risk involved in playing any sport. The longer you play, the greater your chances of getting injured (though I had plenty of kids in youth football who never got hurt in the seven years I coached them). But you're a lot more likely to get injured if you spend your first four years playing flag and not learning how to tackle properly—how to stand, how to take the right angle, how to avoid helmet-to-helmet contact—than you are if you learn early on how to handle contact.

The change that needs to happen if we want to save youth football and make it safer for every kid who plays it is this: we need to start seeing youth football for what it is. It's not about winning. It's not a way for fathers to relive the glory days. It's not a training ground for the NFL or even local high school teams. One kid in a thousand will even go on to play Division I ball in the NCAA. It's not an environment for gung ho coaches who think they're Vince Lombardi or Bear Bryant to teach kids to be hyperaggressive. None of those things is why we play youth football.

Youth football is about learning to play a sport the right way—to hit the right way. It's about learning life skills and developing kids into awesome young adults. It's a tool for childhood development, plain and simple. Think about it. Football is the most team-oriented sport. In baseball, it's mostly about the pitcher and the hitter. In basketball, it usually comes down to the best player taking all the shots. But in football, no matter what play you run, it takes all eleven players to make it work. All you need is a breakdown from one guy, and the play could fail. Teamwork is vital for consistent success in football.

Football is also the most inclusive sport, especially for kids who are big and not very mobile. If you're a squat, burly eleven-year-old, you're not going to make the basketball team. If you don't have a good arm, you're probably not going to last long in Little League, either, because baseball is all about throwing. But youth football has a place for the overweight kids who aren't quick but are strong. It has a place for the skinny kid who has the skill to kick the ball through the uprights. In football, you don't have to be a classically great athlete or have perfect hand-eye coordination to play, have fun, and get dirty. Football players learn discipline, teamwork, and the value of practice.

Football also teaches you how to fail and get back up because on most plays you wind up on your backside. We live in a "participation trophy" society now, where kids get awards for showing up and helicopter parents protect them from the big bad world. The problem is life is at least 50 percent failure! Kids need to learn resilience, to know that they can drop a ball, miss a tackle, blow a coverage, or get knocked down and get up, wipe themselves off, and get back in the game. That's what football teaches. I have taught kids in football camps and youth football for close to two decades and almost every situation, goal, or challenge on a football field correlates to life. We build friendships and relationships that last a lifetime and create experiences that I reflect on every day, long after players have moved on to other things.

I think maybe that's why so many boys fall in love with football— why Dr. Cummings's son Fionn fell in love with it even though his dad did everything he could to discourage the boy's love of the sport. Kids want to find out what they can do. Football does that.

"THE FUNNEST THING I'VE EVER DONE!"

TODAY, MY SON, BEAU, IS twenty-two and a quarterback and running back at Brigham Young University. He had his own issues with a concussion early in 2017, but thanks to the great athletic training staff at BYU and the people at the University of Pittsburgh Medical Center, he's healthy and playing. But even when he was a kid in Fort Thomas, Kentucky, I never had any concerns about him playing youth football. I was going to coach him and implement a head-trauma protocol based on what had happened to me so the kids would learn to address the injury and not be afraid of it because we were going to care for it in the best way we knew. Beau's an example of what I mean when I say that kids fall in love with football. He's also an example of how football is a fantastic tool for developing terrific young adults.

Like I said a while back, at seven years old, Beau decided that he wanted to play in the Fort Thomas Junior Football League, and even though he was too young, the league said that if I coached, he could play.

I agreed. We were assigned to the Red team, and then we went to Beau's first practice. Beau put his helmet and shoulder pads on before we left, and he didn't take them off until we were done, but I'll get to that. We went to practice, and it was against eight- and nine-year-olds. Now, Beau has always been athletically gifted, but he was a late bloomer as far as growth. These eight- and nine-year-olds towered over him.

Of course, Beau wanted to play running back and linebacker, because he wanted to be in on as many plays as possible. So in practice he was right in the middle of everything, and the kid was just getting drilled. They were teeing off on him. He was getting bounced around like a little pinball. Eight- and nine-year-old youth players are a bunch of little weeble-wobbles banging into each other, but he was still taking a lot more than he was giving.

I had been thinking about this happening before we ever got to practice, so I told the coaches that based on what I was witnessing, I did not think Beau would be playing this year. They said that was fine; he could come back the following season. But when practice was done, and we got in the truck, Beau took his helmet off for the first time since he had put it on, looked at me, and said, "Dad, that's the funnest thing I've ever done!"

Just like that, I had a football player. I put the car in drive and thought, *We're back on.*

BECOMING A LEADER

FAST-FORWARD A FEW YEARS, and Beau was one of the best players on all his teams. But I didn't care about that. My job was to help him develop into a young man of character, and football was the vehicle for doing that.

The kid was so gifted and so smart about the game that he would never shut up. But he was also the only player I ever kicked out of practice, because he demanded that everyone else play as well as he played. If you didn't make a block or you dropped a pass, he'd rip you up one side and down the other.

My coaches would say, "Hey, don't be so hard on Beau. You know he says everything we want to say, right?" I did, but I also knew this was an important moment for me as a coach as well as a parent. I have always taught my coaches two philosophies. The first is: "never coach the obvious." Anyone can say, "Throw strikes," or "Make the tackle." That's not coaching. Coaching is giving the player something that will make a difference for him or her, mentally or physically.

But getting Beau on my plan for relating to his teammates and being a leader was going to be a little more difficult than dealing with my coaches because my second philosophy in coaching is: "Coach in the yardstick of their years, not yours." If a kid is eight and I'm thirty-eight, I've forgotten more than he knows. Plus, he is more interested in whose house everyone will be going to for snacks after practice than what I'm teaching him. And no matter what I say, the kid will have forgotten it by the time he walks off the field because he's a kid! I had to help my coaches see through the kids' eyes, not theirs…and I had to do the same with my son.

Beau needed to learn to see through the eyes of his teammates, so he could understand how calling them names and criticizing them was hurting them and the team. So I finally came up with the idea to let him feel the difference in words. I sat him down and said, "Beau, when you get on your teammates about not catching the ball or making the blocks, and you tell them that they suck, it does not inspire them to play hard for you. I want to say some words to you, and I don't want you to say anything. Just see how it feels, okay?" He agreed, so I laid into him. I said, "Beau, you stink; you suck; catch the ball; make the tackle; you're terrible!" That sort of thing. I could see him squirming. He didn't like it.

After I was done I said, "Now, remember how you felt, but now listen to these words." I started saying things like, "Man, you're better than that; you can block him; that's okay, you'll make the catch next time; I believe in you; you'll get it done next time." I let him think for a few seconds, and then I said, "Did you feel the difference? Do you understand what I'm trying to teach you?" He looked up and said yes, and for a moment I did an internal fist pump and thought, *Yes, this worked!* Then he said, "So, I can't get mad anymore?"

I had to laugh. He was ten, and I was forty-two. He could only measure the lesson with his yardstick, not mine. I thought I had made him understand, but it would be a journey. So I said, "I don't want you to talk like that to your teammates anymore. I want you to encourage them, okay?" I also told him if he cut loose on them again, I would kick him out of practice.

Next practice, this kid missed a block—honestly, he had been missing blocks all season long—and Beau got clobbered. He got up and said, "Uh…I know you can make that block." Okay, it wasn't exactly the "win one for the Gipper" speech, but he was struggling to say something nice. I said, "Well, yeah, that's a good start." Then, a couple plays later, the same thing happened, and he snapped: "You suck!" Goodbye. I sent him home. But we kept working on that lesson over another four years together, and the way Beau leads now is a direct reflection of the lessons he learned then.

Today, Beau will stand up in front of his coaching staff and teammates and talk about anything but himself. One time, BYU offensive coordinator Jeff Grimes told Beau, "Stand up in front of the team," and told the other players to say what they thought about him. The only catch was, they couldn't say anything related to football—"He's a baller, you know, great arm," that sort of thing.

Beau told me that the guys all said things like, "Amazing friend, terrific leader, a warrior, man of character." They just went on and on. That made Beau feel great, and it made me feel even better. A coach or a parent has no control once the player enters the white lines of the football field or leaves the front door of your home. All they have is what you taught them, and they have to choose whether to follow it or not.

Well, during Beau's senior year in high school, I was sitting in my office, and I got this email from Mike Code, a health and PE teacher at Beau's school. It read:

Mr. Hoge:

I just wanted to send you a quick message to let you know a couple of things I have observed about Beau. In my 17 years here at Highlands High School I have not seen anyone who treats his fellow students any better than Beau does. He is respectful and nice to everybody in the building no matter how "popular" or not they are. This is very nice to see and as someone who coaches a sport I'm glad we have role models like this. I know you have raised a great kid.

That made me feel about ten feet tall. Beau learned that restraint, that leadership, that ability to lift other guys up, from football. It gave him a place as a young kid to turn from a hothead to a leader.

IT'S ABOUT STAYING ACTIVE

ONE OF THE MANY EXPERTS who really understands the value of youth football is Dr. Rosemarie Scolaro Moser, director of the Sports Concussion Center of New Jersey and author of *Ahead of the Game: The Parents' Guide to Youth Sports Concussion*. She's a neuropsychologist who's not only extremely active in researching ways to keep young athletes safe from head injury but who also opposed New Jersey's bill to ban tackle football before age twelve. She believes strongly that the benefits of youth football outweigh the risks.

"What is the purpose of youth sports?" she said in an interview. "The purpose of youth sports is physical activity, learning team play, socialization, providing strategic thinking. All of these wonderful health aspects. You know, increasing endorphins to the brain through exercise, which improves emotional health. There are so many benefits to it, especially in geographic areas of the United States where there may not be any other after-school alternatives, so parents rely on healthy, positive activities for kids who might otherwise not have activity or get into mischief after school.

"These are the benefits of youth sports," she continues. "Those benefits are not the same as the benefits for professional sports. Thus, we must conduct youth sports very differently, and the problem is when parents and others live vicariously through their children who are play-ing sports. That's a problem. That's a real problem, and if they treat it like pro sports in terms of competition, winning is everything. And I think that's what's happened. If we miss the point of youth sports, if we use the same culture of professional sports in youth sports, we're going to increase the injuries of children. We're not going to take care of them. Safety will not be number one."

She went on. "Banging your head around is not a good thing. Period. I don't dispute that," she says. "It's not healthy. However, saying that tackle football prior to the age of twelve—what is the justification for that? Why isn't it prior to the age of twenty? Why isn't it prior to the age of nine? Do we think that promoting such a bill is really going to help as much as doing other things to improve youth sports, like funding better coaches, health care, athletic trainers, proper equipment, educational programs, and new programs such as those by MomsTEAM? People are taking the wrong approach because once you say ban tackle football, why not go to soccer, equestrian sports, and others that produce a lot of injuries?

"Rather than prohibiting sports," Dr. Moser concludes, "let's just advocate and take a stand to make them healthier and better for the goals that they're there for, which is to improve kids' health in many ways: physical, emotional, social, and intellectual."

Amen! That's the trouble with depending on the research that's hogging the headlines. Apart from being about a bunch of things that are associated but prove nothing, the data can't quantify the lessons that happen every second on a football field. They can't capture the grit a kid learns when he gets back up after a bad play. They can't cap-ture the lifelong friendships with players and the coaches who become like surrogate fathers. And because there's so much money involved in football, people forget that kids engage in activities every day that are just as dangerous.

According to the CDC, more kids die in motor vehicle accidents and in drowning accidents than from any other cause.[8] That's with life-guards and child safety seats more advanced than the space shuttle. Hear anybody talking about banning children from riding in cars or preventing families from building pools in their backyards? I don't. According to Safe Kids Worldwide, there's been a 62 percent drop in the number of bike-related deaths per year in children since 1999 and a 17 percent drop from 2013 to 2014. Still, ninety-eight children ages nineteen and under died from biking-related injuries in 2013.[9] So safety improvements make a big difference, but kids still get hurt. Why? *Because there is no perfectly safe activity*.

By the way, for comparison, according to the National Center for Catastrophic Sports Injury Research, there were six fatalities directly related to football, and ten fatalities indirectly related to football, during the 2014 season. The indirect fatalities were all related to heatstroke, cardiac problems, or water intoxication.[10] And for boys and girls ages nine and under, concussions happen most often while playing on a playground or riding bikes.[11]

THE REAL CHILDHOOD THREAT

IF YOU WANT TO BAN one thing, with a 100 percent certainty that you'll protect kids, don't ban football. Ban sugar. Childhood obesity is a huge problem in this country, and you want to take away one of the best sources of strenuous outdoor exercise for kids?

Does it make sense that we're ready to ban or restrict youth football because of a CTE "epidemic" based on a few cases who were mostly pro football players and an epidemic of parental fear based on a lot of bad science that hasn't been replicated while ignoring the real, proven dangers of obesity, overconsumption of sugar, and a sedentary lifestyle in our kids?

No, it doesn't. People are targeting football because they think the NFL is Big Tobacco, because it's convenient, because it lines their pockets, or because it's easier than actually parenting and making tough choices.

Let's talk about childhood obesity. It's been linked to a huge range of serious health problems, from type 2 diabetes to asthma to cardiovascular disease. Obese children have more problems at school and miss more school, have more self-esteem problems, and are more likely to be obese as adults, which reduces their life expectancy. And what's one of the major causes of obesity? This passage from a comprehensive 2015 study says it all:

> One of the factors that are most significantly linked to obesity is a sedentary lifestyle. Each additional hour of television per day increased the prevalence of obesity by 2%. Television viewing among young children and adolescents has increased dramatically in recent years. The increased amount of time spent in sedentary behaviors has decreased the amount of time spent in physical activity. Research…indicates the number of hours children spend watching TV correlates with their consumption of the most advertised goods, including sweetened cereals, sweets, sweetened beverages, and salty snacks.[12]

Sitting on the couch, eating Red Hot Flaming Cheetos, playing video games, and gaining weight certainly sounds healthier than running around with friends playing football, doesn't it? But it's not only obesity that's dangerous to kids. The amount of sugar Americans eat has more than doubled since the 1950s,[13] and studies have decisively linked eating too much sugar to everything from memory problems[14] to the beginnings of cardiovascular disease and high blood pressure.[15]

That's right. Obese, inactive, sugar-addicted kids are beginning to develop early signs of heart disease. I don't know about you, but I'd rather accept a one-in-a-thousand risk of my kid getting a concussion on the football field than the certainty of my kid sitting around and rotting from the inside out.

The cure? Exercise, for starters. To quote a 2012 study, "Taken together, conclusive evidence exists that physical inactivity is one important cause of most chronic diseases. In addition, physical activity primarily prevents, or delays, chronic diseases, implying that chronic disease need not be an inevitable outcome during life."[16] In other words, if you want your kids to be healthy, get them moving. For millions of boys (and some girls), that means playing football. Football, at its heart, isn't really about tackling. It's about running. That's another problem with researchers and policymakers who've never played the game: they don't get that in football, you mostly run your tail off.

Practice? Running. Drills? Running. Games? Running. In football, they start and stop, do quickness drills, and are always on the move. A game is one long interval training session. No wonder players are exhausted after practice.

To play football and be safe, players have to get in terrific physical condition. They're constantly doing sprints and drills to improve explosiveness and quickness. That burns tons of calories, which helps keep their weight under control and prevents obesity. Older kids get into strength training and plyometrics to improve everything from power off the line of scrimmage to jumping ability, and that extra muscle and lean body mass means better blood sugar control, less inflammation, and improved mobility so kids can avoid collisions and prevent injuries.

Football even helps you invest in your health after the season is over because you want to be ready for next year. It helps build a healthy lifestyle for kids, which is really important when kids have lots of entertainment choices that involve them sitting on their backsides.

Playing sports also improves mood and concentration (which is great for schoolwork), boosts self-confidence and self-esteem, and promotes better sleep. Wait, there's more! Student-athletes are less likely to use illegal drugs,[17] tend to make more money as adults than nonathletes,[18] and have less stress and better mental health as young adults.[19] Sports in general and football in particular are forces for good in the lives of millions of kids and their families.

"I feel the benefits of football are enormous," says Dr. Collins from UPMC. "One is that a lot of kids that play football are actually by definition at risk for obesity. Without playing sports, I think that there's a very strong scientific argument that these children could be at risk for other health-related consequences of being in a larger weight category and a larger size category. Let alone the fact that [football] creates teamwork and work ethic and camaraderie and social skills and competition.

"What I often see in my practice is the influences of non-sport participation on anxiety," Collins continues. "Anxiety is a medical condition that can create a whole host of problems, including migraines, cognitive issues, attention deficit problems, and sleep issues. By being in good physical condition and having structure and having competition and having an outlet for anxiety and stress, I think the benefits of that are just tremendous. That's not something a lot people talk about, but it's something I see in my clinic all the time. I'm treating a lot of kids who are anxious but not having concussion problems, and by them not participating in sport, that anxiety actually worsens, which results in headaches and dizziness and problems that actually mimic the effects of concussion."

So, by not letting our kids get out and play and be kids so we can avoid them getting head injuries that are unlikely to happen anyway, we're actually raising nervous, anxious kids who are developing the symptoms we're working so hard to help them avoid. Does that sound healthy?

LET KIDS BE KIDS

IT DOESN'T BECAUSE IT'S NOT. Are there risks in playing youth football? Of course. But there are also risks in riding bikes, jumping in a bouncy house, going on a roller coaster, and going to the pool, and nobody is talking about banning swimming or calling it child abuse.

Of course youth football has problems. There are leagues that emphasize winning and crushing the competition to the point where it stresses the kids out and makes them hate the sport. There are poorly trained and flat-out bad coaches who teach kids the wrong techniques. That's got to be wiped out, coast to coast. There are parents who forget that the whole point of youth football is to help kids gain confidence, resilience, and leadership skills while making lifelong friendships. But the solution is to change the culture of the game, train better coaches, and educate parents, not to ban the game.

Yes, there are health risks. But as I think I've shown, they're grossly overstated and not very well supported by science. I asked Dr. Mark Lovell about the risks, and he said, "Real science is going on. It just doesn't happen on a twenty-four-hour news cycle. I'd like to see everybody calm down and stop taking their kids out of sports because that's going to have negative consequences in terms of diabetes and obesity. We have an obesity problem far worse than anything that could come up with concussion.

"Lately, parents will come in and say, 'I don't want my kids playing sports,'" Lovell continues. "I say, 'Okay, what are they going to do instead?' They'll start talking about music or the chess team. That's not going to do it. One woman came in—her kid was twelve years old, and he had a mild concussion. She said, 'I'm never letting him play soccer again.' I replied, 'Well, there is no evidence for doing that if we handle it well.'"

Dr. Lovell pointed out that while putting kids who get repeated concussions back into play might turn a temporary dysfunction into a long-term one, that's not the definition of cautious, smart science. And that's not what anyone is suggesting. What I and experts from doctors to coaches are recommending is that we do what's best for kids' physical, mental, emotional, and social health based on good science, reason, and solid parenting smarts. And that means letting them play sports.

CHAPTER 10

HEADS UP!

Youth sports have never been safer in terms of prevention and management. This was in the New England Journal of Medicine: *the most common causes of concussions and head injuries in kids and young teenagers are automobiles, falls of all kinds (including on playgrounds), bicycles, and self-propelled scooters. Should we keep kids off of playgrounds? Should we eliminate bicycle riding? Should we eliminate scooters? These are all much more dangerous venues in terms of serious injuries than football fields.*

—DR. JOE MAROON, PITTSBURGH STEELERS TEAM NEUROSURGEON

CHAPTER 10 PLAYBOOK

- Why the people who insist that youth football hasn't changed to become safer are wrong

- The truth about injury and concussion risks in youth football

- The origins of the Heads Up Football program and how it does make the game safer

- The need for consistent national youth football coach training and standard head trauma protocols

- How equipment is changing to make the game safer

It's BAD ENOUGH THAT WE have attacks on youth football fueled by emotion and the hunger for the spotlight. What makes it worse is when so-called experts make statements based on nothing. Back in March of 2018, that happened at a San Diego fundraiser for the BU CTE Center put on by the family of the late Junior Seau, the beloved star who committed suicide at forty-three and was later diagnosed with CTE by the National Institutes of Health.

I have nothing but respect for the passion and efforts of the Seau family; they're terrific people who want to honor their loved one and help prevent other players from suffering. But I take serious issue with something that was said by the event's keynote speaker (who, by the way, was a representative from the Concussion Legacy Foundation and isn't a medical doctor) during the event: "We want to educate parents and coaches. If you love football and think it's the greatest sport in the world, your child would be so much better off playing flag, or seven-on-seven, or another sport until you expose them to tackle in high school. That's the best way to prevent CTE, by a long shot."

Really? Show me the research that says keeping kids from playing tackle football before a certain age will prevent CTE. Show me the research that shows definitively that football even *causes* CTE! You can't because it isn't there.

That same speaker said even more inflammatory things: "Children get hit in the head because adults direct them to do it. They don't do this to themselves because it hurts to get hit in the head. Then we put helmets on them so they don't feel the pain."[1]

This is another example of someone talking about youth football who has no clue about how we practice, teach, and play in Pop Warner and USA Football. How do I know this? Because I asked USA Football officials if the keynote speaker had gotten any youth football coaching certification, and their reply was, "He has not completed USA Football youth-coach certification, which is part of our Heads Up Football program."

I think the earlier comment was based on an infamous ESPN video that showed parents encouraging their kids to do a drill where they ran into each other head-on. There might still be morons who coach or teach like that, but everywhere I go, improvements in drills and tackling techniques are being implemented. If you see coaches or parents coaching like that, get your kids out of there and demand immediate changes.

But I get the fear. As parents, our first instinct is to err on the side of protecting our kids. Remember, even Dr. Cummings, who's been so invaluable in writing this book, fell victim to the fear. He was determined to keep his son from playing football because of worries about brain trauma and CTE—and he's a brain doctor! If it took Dr. Cummings three years of research in his own field to uncover the truth about the sensationalist claims and terrible science, those of us who aren't doctors don't stand much of a chance.

But that's our job in the end: to do what's right for our children based on reason and good information, not to knee-jerk away from things that are actually beneficial because we're scared or fear a public rebuke. As Dr. Cummings told me, "I didn't reach these conclusions because my son plays football; my son plays football because I reached these conclusions."

That's the same thinking that, despite all the nonsense about vaccines causing autism, leads the majority of parents to vaccinate their kids. We can overcome fear and make good choices if we have good information. Providing that information and encouraging parents to look for it from other sources is why I wrote this book.

TEACHING FOOTBALL THE RIGHT WAY

BACK IN 2015, THE AMERICAN Academy of Pediatrics (AAP) Council on Sports Medicine and Fitness reviewed the published research on injuries related to youth tackle football and the risks of contact. Its official statement said that while delaying contact or eliminating it completely from the youth game would probably decrease the number of concussions and other head injuries, it would be better to address those risks by improving adult supervision of the sport, changing rules to minimize dangerous contact, training coaches to teach proper tackling techniques, instituting a zero-tolerance policy for dangerous contact, and having certified athletic trainers present at games and practices.

The AAP called for more study of safer tackling techniques and other measures but didn't propose eliminating tackle football.[2]

The position of the AAP was the same one I've already made: eliminating contact when children are younger might reduce the risk of head injuries by a fraction, but when kids reach high school and start playing contact ball against kids who are bigger, stronger, and faster, they will be more likely to become injured because they don't know how to tackle.

Efforts to make football safer have been going on since the 1920s, when the first hard helmets and leather pads were introduced. (When Rutgers and Princeton played the first ever college football game in 1869, nobody wore helmets at all.) After that, we got face masks in the 1930s, padded plastic helmets in the 1950s, face shields in the 1990s, and so on. The game has always been working to advance player safety. But as any competent coach will tell you, while equipment and technology grab most of the headlines, when it comes to youth football, it's coaching techniques and rules, not helmets, that offer the most safety benefits.

Conversely, the greatest risks in youth football don't come from the simple fact that ten-year-olds might be allowed to tackle each other but from poorly trained, unsupervised, or overly macho coaches who treat little children like budding NFL players. Writing in *USA Today*, Thomas P. Dompier, an athletic trainer, sports-injury epidemiologist, and father, got to the heart of the issue:

> Today's helmets are tremendously effective at preventing eye, dental, skull and other facial fractures, and we seem to forget this benefit simply because they're unable to prevent all concussions, which is impossible for any helmet.
>
> Youth football remains the Wild West when it comes to organizational structure. You have USA Football, the national governing body, but there are also other national

organizations like Pop Warner and American Youth Football. By my estimation, those two organizations account for only a little over half of all youth football programs. Many leagues are independent or unaffiliated with any national organizations.

For example, my son played flag football for an unaffiliated recreational league in Indiana. In that league, as a 7-year-old, he was required to wear padded football pants, but not shoulder pads or a helmet. Despite wearing minimal equipment, he was taught to block and "tackle" as if playing tackle football. He was even taught the local high school football team chant.

Clearly that community sponsored recreational program, like so many others, was designed to feed quality players into the competitive high school program. My wife, also an athletic trainer, and I removed him from that league because it was not safe. Neither my wife nor I are encouraging our son to play tackle football. However, if he wanted to play, we would only let him join a league with sound practice and game policies, required coaching education, and a proper helmet that is effective for what it was designed [for], preventing death from skull fractures.

Proposed laws include banning tackle football below the age of 12 or 14. The main premise is that youthful brains are still developing and more susceptible to trauma and this would limit players' exposure to subclinical head impacts over a football career.

However, these bans would not address uneducated, overly competitive coaches, scholarship-seeking parents, or organizations competing to make money and/ or provide athletes to high school programs. Without extensive forethought, guidance and policy as to how flag football should be implemented, these bans would only exacerbate the unsafe conditions of the youth league to high school pipeline because they remove the protective equipment, without removing the bad actors who still see these programs as preparation for the high-contact version that will likely follow.[3]

Exactly right. I think the image many parents and members of the news media have of Pop Warner coaches is a bunch of frustrated would-be NFL players who throw kids to the wolves out of some delusional love of the game and the feeling that a few concussed fourth graders is a small price to pay for gridiron glory. Nothing could be further from the truth.

In fact, safety is part of the law governing youth football. For example, in 2009, the Lystedt Law was passed in Washington. It's named after a Seattle middle school player named Zack Lystedt, who took a head impact while playing as a thirteen-year-old in 2006, suffered an undiagnosed concussion, went back in the game, collapsed later that night, and spent the next three months in the hospital with brain swelling and bleeding. To this day, he still has physical symptoms and gets physical therapy. His law mandates that any athlete younger than eighteen who's suspected of having sustained a concussion has to come out of practice or a game and can't return until cleared by a medical professional.

That's just one of many, many steps that have been taken in recent years to make the youth game safer. The idea that parents, coaches, and governing bodies like USA Football are just throwing kids into the brain smasher is ridiculous. So let's look at how and why youth football is safer than ever in four areas: USA Football's Heads Up Football program, coaching improvements, rule changes, and equipment.

HEADS UP FOOTBALL BY THE NUMBERS

I KNOW ALL ABOUT THE *New York Times* "gotcha" story that said that the safety improvements touted by USA Football about Heads Up were wrong. And some of the numbers *were* wrong, but the story implied that the program did nothing to reduce head injuries, which is completely mistaken.

First of all, I can tell you from having coached for years that most injuries occur during practice, not games. I had been using Heads Up techniques as a coach for years before I presented them to USA Football, and I saw firsthand how much safer the kids were and how much better they played when they used them. They really do work, and evidence backs that up.

If you dig into the story instead of just reading the headline, you find that, for example, practice injuries in leagues following Heads Up guidelines dropped 63 percent. That's significant. As part of the Heads Up program, USA Football trains player-safety coaches for schools all over the country, and a study published in 2016 found that high schools with trained player-safety coaches had 88 percent lower practice concussion rates, 43 percent less time lost to practice injuries, and 57 percent lower injury rates in games.

USA Football has also done case studies with specific football programs and has found safety greatly improved. Virginia's Fairfax County Public Schools, the tenth-largest school district in the country, has used Heads Up Football since 2013, and in that time, the district has reported a 43.3 percent decline in concussions. True, as reported in the *Times*, the district has gone beyond the Heads Up guidelines—restricting full-contact practice time to ninety minutes per week, for example—but that doesn't diminish the positive effect of Heads Up. In another example, from 2014 to 2015, South Bend, Indiana, high school football programs reported a 40 percent reduction in concussions from football from 2014 to 2015, the first year the school system implemented Heads Up Football district-wide.[4]

So Heads Up does work. But there's a lot of suspicion attached to it because it's a product of USA Football, which is connected to the NFL. The bad press the NFL has gotten over the issue of denying the dangers of concussion (some of it deserved, as I've said) has led some people to conclude that USA Football is just a puppet of the league and that Heads Up is just an attempt to whitewash (or *brain*wash) the controversy over brain injury and long-term damage in youth football players. It doesn't help that Heads Up launched with a $45 million grant from the NFL Foundation, either.

However, as I said, I served on NFL's Return-to-Play Subcommittee and on the board of directors of USA Football for four years. I know how dedicated USA Football and the NFL are to improving coaching standards, instituting rules to reduce contact (especially for the smallest players), and using the latest safety equipment. Ever since Heads Up Football rolled out in April 2013, the mission has been to improve safety for youth and high school players by teaching proper tackling, certifying coaches in safety fundamentals, making sure every youth league has a player-safety coach, and teaching coaches, parents, and players how to recognize head injuries, including concussions, and treat them appropriately. It also addresses other risk factors like heat and hydration, as well as how to handle sudden cardiac arrest.

Through 2016, more than 142,000 youth and high school coaches earned their certification in Heads Up Football. It's a comprehensive program, and while it's not perfect, it is making a difference. That's not just my opinion, either. Dr. Bailes has said in the past that football is the safest it's ever been and believes youth football is taking all the right steps. "Six years ago we eliminated hit-contact drills in practice, so we've had no-hit contact in practice for the last six years," he says. "Last year we eliminated the kickoff for younger age groups. We have limited any contact at all to 25 percent of practice hours. So, if kids practice eight hours a week, they can only have any contact for two hours, and not to the head."

Dr. Bailes also believes the fears about young players developing CTE to be badly overblown. "As far as we know…the real risk is in those who have played for a long time," he says. "There have been a few cases of some CTE changes in the brain or some tau protein deposits in a handful of those who have played high school or college football. But the vast majority, 98 percent plus, are those who have played professionally for many, many years."

WE ARE THE GATEKEEPERS

Dr. Bailes is correct, but it's still up to youth football to protect young players against all potential health risks, even ones with a low probability of happening. That starts with the eighteen thousand or so Pop Warner coaches. They're amazing, but they are all volunteers and some need training in how to coach to reduce head injuries, which is what Heads Up Football is great for. I also know of a lot of organizations that are not a part of Pop Warner or USA Football but that have stayed up to date with the changes and improvements in practices and games. Not every independent league is that way, but more are seeing the value in the way we teach and play the game now.

The thing is, safety is not just the responsibility of coaches. That's why parents need to be involved and engaged. Go to practices. Watch what happens. Insist that your youth programs follow the correct practice techniques, head-trauma protocols, and hydration rules. If your coaches and league officials can answer all your questions and follow through on the field, your child is safer there than on the couch eating a doughnut and playing Xbox. Proper coaching is the most important safety measure of all.

Unfortunately, I didn't get good coaching as a kid; I was twenty-one before I really knew the proper techniques to play the game. Chuck Noll, the legendary head coach of the Steelers, used to talk about three principles from the day he started coaching to the day he stopped coaching:

1. Same foot, same shoulder.

2. Rising blow.

3. First contact wins.

That's how I learned how to play the game right. Basically, I was coaching using Heads Up techniques years before I ever presented them to USA Football. A few years ago, Jim Mora Jr. and Northwestern University head coach Pat Fitzgerald were on staff with me for USA Football's advisory committee on safety. It was our job to give youth football leagues some direction, because some of them weren't giving their coaches a lot of instruction. It was mostly, "Just go out and do the best you can."

I was on a conference call about our ideas for assisting youth programs. When I hung up, the phrase "better and safer" kept ringing in my head, and I looked up and there was one of my old Steeler playbooks. I could hear Chuck Noll say, "If you want to be a better, safer player, this is how you do it." That's when the "same foot, same shoulder," "rising blow," and "first contact" techniques popped into my head.

I sent those principles to USA Football, and other than one change that LaVar Arrington deserves a shout-out for (we removed kids getting their heads in front of a ball carrier, which protects their necks, forces them to use their shoulder pads, and teaches them to wrap up the player with their arms), that became Heads Up Football.

Let's take the first one: "Same foot, same shoulder." You're in a coiled position every time you're in a position to block, carry the ball, or make a tackle. That's the core position that you always need to be in to be successful as a football player. You can't be standing up tall and get out of a break. Your hips have to sink low and your knees have to be bent to get in and out of breaks efficiently or to run good routes. It works for quarterbacks, too. To throw the ball successfully, your knees have to be bent, and your hips and feet are essential. Standing upright to throw the football doesn't work.

"Rising blow." If you want to make a block, carry the ball, or tackle, you have to be in that coiled position so you can deliver a rising blow. That's where your power comes from. But that's also protection. If you're standing upright, your joints, especially your knees, are weaker. But if you have your knees bent, your hips are down, and your shoulder is in line with your feet in a coiled position, you're powerful and protected.

That blew my mind. That approach helps you as a blocker, a tackler, and a runner. It helps you across the board. Football is not played up around the rim like basketball. Football is played with a low center of gravity. The greater leverage you have, the better technique you have, and you are a better, safer player.

"First contact wins" means exactly that. Next time you watch a game, watch the trenches—the offensive and defensive lines. The first player to get his hands on the other guy wins that encounter 90 percent of the time. Being quick is vital in football.

Coach Noll made everybody do this stuff, from the punters to the quarterback. So when I had Beau and started coaching youth football, I thought, *How cool is this going to be to teach seven-year-olds how to play the game right from the very first time they enter a football field?* How much better would I have been had I learned how to play the game fundamentally from the beginning?

Back when I was a kid, safety was wearing a helmet, period. We did tackling drills by tackling our coaches. Think about that. We were tackling grown men. They would run the ball and we would tackle them. But we didn't get any real instruction: "Wrap your arms up, put your head through it," that sort of thing. It was about "teaching boys how to be men." But boys aren't men. They're boys, still developing, and you have to teach them in a way that accounts for that—plus the fact that boys come in all shapes and sizes, from skinny and fast to slow and strong.

WE'RE CHANGING HOW COACHES THINK ABOUT THE GAME

So I DECIDED TO IMPLEMENT a head-trauma protocol. But I found a conflict I didn't expect between being tough and playing football. A head injury is not one where you physically can't play, so it's difficult to understand why you have to sit out. The sensitivity is a conflict with toughness. But what's wrong with being tough and smart? You can blend them. So we did.

Remember my youth football head-trauma rule from early in the book? Every year for my seven years of coaching Beau, I started the season by saying, "Men, this game is a tough game for tough people. It's not for everybody. But it's also a smart game for intelligent people, and we're going to be smart. So if you guys get hurt, in any way, but specifically a concussion, I'm going to remove you, and you are not going to play the next week. Period. Just because you're not playing does not mean you're not tough because you're still going to be tough. But you're also going to be smart. We're going to take care of that injury."

Those seven- and eight-year-old kids were like, "Okay, that's cool."

And until those kids hit twelve or thirteen and the pads started popping, we had a grand total of two concussions. Fast-forward a few years and we're launching Heads Up Football. I have a pilot program of two hundred coaches from all over the country, from some of the biggest programs in USA Football, and we're introducing Heads Up to them. This kid—he's maybe twenty-three or twenty-four—gets up and starts telling the room about all the techniques that won't be allowed anymore. "Biting the football?" he says. "Done. Leading with your head? Done." He's going down a list of all the classic blood-and-guts techniques, and these coaches were not buying it. I could see it. Everybody in that room was thinking, *Kid, I've been coaching longer than you've been alive.*

Then one coach raised his hand and said, "Who are you? You know, I've been coaching like this for twenty years." Everybody started butchering this poor kid, and I wanted to help him out. I was standing there with Scott Hallenbeck, USA Football CEO, and I said, "I'm going up front." I walked to the front of the room and said, "Hey, guys, time out. Let's start over. Tell me something. By raise of hands, who knows Chuck Noll?" Everyone raised a hand. I said, "Keep your hands up if you believe he's one of the greatest coaches of all time." I played for him for five years, so I had my hand up. Everybody kept his hand up.

I said, "He was the greatest teacher I've ever been around. The guy is a legend. What we are showing you is what Coach Noll used to teach to help everybody on the Steelers become as good a football player as he could be, regardless of position." Then I got serious. I said, "Men, we're being targeted. We need to give direction at this level to help kids play the game in a better, safer way. At the end of the day, what gives these kids the most joy? It's not winning. It's about seeing a kid smile when he feels what it's like to do something well. That's what it's about. Kids love having success, and you can teach that every day in youth football. Plus, win or lose, the kids are still excited about going to get pizza with their buddies and talk about the game. This helps breed success in all our kids. These principles will help us grow the game and help our kids become safer football players."

Now everybody's hands were down, and there was a totally different atmosphere in that room. They were in. But we've had to get past the idea that football is all about being macho. Maybe that's true for the professionals, though you heard from Ben Roethlisberger earlier that even the pros can be—and should be—tough and smart. But even if you believe that the sport is about toughness, these are kids.

Football will not be a career for most of them. It'll be a part of their childhood that will lead to something else. They should be learning to use their brains, not rattling them. They should be learning to be strategic and memorize plays and develop their hand-eye coordination and be great teammates. That's what youth football is for, and getting that word out has meant reprogramming a lot of coaches.

THE BIGGEST THREAT IS IGNORANCE

BUT THE BIGGEST OBSTACLE to good coaching is still ignorance. People still tell me, "Football is terrible; it's constant banging." Again, I'm not going to sit here and tell you that kids taking constant blows to the head is a good thing because it's not. But that's not what's happening. There are fifty-two weeks in a year; we practice and play anywhere from eight to twelve of them. Everything has been redesigned to minimize impacts. You don't need to practice four or five days a week in youth football, so in our league we only practiced two days a week. I had one fifteen-minute live-contact practice once every two weeks. We played on Saturday, and everyone played.

That was the environment in 2009 when I went to Congress. I was the last one to speak, and I challenged them. I talked about how ignorant we were about football and concussion and CTE. I was speaking from personal experience as a parent, player, and coach. I said that yes, we needed better care, but we also needed a concussion protocol at the youth level because there was so much ignorance about this injury. You had Roger Goodell; DeMaurice Smith, executive director of the National Football League Players Association; a few owners; some doctors; and me in the chambers. When I finished, Rep. John Conyers Jr., chairman of the committee, said, "Merril, do you want to explain ignorance to me?"

I said, "Yes, sir, I will explain ignorance to you." I told this story: The week before, I had a kid, Griffy, who was a little wobbly after he got hit. I knew Griffy. Griffy didn't walk like that. I knew that he had gotten his bell rung, and I pulled him from the game. His brother, Jake, would coach with us on Saturdays sometimes, and he happened to be there. I told him, "Take Griffy over to the sideline and make sure he doesn't get any worse. If he gets emotional or throws up, we'll take him to the emergency room." I knew Griffy wasn't really that bad but wanted to teach his brother what to look for after a hit to the head. Everything is a teaching opportunity, and we're all safer if we're all watching out for each other.

Five minutes later, Jake came up to me and told me Griffy was ready to play. I said, "Jake, get his pads off. He's done." Jake started to argue with me, saying that we needed Griffy. And we did. He was one of my better players, and we were playing one of the better teams. But that didn't matter one bit. I said, "Jake, he's done. I'm not putting him back out there. Get his pads off."

Story over, I looked at that House committee and said, "Let me ask you something. Do you think Jake doesn't love his brother? Do you think he was going to throw him out in harm's way? Jake doesn't know what I know. But here's the danger. Jake could be a head coach anywhere in this country, coaching your kid, putting your kid back out there in a dangerous environment. That's ignorance. We need to change the ignorance. We need to get a protocol and help people who don't know what I know. We remove kids from harm's way during that two-week window and have them evaluated by a medical doctor." Dead silence. If I'd had a mic, I would have dropped it. Conyers had no response.

This has taken time. It's just like seatbelt laws when they were implemented. Guys who had been driving bareback for forty years were like, "To heck with that; I ain't never gonna put no seatbelt on." Now even those guys won't get into a car without putting a seatbelt on. It's become normal, and they've seen the benefits.

It takes about a decade to change people's minds, and we're on our way. The kids who learned these things in Pop Warner and high school will be the ones who change it. We have a protocol: if we remove kids who suffer a head trauma and they don't play the following week, we have just basically taken about 99 percent of them out of the danger zone. Just think of that. If you educate everybody to coach a certain way, practice a certain way, and follow that protocol, you're going to protect a lot of kids.

Chris Fore, the longtime athletic director and high school coach you met in chapter 8, agrees that coaching is the X factor. While he's seen some great coaches, there are a lot of bad apples, too. "I started coaching this game in the nineties," he says. "The youth football in my community was very good. The coaches were very good where I was born and raised down in San Diego County. But when I left that nest and saw youth football in other areas I said, 'Whoa. There's some *bad* coaching going on.'

"The thing is, my wife and I made a decision before the word *concussion* was on the national mindset that my kids would not play tackle football until junior high. One of the main reasons for that isn't the physical part of it. For me, it's more the mental aspect of it because it's a five-day-a-week thing. I've seen so many kids who play youth football forever and get burned out quick in high school, or they're not playing any other sports. I love the fact that my son plays baseball, basketball, flag football, and soccer. I don't think he would be able to do all that stuff if he was playing tackle football because it just demands so much."

But USA Football is wide open. Come to a practice. Look what's happening at the high school level. Ask questions. These doctors have never even done that, and they have no concept of what's happening on a football field, but they're going to guide football?

IF THE RULES DON'T WORK, CHANGE THEM

BACK IN THE DAY, we used to run something in practice called the "Oklahoma drill" (it was called that because a University Oklahoma coach named Bud Wilkinson developed it). Two players would line up three yards from one another surrounded by blocking bags, creating an area about nine feet by three feet. Then, at the sound of the whistle, the players would charge at each other until one guy went down. It was gladiator stuff. It was brutal.

That's the old-school football that so many coaches fought to keep, and we've done away with that. There was a game we used to play as kids called British bulldog. You get a hundred kids on one side of the football field, with one kid—the bulldog—out in the middle. You yell, "British bulldog!" and everybody runs across the field and tries to avoid getting tackled by the bulldog. Once you're tackled, you become a bulldog and try to take down anyone left. You keep doing it until there's only one person left standing. That's what you did. You kicked the tar out of each other.

Not anymore. Coaching is critical, but so are rules designed to keep kids safe. In 2017, USA Football handed down a major practice rules change. Practices can feature contact for no more than thirty minutes. Each team now has six to nine players on the field, not eleven, and the field is smaller. Kickoffs and punts are gone, which means no more kickoff and punt returns (something the NFL is considering). Players have to start each play in a crouching position, not the classic three-point stance. And in practices, players other than linemen who line up more than three feet apart cannot tackle at full speed or head-on. The rules are the first to earn the endorsement of the American College of Sports Medicine, the American Medical Society for Sports Medicine, and the National Athletic Trainers' Association.

In practices, coaches even use a five-part scale for the intensity of impact that's all about minimizing actual contact while still teaching kids how to hit:

- Air: Players run a drill unopposed without contact.

- Bags: Drill is run against a bag or another soft-contact surface.

- Control: Drill is run at assigned speed with a predetermined "winner" assigned by the coach. Contact remains above the waist, and players stay on their feet.

- Thud: Drill is run at competitive speed until the moment of contact. There is no predetermined "winner." Contact remains above the waist, and players stay on their feet.

- Live Action: Drill is run in gamelike conditions and is the only time that players are taken to the ground.[5]

Speaking of tackling, one of the biggest rule changes involves how to tackle. USA Football has incorporated the shoulder-first tackling common in rugby—a sport that has a head-injury rate higher than that of the NFL but where players don't wear protective headgear.[6] Rocky Seto, the former Seattle Seahawks coach, brought rugby technique to the Seahawks, and when Pete Carroll took them to a Super Bowl win, everybody wanted to know what Seto had done to make a difference.

Basically, the idea is to keep players from having helmet-to-helmet impacts. The tackler is taught to get low (thank you, Coach Noll), get his lead foot in between the ball carrier's feet, and drive his front shoulder into the other player between the chest and hips and then take down the player's center of gravity by wrapping up his knees. Down he goes, and the helmet—and thus the head—never comes into play. It takes practice, but done right, it's a clean, solid tackle. As we teach it, more and more kids will learn to tackle while keeping their heads out of the line of fire. Go to the USA Football website, and you'll see strict guidelines on handing off, orchestrating practice, handling injuries, and so on. That's how you keep kids safe, folks!

Something nobody is talking about: hydration and exertional heatstroke (EHS). High school teams run two-a-days in the summer heat and humidity, wearing heavy gear. Those are punishing conditions, and every year kids die from EHS when they get overheated and can't cool down. In fact, as of 2015, EHS was the third-leading cause of sudden death in high school athletes.[7] But last time I looked, nobody was looking to ban youth football because of that.

Heatstroke and hydration illnesses are 100 percent fixable. According to the University of Connecticut, between 1980 and 2015, there were forty-four exertional heatstroke-related deaths during preseason high school football practices. But in states that have adopted new mandatory guidelines designed to help high school players acclimate to the heat gradually, there have been zero heat-related deaths since 2016.[8]

USA Football now has precise situation guidelines for helping players adapt to the heat, along with rules about practicing (and not practicing) in certain temperatures and guidelines for keeping players hydrated. See? We're even changing the rules to address things parents aren't freaking out about.

THE FUTURE IS NOW

EQUIPMENT IS THE LEAST IMPORTANT aspect of safety because there's only so much you can do to defy physics. But even with limitations, changes can always be made to gear to help sports become safer.

For example, there's a condition called *commotio cordis*, which means "concussion of the heart." Kids playing Little League baseball would get hit with a pitch in the chest at a specific point in the heart's electrical cycle where it's vulnerable, and they would drop dead. No undiagnosed cardiac condition, just gone. Terrible stuff. Then researchers from the Tufts University School of Medicine fired baseballs at a group of young pigs at different points in the EKG to find where that vulnerable point was, and that study showed that safety baseballs reduced cardiac events.[9]

When they figured out what was causing the deaths, they made the baseball a little softer. It doesn't affect the game, but now if kids get hit in the chest, the ball doesn't transfer the same energy to the heart muscle, and there's no arrhythmia. Plus, a lot of ballparks have installed automatic electrical defibrillators, just in case.

Changing equipment isn't the solution by itself, but it certainly helps. After I was done playing, I started thinking about NASCAR helmets and safety gear. A NASCAR helmet is better than a football helmet because it's built to absorb impact. A football helmet is meant to *withstand* impact. Also, there's a cost issue. If a NASCAR helmet's in an accident, you hope it survives the one crash and get a new helmet. You can't do that in football, especially in youth football, where budgets are so tight.

So the trick has been to build helmets that absorb and deflect impact and to deploy sensors and accelerometers to determine how much force we need to deflect away from vulnerable young brains. Serious work with sensors began with Kevin Guskiewicz at the University of North Carolina, who began putting sensors in the helmets of college football players in 2003 and continued with Dr. Stefan Duma,

Harry C. Wyatt Professor of Engineering and founder of the Virginia Tech–Wake Forest Center for Injury Biomechanics. Duma changed the game when he put accelerometers in the helmets of six- to eight-year-old Auburn Eagles football players in 2011 and recorded impacts as high as 50 to 100 g's. For reference, the danger zone for a possible concussion is around 98 g's.

The research led to Pop Warner and USA Football adopting the new rules and coaching methods I've told you about, resulting in Pop Warner head impacts dropping by 50 percent.[10] It also began a sort of arms race in the world of football headgear designed to better absorb and reduce the violent kinetic energy delivered to the head during an impact. Companies like Schutt are testing helmets with advanced concussion technology: more points of contact that secure the player's head more firmly and keep it from being jerked around after a hit, which is the action that commonly causes a concussion.

Riddell is marketing helmets equipped with its InSite impact-response system. The helmet is fitted with a sensor array that measures the force of impacts, and if it detects g-force above a certain limit, a transmitter alerts the coach and athletic trainer that the athlete needs to come out of the game for evaluation.

Then there's Seattle start-up Vicis, which is taking on Schutt and Riddell with its ZERO1 helmet. Its key design feature is a layer of shock-absorbing columns (often compared to the bumper of a car) beneath the softer outer layer that can absorb impacts from multiple directions. The ZERO1 actually beat out thirty-three other helmets in NFL lab testing to determine which helmet reduced head-impact severity.[11]

"There's a lot of activity in this space, as you can imagine," Duma told me. "There are new helmet designs coming out almost weekly from different manufacturers. The major changes have been to soften the outer shell and look at new layers of materials in the helmets. Manufacturers work very hard to optimize the design to reduce linear and rotational accelerations.

"In a general sense, football helmets are about 95 percent as good as they can get," he continues. "The very best ones are the ones that are out right now. I think they're about as good as they're going to get because there's only so much you can do with the space limitations."

Duma's team took their youth football impact data, ran it through a mathematical concussion-risk algorithm, and created the Summation of Tests for the Analysis of Risk (STAR) system for grading helmets based on their ability to reduce brain acceleration during different types of hits. That rating system is now widely used with every major brand of football helmet.

For good reason, too: according to the data, a 150 g hit in a one-star helmet only delivered 75 g's of force to the head of someone wearing a five-star model. That's the difference between "getting your bell rung" and ending up in the ER. However, Duma and his team continue to work to learn more about keeping players safe.

"We're instrumenting youth football teams," he says. "We started as young as seven years old, through grade school, middle school, and high school. We're trying to better understand how the game changes. How do we develop those products? There's a lot of work in age differences. There's a lot of work on how you construct practices. How much practice time should there be? Should we do two a day? Should we not do that? Should we limit different types of practices? We do a lot work with the sensors and with video to quantify the different events and then to provide guidance to organizations like the NCAA and Pop Warner, in terms of how to construct better and safer practices.

"I think if you really look at football in the past five years, there's been dramatic change, more than any other sport," he concludes. "That's not only in the NFL but certainly at the college and youth levels, too. There have been really dramatic changes in how the sport is played. I would point to that as pretty strong evidence that change can be made. If you look at the youth levels, just in the past five years, they've dramatically reduced the amount of practice time. That's removed about 50 percent of the head-impact exposure. If you look at any sport, I'd argue that no other sport has made that kind of change that quickly. The NFL is doing everything they can to eliminate helmet-to-helmet contact. College football is ejecting players. Those are pretty dramatic steps. I'm not sure there's a lot of additional room without really changing what the game looks like."

State-of-the-art gear can be expensive, beyond the means of many youth and high school programs. But as technology improves and competition grows, prices come down. As other innovative start-up companies join Vicis in challenging the entrenched helmet companies, prices will drop. Who knows, maybe more cash-strapped youth leagues will start using the sixty-dollar Guardian Cap, a foam shell that covers the regular helmet surface and supposedly reduces head impact forces by 33 percent.[12]

The point is that good things are happening in coaching, rules, science, and technology. Despite the scary hype, youth football has never been safer. Now, let's finish our journey by looking at how we're going to protect all players in the coming years.

CHAPTER II

FROM THE CLEATS TO THE HELMET

Football is a great deal like life in that it teaches that work, sacrifice, perseverance, competitive drive, selflessness, and respect for authority is the price that each and every one of us must pay to achieve any goal that is worthwhile.

—VINCE LOMBARDI, PRO FOOTBALL HALL OF FAME COACH

CHAPTER 11 PLAYBOOK

- How Walter Payton inspired me to become the player and man I am

- The bright future of football because of science, technology, culture, and awareness

- There are six kinds of concussions, and we know more than ever about how to treat them and get players back on the field

- Nonpharmaceutical approaches, such as diet and supplementation, can make the brain resistant to impact and help speed recovery from trauma

- Football is a positive force for turning children into terrific adults

AFTER WE LAUNCHED Heads Up Football, you would think the press would have been full of stories saying, "Look at everything youth football is doing to become safer." Instead, it was, "Look at all the head trauma in football." The public has the idea that football hasn't responded to the need for a greater emphasis on safety—that, from Pop Warner to the NFL, the powers that be have just ignored the issues.

Nothing could be further from the truth. From the cleats to the helmets, every aspect of football has been altered by a deep concern for safety, with some advances trickling down to the youth game and others trickling up to the NFL. In this concluding chapter, let's look at all the ways knowledge is making football safer and its players healthier and how the game enhances the life of just about every kid who plays it.

SWEETNESS

As I REFLECT ON MY CAREER, what always stands out are the people my path has crossed. As a kid, I dreamed of playing in the NFL, and I had my dad make me a wall of cork in my bedroom so I could pin my goals up. People always told me, "Write your goals down," so I thought if I was going to write them down, why not put them up so I could see them every day? My bedroom was the place I started and ended each day, so that wall of goals was my life.

At the top of the wall, I had my number one goal: "I will play in the NFL." Surrounding that was a picture of the Pittsburgh Steelers, my favorite team, and my favorite player, Chicago Bears running back Walter "Sweetness" Payton. When I was a kid, Payton's training methods were legendary. There was a sand-based hill he would run almost every day—eighty yards long, with a forty-degree angle. That's like running up the pitched roof of a house for 240 feet—*on sand*. Just walking up something like that would leave most people gasping for air! But Payton would run up it as fast as he could and then rest while he came back down, sometimes as fast as he went up.

Then one day, when I was fifteen, I saw an interview with Payton. I don't remember it perfectly, but it went something like this. The interviewer asked Payton, "What makes you better than anyone else?" Payton paused, and then he said something like, "I want it more than they do every day of the week. When I train in the offseason on that dirt hill at six in the morning, I want it more than they do. When I practice and there aren't 65,000 fans in the stands, I want it more than they do. Then at one o'clock on Sunday, I want it more than they do." Those words changed my life. From that day on, when I trained, practiced, and played, I wanted it more than anyone else. That became my mindset, too.

We all have people we look up to and admire, and I looked up to Walter Payton. I'm sure that my dream to be a pro player like him helped me deal with peer pressure and make good choices growing up. My mom bought me a Bears lamp when I was thirteen, and it still lights up a corner of my office.

So you can imagine what it was like when I was drafted by the Steelers and then looked at our second preseason game, and we were playing the Bears in Chicago. For that moment, my goal of making the team was secondary to meeting my hero. In 1987, when I was a rookie and Payton was in the final year of his Hall of Fame career, teams would cut players every week, sometimes daily. There was no limit to players you could bring to camp, so a lot of guys got cut, and it always gets your attention when somebody isn't there the next day. My first preseason game was against the Washington Redskins, and I had impressed enough as a running back and special teams player that I'd avoided getting cut. I would play in the Bears game.

The night before the game, I was going over my notes—not of the game plan but of what I would say to Walter Payton when I met him. Because I was young and dumb, I asked Frank Pollard for advice. He was in his ninth year as a running back and had taken me under his wing, so I knocked on his hotel room door. When he answered, I asked him if he thought I should approach Payton before or after the game. Frank got a very odd look on his face, took a deep breath, and said, "Neither. What's more important: meeting Walter Payton or making this team?" It was like being sucker punched, but he was right. Still, that didn't stop me. I was a fan obsessed.

The evening of the game came. I had flown my dad in to film the moment I met Payton; my mother had passed a little over a year earlier, and I thought it would be a good way to get his mind off it. He sneaked in a video camera, and his only job was to find me after the game as I introduced myself to my hero. No big deal, right? Fast-forward to the fourth quarter, and with fifteen seconds left, the Bears were crushing us 50–0. Was I concerned? No, all I cared about was telling my idol about his impact on my life. Just before we were about to run our last play, I looked over to the Bears' sideline, and there Payton was with fullback Matt Suhey. *Perfect—get this last play over, and I'm right over there as fast as these feet can get me there.*

We ran a pass play, and like every other play that day, it didn't work. Game over. I could go meet Walter! I spun around and saw that players were going in a million directions—across the field, to the locker room, into the stands, you name it. I couldn't find him. Well, I had not come this far to miss meeting my hero; I would go into the opposing locker room if I had to. I started to head to the tunnel, but on my way I looked left, and there was Walter Payton walking all by himself at the fifty-yard line.

I took off like a cheetah looking for its first meal. But when I came up to him, I was taken aback. In my mind, Payton was a giant, but in reality, I was bigger and taller than he was! That floored me. When you see a man run the ball like he did—with such balance, grace, and power—something is different about him. Well, I pulled it together, stuck my hand out, and said, "My name is Merril Hoge." I told him he had been my hero and told him about the lamp, the hills, and the stairs. The trouble was, I didn't know how to wrap up, so I asked him for an autograph.

I know. An autograph, right after a game? Like he had a pen in his jersey? I still roll my eyes at that. But he was incredible. He looked at me and said, "Merril, thank you for taking the time to come over and tell me those amazing things. That's the nicest thing I have ever been told." Then, because he didn't have a pen, he took off his wristbands and elbow pads and gave them to me, shook my hand, and walked to the tunnel, leaving me on cloud nine. I've never forgotten that.

Walter Payton gave me his time and genuine kindness at a time when I'm sure all he wanted was to get to the locker room and shower. I've never had the talents of Walter Payton, but his example helped me get *everything* out of the talents I did have. More important, his lesson of being kind and humble helped make me the man I am. Life is about preparation, accountability, work, but it's also about treating people with respect and gratitude.

The point is that the experience of playing football, no matter the level, shapes who you are and how you live your life. If you work hard and keep your head on straight, it will teach you everything you need to know about living well. I want as many kids and adults as possible to have that experience, so let's wrap up this journey by looking at the future of our great game and why it's getting better and better every year.

DIAGNOSTIC ADVANCES

FRED MCNEILL WAS A LINEBACKER for the Minnesota Vikings from 1974 to 1985. After his career, which included playing in two Super Bowls, he went to William Mitchell College of Law, graduated at the top of his class, and became a partner with a Minneapolis law firm. But he was later diagnosed with dementia and then with ALS and died in 2015. However, Fred's legacy lives on because thanks to him, scientists believe that we might one day be able to diagnose neurodegenerative diseases in living patients.

Normally, a formal diagnosis of a condition like CTE requires dissection and microscopic examination of a person's brain—which, obviously, can only happen when that person is dead. That's still the case. But an experimental scanning tool first tested in 2012 uses a radioactive tracer substance to bind to tau proteins, allowing a positron emission tomography (PET) scan to detect the distinctive pattern associated with CTE while the patient is on the right side of the grass. A scan found that pattern in McNeill's brain.[1] If the result stands up to scientific scrutiny, it's a big deal.

But I'm speaking in qualifiers because they're justified. First of all, according to the doctors involved in the pilot study, the signs detected by the PET scan look a lot like the signs of depression. Also, finding a tau pattern in McNeill's brain doesn't mean he had CTE or that CTE led to his ALS. Experts have expressed doubt that a person can be diagnosed with CTE simply by a positive tau stain, considering that the same protein can appear in healthy brains.[2] The scan result is just a correlation in a single case; it's not confirmation of anything. It's a step. That's all.

Still, it's an encouraging step. If you remember UCLA's Dr. Kristen Willeumier from chapter 7, you might also recall that she and her team have been doing great work helping current and retired athletes recover from some of their mood, behavioral, and cognitive problems. Well, she worked with Fred McNeill on the scan research.

"Fred came to see us back in 2009, when we started our big NFL study," she says. "He was a first-round draft pick, very bright man, went to UCLA. I don't know the exact number of games he played, but had a very good career, and when he left the NFL, he went to law school and graduated valedictorian for his class. He's clearly a smart man.

"Fred became a partner in his law firm, but when he came to see us, he was in his mid-fifties and clueless about what was going on in his brain," she continues. "He knew we were running this brain-imaging study in professional athletes, and he had symptoms of depression and some issues with his memory. We scan him, and he's got frontotemporal-lobe dementia and doesn't even know it. We immediately put him on a brain-rehabilitation protocol because we were saying, 'Wow, the damage here is severe; we really need to help steer his life in the best direction possible.'

"We ended up working with Fred for seven years, and I think of him as a success story, not a failure, because although he did pass away from ALS, we were able to help him maintain brain function and maintain connection with his family," Dr. Willeumier goes on. "He was one of the players I sent over to Dr. Omalu, and he happened to be the player who was shown to have CTE in his brain while living. Then Dr. Omalu autopsied his brain and confirmed that he had CTE."

Even though we need a lot more long-term research to determine where tau comes from and what causes CTE, we can never have too much accurate information about what's going on in our brains, especially while we're alive enough to do something about it. That work, Dr. Willeumier says, is continuing.

"Now there's a player in the study, forty-five years of age, who was a center for the Green Bay Packers," she says. "He played a few years in the NFL, left due to an injury, and had two master's degrees, but Dr. Omalu's studies showed the presence of CTE in his brain." Kristen tells me that other researchers are looking for tau markers in the cerebrospinal fluid, the stuff surrounding the brain inside the cranium. And while everything is at its early stages and has to be looked at with caution, the idea that we might be able to detect the physical signs of neurodegenerative diseases early, while they might still be treatable, is exciting.

IMPROVING HELMET TECHNOLOGY

I TOLD YOU ABOUT MY CONVERSATION with a NASCAR official about helmets and the fact that while NFL helmets are designed to withstand impact (so you don't destroy your helmet after every play), NASCAR helmets are designed to absorb and deflect the force of an impact and be destroyed in the process—which is fine, since once you crash you're pretty much out of the race for the day anyway. But what a lot of people don't know is that the NFL has been paying close attention to helmet safety and conducts annual tests on helmets to determine which ones players may and may not use. In the past, players could wear any helmet that met the current certification standards of National Operating Committee on Standards for Athletic Equipment.

Not anymore. For example, based on the results of the league's 2018 study, which is done by an independent testing lab in Ottawa, Canada, called Biokinetics, the league has banned ten helmet models, including helmets from Riddell, Schutt, and Rawlings.[3] To help players choose the safest helmet, each team also posts a poster in its locker room that clearly shows which helmets have been shown to best reduce head-impact severity. At a glance, players can quickly see which helmets performed best and which ones are prohibited by the league.[4]

That's great, but what about truly new helmet technology that helps protect players? That's in the works, too. In addition to its InSite impact-response system, helmet giant Riddell has rolled out the InSite training tool, which coaches can use to create individual player head-impact profiles and improve brain safety for each player using specialized training techniques and practice plans.[5] And while I already mentioned the Vicis ZERO1, which the NFL considers the state of the art in helmet safety, there's something genuinely futuristic going on out in Boulder, Colorado.

Chris Yakacki, a professor of mechanical engineering at the University of Colorado, cofounded a company called Impressio that is developing a helmet padding made from something called liquid-crystal elastomers (LCEs). The substance, which Yakacki calls "reverse flubber" because of its tremendous ability to absorb the energy of an impact, can also become soft and absorbent in the direction of an impact while staying rigid in the other direction. Yakacki, who's already gotten some outside funding to turn his LCEs into helmet tech, believes the padding could revolutionize helmet technology.[6]

The NFL is also experimenting for the first time with position-specific helmets.[7] In theory, such a helmet might be designed differently to protect the head of a quarterback, who's more likely to strike the back or side of his head after a sack, versus an offensive lineman, who's probably going to get most of his impact at the front of the head. The whole thing's still pretty experimental, but the innovative spirit is promising.

SIX KINDS OF CONCUSSIONS

SPEAKING OF INNOVATION, EVEN AFTER an athlete experiences a mild brain trauma, there are more and better ways to treat it than ever before—certainly more than when I was playing. When the subject is concussion and post-concussion syndrome, the leading expert in the country is probably Dr. Micky Collins, who (in case you've forgotten) runs the University of Pittsburgh Medical Center (UPMC) Sports Medicine Concussion Program.

I have a personal story about the work they do at UPMC. I've already told you that my son, Beau, suffered a concussion in 2017 at BYU. But really, his concussion history goes back farther. He got his first major concussion when he slipped in the shower in 2015, his freshman year. He then got a concussion against Wisconsin in 2017, but during his recovery from that one, he did very little physically or athletically. He got back to his baseline cognitively and felt better before being cleared to play a couple of weeks later. In his next game, against Utah State, he suffered his second concussion in two weeks. That hit too close to home for me, and I knew I had to get him to Pittsburgh to see Micky Collins at UPMC.

I told Dr. Collins about what had happened during the last several weeks, but I had forgotten about the shower accident. After he did his evaluation of Beau, he came to me and said, "Merril, this has been going on longer than two weeks." The light bulb went off, and I told him about Beau slipping in the shower. The point is, Dr. Collins knew right away that there was more to Beau's condition. He and his team really know concussions.

Beau picks up the story about what happened when I took him to UPMC. "A few days [after my concussion], my dad and I were on a plane to Pittsburgh to see Dr. Collins," he says. "One of my fears going to UPMC, and talking to doctors in general, was that they were going to tell me I could not play football anymore. However, five minutes of conversing with Dr. Collins helped reassure me that I would not only be able to play again, but that when I did my brain would be fully recovered.

"I had done several tests before talking with Dr. Collins, so once I was with him he and his team had already pinpointed what type of concussion I had," Beau continues. "This was news for me, as I had no idea there were even categories for concussions. I fell into the category of a vestibular system concussion. He had asked me if I had been more prone to getting carsick since my concussions, and I absolutely had. Just driving from the airport to UPMC, I had gotten carsick on some of the windier roads my dad and I had been driving on.

"Once Dr. Collins and his team zeroed in on that, they were able to give me specific exercises that actually made me feel symptomatic," he goes on. "He explained that this was the purpose of the exercises—it was a good thing I was starting to feel sick from them. As I continued with the exercises, I began to be able to do them faster and for longer, as Dr. Collins predicted. The reason for this, as they explained to me at UPMC, was that my vestibular system was essentially recalibrating. Within five days of visiting UPMC, and with my trainers at BYU helping me perform the exercises as specified, I felt 100 percent again, physically and cognitively."

Beau and I walked out of UPMC empowered and excited. Before we got in the car, I said to him, "Twenty-two years ago, they retired me and gave me eighteen months to recover with no cognitive treatment plan. Now they have treatments to repair and help you recover without being vulnerable when you return!" As a dad, I could not be more confident and happy for Beau because I know he was concerned they would tell him he couldn't play anymore. What a blessing it is to have these treatments and protocols in sports today.

A MULTIDISCIPLINARY APPROACH TO CONCUSSION TREATMENT

ASIDE FROM HELPING BEAU get back on the field, Dr. Collins's methods have helped hundreds of players fully recover from concussions—including NFL players like Denver Broncos safety Su'a Cravens, who sat out the entire 2017 season due to post-concussion syndrome.[8] That's the difference twenty-four years of research and learning can make. Back then, post-concussion syndrome ended my career; today, players can make a full recovery because we know more.

The approach at UPMC relies on multiple therapeutic approaches that address the many complex aspects of any concussion:

- **Neuropsychologists** identify symptoms and conditions that could impact recovery, design treatment programs, and quarterback (pardon the pun) the rehabilitation program.

- **Vestibular physical therapy** addresses symptoms related to dizziness and balance.

- **Exertional physical therapy** uses strength training and aerobic exercise to rehabilitate the vestibular system.

- **Primary care sports medicine, physical medicine, and rehabilitation** helps manage conditions that need medical care, such as anxiety, sleep disorders, and headaches.

- **Behavioral neuro-optometry** addresses vision problems.

- **Orthopedic/neurosurgery** treats ongoing symptoms, such as neck pain and headaches.

- **Neuroradiology** uses advanced imaging to locate problems, including bleeding in the brain.

With this strategy, Dr. Collins and his team have revolutionized concussion and post-concussion treatment, including identifying six distinct types of concussions and developing treatment methods that go far beyond the "lie down in a dark room" ideas of years past. I talked with him, and he told me all about his approach.

"For the first five years of my existence at UPMC, we were doing extensive research looking at really understanding the phenomenology of this injury," he says. "Were the grading scales accurate? Were boys the same as girls? Was loss of consciousness more important than other symptoms? What symptoms predicted the best outcomes? How long did it take patients to recover? What are the effects of repetitive concussions in terms of neurocognitive function? We just published, published, published, published, published. What we learned is that this is a very heterogenetic injury. It's different for everyone—and by the way, the grading scales don't work.

"Fast-forward after hundreds of scientific papers, thousands of patients, extensive experience, collaboration with other places around the country, and this is what I have done full time, sixty hours a week, for the past eighteen years of my life," Collins continues. "We're really to a point now where we understand that there are different types of concussions. We understand that some of the subtler symptoms are what is really important. Take dizziness. If you have dizziness, that is six times more predictive of a poor outcome than any other symptom, including loss of consciousness.

"We found that there are different risk factors for injury," he goes on. "It's not necessarily how hard you get hit in the head; it's what you bring to the table when you get hit in the head as to not only how bad the concussion is, but what type of concussion you have. We've learned that. We've learned that boys are different than girls in terms of recovery. Kids take longer to recover than adults. We've learned that active treatments are critical. We [learned] the phenomenology of the injury through science. What were three thousand patients a year became five thousand patients a year became ten thousand patients a year and are now eighteen thousand patient visits a year to our clinic.

"I was really understanding this injury better," Collins says. "I understand what predicts what. I understand how to measure the injury. I understand how to look at it, but how do we treat it? But I was beating my head against the wall because patients weren't getting better very quickly. We were finding that recovery takes longer than people realize. Nobody was talking about [treatment]. It was identify and manage.

"From that day forward, the real focus of our program has been actually *treating* concussions," he concludes. "That's when we started to really understand that there are different types of concussions, different physical therapies that work, and that you have to apply these physical therapies in certain ways. Everyone's looking for a magic bullet, and it doesn't exist. The magic bullet is good clinical evaluation, asking the right questions, doing the right physical exam, using the right tools, understanding how to interpret the results, understanding the risk factors, understanding the psychology of the athlete, and then applying all of that stuff in an individualized, evidence-based treatment program."

Yes indeed. But what about those six kinds of concussions? They are as follows:

1. Cognitive: difficulty thinking

2. Problems with the vestibular system, the part of the brain that interprets movement and interprets the position of the body in space

3. Ocular, which affects your eyes' ability to work together

4. Migraine

5. Neck or cervical issues

6. Anxiety and mood problems

That sounds complicated, and it is, because as Dr. Collins says, those different types of concussions are like interlocking circles; you can have patients with symptoms of more than one type of concussion, sometimes all six. But what makes the UPMC program so amazing is that they've got this. They're experienced, they're scientific, and they know what to do.

"For each of those circles, you have different risk factors, different symptoms, different findings with neurocognitive testing like ImPACT, different findings with the physical exam, and most important, different treatments," he says. "So for each of those circles, we have totally different treatments. I'll tell you that for all six, activity is good for you, not bad. But it needs to be prescriptive activity. We do not recommend dark rooms, passive treatments, taking naps, or complete rest. We recommend prescriptive, active rehabilitation.

"Let me explain why. For example, the vestibular system is one of the more common types of concussion," Collins continues. "When you affect that system—and concussion at the end of the day is an energy problem with the brain—that energy problem will cause that system to decompensate in certain individuals. Patients with a history of car sickness are more likely to have a vestibular problem following concussions than patients who don't have a history with car sickness because that system is weak in that individual.

"When patients have that problem, the signal comes through abnormally or slowly, and it produces this foggy, dizzy feeling, like you're one step behind, detached," he goes on. "You become environmentally sensitive. You don't like car rides, busy environments, or busy locker rooms, and when you move dynamically you don't feel well. Now, the only way you treat a vestibular problem is by exposure. Rest actually can make it worse because you're not treating the problem. You have to retrain that system to get it better. So we've now developed exertion programs. We use physical therapy, first of all, to desensitize that system. We actually prescribe certain exercises depending on what type of vestibular problem you have.

"When you have an ocular problem, we have to retrain the visual system, and we do that by rehab, not by rest," Collins concludes. "When you have a migraine, you have to make sure that patients aren't napping, are exercising in specific ways, and are regulating their diet and hydration. For every one of those circles, we have totally different approaches. You need to go to a clinician who understands how to answer the question of where the aberrancy is coming from. That's why this is becoming a specialty injury. That's why you need to go to a clinic that understands how to assess this and approach it."

Dr. Collins really knows his stuff. But as he told me, the real key to making progress is awareness, understanding that concussion isn't a black box, a mystery that can't be diagnosed. Success in treating it is about information and good, solid science. From his perspective, we're making a lot of progress.

"The pendulum has swung from an awareness standpoint," he says. I've always said this, but awareness with no solution is hysteria. Awareness with a solution is good clinical management and treatment. That's where we need to go with this injury. We have a much better under-standing now of how to properly assess, treat, rehab, and individualize the care of this injury. That's the story that needs to be told.

"Let's say you have a knee injury," Collins continues. "You go to an orthopedic surgeon; he looks at your knee, does a physical exam, runs some tests, and says, 'Yep, you have a knee injury. This is the type of knee injury you have, this is the rehab we're going to do, recovery's going to take this amount of time, and you're going to be able to get back to play safely.' My goal is getting to the point of that conversation with my patients.

"We're getting close to that," he insists. "'Yes, you have a concus-sion, this is the type of concussion you have, this is the active rehab we're going to do, this is the expected recovery time, and yes, you're going to get back to play safely.' If we can have that conversation, it changes the conversation of the public perception of [concussion]. I think we're as close to having that conversation with parents as we've ever been in terms of this injury. I just think sports are a wonderful thing for kids, and for every patient I see it's my goal to get them back to play. I think this is a treatable problem a great majority of the time."

And there's more great stuff happening in concussion rehab beyond what Dr. Collins is doing. Penn State researchers have found that an FDA-approved "cooling helmet" relieved athletes' concussion symptoms like nausea and dizziness and improved cerebral blood flow, while an oral supplement made from pine bark improved cognitive function in patients three to six months after a concussion.[9] Mean-while, Israeli researchers have found that hyperbaric oxygen therapy brings relief for post-concussion syndrome where other therapies like rest and medication fail.[10] Bottom line, our understanding of concus-sion and post-concussion syndrome and our ability to successfully treat both is light-years beyond where it was when I played.

NUTRITION, LIFESTYLE, AND NONPHARMACOLOGICAL APPROACHES

HOWEVER, EVEN WITH ALL THIS wonderful technology and research and treatment, I think we can agree that the best way to deal with brain trauma and neurodegenerative disease is to help the body heal itself, either as a way of recovering from damage that's already happened or becoming more resilient to future insult.

One of the best ways to do the first is through lifestyle and nutrition, and for a look at that, I want to circle back to Dr. Willeumier at UCLA. Remember a few chapters back when she told us about the link between cognitive symptoms and obesity, and how getting athletes' BMI down and getting them on a better diet made a huge difference in their condition? She elaborates here on things that every athlete—every person—can and should do for better brain health and better resistance to conditions like CTE.

"You're at a disadvantage if you've played a collision-based sport or a contact sport and you're not proactively doing things to support your brain health. I promise you, there's a lot more that people can do than they realize," she says. "What was really fascinating about our work is when we started seeing how awful players' brains looked, in good conscience, we could not *not* help them. I actually ran—and to this day I can't even believe I did this—an NFL weight-loss group for two years. Everybody who participated in our study was welcome to come and be a part of it, and every two weeks, I taught them about brain health.

"I taught them how to eat properly to support their brain," Dr. Willeumier continues. "We put them on nutrient protocols to support their brain. We got their psychiatric issues addressed, because many of them had comorbid issues that needed to be handled. Everyone got their sleep apnea addressed. That's just a problem that happens to certain players, especially because they tend to have a larger body mass index—I mean, six-foot-five, 365. We made sure that in addition to getting their weight down, we got those issues addressed.

"We had some players do neurofeedback," she goes on. "We did EEG, looking at the electrical activity of the brain, and a lot of our players had elevations in delta brainwaves, which are the slow, sleepy brainwaves, which explains the cognitive impairment. For the players who were open to it, neurofeedback helped correct some of those electrophysiological deficits. We had some players do hyperbaric oxygen therapy, which can help stimulate angiogenesis, the growth of new blood vessels. We also made sure we corrected any sort of hormone deficiencies.

"There's actually an extraordinary amount that you can do, even getting them exercising again," Dr. Willeumier says. "I had to be very creative because a lot of these players are like the walking wounded. I got some of them in the swimming pool. I was very creative at strategizing ways that a particular player might need help, and I geared a program specifically for that issue. And we published a paper showing that we could reverse brain damage in these players through diet and lifestyle alone, because the excess weight on the body causes inflammation in the body and the brain. Reducing that inflammation—helping them get to a healthy body mass index—actually helps the body. It decreases insulin resistance."

Dr. Willeumier's work represents the leading edge in actually *healing* the brain. Along with the reduction in BMI and improved cognitive function she saw in her research, she also saw improvements in blood flow to the regions of the brain that had reduced blood flow at the outset of the studies. That's amazing stuff that nobody's talking about, but it's real.

"Our goal was to put players in a state where their bodies can do that restorative work," she concludes. "That's why we needed to work the nutrient therapies, and I saw so many players get better. That was the exciting piece for me. Not the brain damage piece but the restorative recovery piece. That's what I like to telegraph when I speak on this topic because I think it's really the more empowering message."

Hope is a word nobody talks about in the context of neurotrauma and CTE, but it's a word worth using. We're not talking about an inexorable slide into dementia and death but in many cases a set of known conditions that respond to simple therapies like weight loss, exercise, good food, and rest.

But there's another piece to this hopeful picture—supplements and nonpharmacological treatments—and there's no one who knows more about the possibilities there than Dr. Maroon. For twenty-five years, he's been promoting total-body wellness through things like exercise, an anti-inflammatory diet, using your brain…and supplements. He's a towering figure in brain health and concussion, and while the movie *Concussion* defamed him as a shill for the NFL, I know the truth: Joe Maroon is a pioneer.

He also knows how to speak his mind when he wants to. When he was asked about the early retirement of the 49ers' Chris Borland due to CTE fears, Dr. Maroon didn't pull any punches. "There are more injuries to kids from falling off of bikes, scooters, falling in playgrounds than there are in youth football," he said. "I think it's never been safer. Can we improve? Yes. We have to do better all the time to make it safer. I think if a kid is physically able to do it—and wants to do it—I think our job is to continue to make it safer. But it's much more dangerous riding a bike or a skateboard than playing youth football."[11]

Dr. Maroon is a recognized expert in football-related brain injuries, but when you talk about the future and ways that we can both treat neurotrauma and make the brain resistant to it, you have to come back to his research into supplements and other alternative therapies. That word *alternative* gets a bad rap, but a prevailing theme of Dr. Maroon's work is that the traditional drug treatments for mild traumatic brain injury aren't very effective. However, the research he has led on this topic shows that other therapies do get results. Here are some of the highlights of that work and what the results mean:

- Research from 2011 found that supplementing with fish oil can prevent brain inflammation following MTBI, which ties into the theory that CTE is a product of untreated, chronic inflammation, not impacts. Fish oil supplementation also appears to have benefits for post-concussion syndrome.[12]

- Another 2011 study found that consuming plant extracts like curcumin (the active component of turmeric), quercetin (an antioxidant found in red wine, apples, and berries, among other foods), and catechins (found in green tea) suppresses immunoexcitotoxicity—the inflammatory immune system response that, as we talked about in chapter 7, may well be the mechanism behind CTE—and promotes neuro-recovery.[13]

- Work from 2018 sits on the cutting edge of healing science surrounding CBD or cannabidiol. Dr. Maroon's research shows that phytocannabinoids have powerful neuroprotective and anti-inflammatory properties and may be effective treatments for a huge range of neurological conditions.[14]

The common theme in Dr. Maroon's work is inflammation. His work looking at how botanicals, supplements, and other therapies affect the brain's immune and inflammatory response is the heart of the alternative CTE hypothesis I've already presented in this book. Dr. Maroon was thinking about immunoexcitotoxicity as a possible cause of CTE and other neurodegenerative disease long before most other scientists had it on their radar screens. That makes sense because the closer you look, the more the "contact sports" theory breaks down.

"We can say with a high degree of confidence that CTE is not exclusive to contact-sports athletes," Maroon says. "If people with 'pedestrian' injuries like falls, car accidents, bike accidents, and the like are also getting CTE, then the population at risk widens considerably to include the over 2.8 million people who sustain head injuries each year.[15] That being said, CTE is still rare, and it is true but uncommon that people with head injuries can develop neurodegenerative diseases. Because of this, it is vital that we examine how other factors are contributing to the problem—factors like inflammation, which has been well established in neurodegenerative diseases."

Now, his years of work exploring that inflammatory connection have been backed up by a terrific study out of Toronto. The work found a strong relationship between inflammatory markers in the blood and the MRI scans of athletes who had been concussed (and, even better, a decrease in t-tau, considered a potential biomarker for CTE). In other words, the findings are strong support for the idea that MTBI is associated with inflammation, oxidative stress, and cellular damage caused by the brain's impaired ability to get rid of waste products—*not* with the buildup of tau.[16] Coffin, meet nail.

In fact, BU hangs its own impact hypothesis with one of Dr. McKee's own papers from 2016. In the work, the researchers propose their own chronic inflammation theory of CTE.[17] But wait, if inflammation is the root cause of CTE, not repeated SCIs, why not prevent or treat the inflammation? After all, it's well established we can treat cardiovascular disease by curbing inflammation, so why is it such a stretch to apply that to CTE? Maybe it's because proposing a simple, effective treatment for this dreaded disease wouldn't attract the same headlines as "All football players are going to lose their marbles."

THE TB12 METHOD

However, we're still talking about *treating* neurotrauma. But what about *preventing* it? Can we do that? The answer appears to be yes. Recent research shows that Alzheimer's disease might even be preventable, at least in some cases, by reducing inflammation in the body.[18] Not only that, but reduced blood flow to the brain may also be a vital part in the development of this terrible disease. So there's a precedent for making our brains resistant to the worst neurodegenerative diseases.

You might have noticed a common theme in this chapter: sugar, obesity, dehydration, inflammation, and poor blood flow destroying your brain. Logically, doesn't it follow that by making better choices about the food you eat, being active, and maintaining a healthy weight, you can prevent a lot of bad things from happening to your brain? Of course. And no one has attracted more public attention on this topic than Alex Guerrero and the cutting-edge techniques he employs at the TB12 Center in Foxboro, Massachusetts.

In case you've been living on Mars, TB12 refers to Patriots superstar quarterback Tom Brady, who the TB12 Center is named for. One day, Dr. Cummings called me and said that his pediatrician told him that he follows the TB12 Rule when it comes to his patients playing football. He asked the pediatrician, "What's the TB12 Rule?" His son's doctor explained that because Tom Brady didn't play football before high school, he advised parents that their kids shouldn't play before high school, either. I didn't remember ever hearing that and thought the so-called TB12 Rule didn't exist.

Coincidentally, Dr. Cummings had sent me a link of Tom Brady appearing on *The Late Show with Stephen Colbert*, and I watched it. There he was, TB12 himself, in living color, talking about letting his kids play youth football and how fun it would be to coach them.

Mystery solved. The TB12 Rule *was* a myth! But like so many other myths, if it was repeated often enough, people would believe it.

I decided to reach out to Tom's team for this book. I discovered the cutting-edge work the TB12 Center is doing to keep young athletes healthy and make all athletes' bodies more resistant to, among other things, brain trauma.

Tom is the star, but when it comes to healing in general and preventing brain injury in particular, he shares the spotlight with Alex. Now, if you do know about Mr. Guerrero, you know he's controversial. Because his therapeutic approach is based on pliability, holistic nutrition, and reducing inflammation, he's been called a quack and worse.[19] But ask any of the many athletes who have found their health and careers turned around by his methods, and you'll hear a different story.

Alex's TB12 method represents the ultimate expression of our alternate CTE hypothesis—and it works. With diet, exercise, supplementation, and other measures, the brain can be made resilient to the cascade of immune compounds that lead to chronic neuroinflammation and, eventually, CTE. Joe Maroon, Peter Cummings, and I sat down with Alex to talk about it.

"Our whole approach is to try to maximize blood flow, to get as much circulation to the nervous system as we possibly can as quickly as we possibly can," he says. "Hydration levels, electrolyte levels, trace mineral levels—we look at it all. We can, one, bring down inflammation, and two, increase blood flow. That's been the premise of all the work we've done at our center for years now."

That's what Alex calls *prehab*, putting the body in a state where you don't get an off-the-charts inflammatory response to an insult as easily. To get there, he also promotes about four grams of daily fish oil supplementation just like Dr. Maroon, along with something near and dear to my heart: a low-sugar diet.

"The idea is to really control inflammation rates systemically," Alex says. "We do that by looking at somebody's ability to maintain insulin stability. The more stable we can keep their insulin levels, the lower their inflammation rates. Diet is a big part of that, and we try to minimize, if not eliminate, the amount of proinflammatory foods in some-body's diet. These are the four Ws: white sugar, white flour, white rice, white liquid, meaning milk and cheese. If you can start there, that is really helpful in starting to bring these inflammatory rates down.

"Again, the idea is to maintain insulin stability and find out what your balances are," he continues. "Moderation in all things. Too much of a good thing is just as bad as not enough of something. So we look at lifestyle and diet because we want diet to become a lifestyle, and the best way that we can do that is to give our patients goals. We set goals at fourteen-day cycles because I think anybody can do anything for two weeks. Interestingly, once you do something for fourteen days, you start to develop new neural pathways for that behavior.

"Insulin stability is important, and exercise is important in main-taining that, too," Alex goes on. "But exercise also can increase levels of inflammation, so that's where pliability comes in for us. We tell people that they can't do any strength training or functional movement at the expense of pliability. We're trying to create new neural pathways of movement but good correct functional movement. To do that, you have to have good muscle-pump function, and to have that, your muscles need to be able to contract at 100 percent. They have to contract and relax, getting the lymphatic system to move the metabolic waste and then cre-ating a great muscle pump so we get greater oxygenated blood flow."

But does all that work for the athletes Alex trains? Yes. "I have a lot of clients who play contact sports," he says. "Soccer, where they're heading the ball a ton, and they live good lifestyles. And guess what? They don't have headaches. They don't have these subconcussive issues. I don't see them."

Brilliant stuff. What Alex does to make the body withstand injury also applies to the brain. He's become the go-to post-concussion rehab guy for Patriots players. No doubt these approaches have played a major role in Tom Brady becoming the greatest quarterback of our time.

TEACHING KIDS TO LIVE A HEALTHY LIFESTYLE

THE BEST THING ABOUT ALEX'S WORK? You don't need a hyperbaric machine, and there are a lot of things you can do at home yourself or with your young athlete. "What we wanted to do is teach parents how to do some pliability with their kids," he says. "You've got your son, and he's getting ready to go play some football, and you spend ten minutes doing some pliability work on him before he goes to practice or a game. That's bonding time that kid will have with his parent that he will never forget. They're going to bond through that hormone stimulation. That's why our clients absolutely love us. What we do is bonding."

I love it. Alex also focuses on teaching kids about proper nutrition and making good lifestyle choices. That's genius, but learning those lessons early can help them stay healthy and active as adults for decades— just like Dr. Maroon, who's still doing triathlons in his seventies.

"We're just telling kids to do the same thing we tell our adults to do but on a smaller scale. So, some of our kids go to private schools. Some private schools don't allow them to bring lunch; they have to eat the school food. The school food isn't great. So I'll say, 'Okay, you can control breakfast, and you can control dinner. So eat whatever you want at lunch, and don't feel guilty. But for breakfast, you can do x, y, z. For dinner you can do x, y, z.' And they can do that.

"But where we really start to work with the kids is on the prehab component," Alex continues. "I tell them, 'If you're going to work out your body because you want to play your sport, how important is your brain to your body?' The kids always look at me like, 'What?' Then I ask, 'Do you think you should work your brain out like you work your body out?' That makes sense to them. Then I'll say, 'Your brain is like a muscle, so if you want to be a good football player, you've got to work your brain the same way you work your muscles.'"

Those workouts are a battery of cognitive exercises. "We put them on our TB12 brain HQ exercise program," Alex says. "I can have them do five, fifteen, or thirty minutes a day. And it's fun. I have them do cognitive exercises, which the parents love because of what it does for kids on the scholastic side. I can take a kid who has some attention issues and focus his exercises a little bit more on the attention area of his brain. The kid doesn't know. But I get parents who come to me and go, 'Ever since he started doing these exercises, his grades are better. His teacher reports that he's able to pay attention in class better.' We can do attention, memory, processing, speed, people skills, navigation skills. The kids will do their exercises because we sold it to them from a brain-fitness perspective and not by saying, 'This is homework.'"

But what I love most about TB12 for kids is that he treats kids like kids, not little adults. They want to play video games and stuff because they're kids! So Alex doesn't deny them what they love; he preaches balance. That's how you get compliance. "I teach them the value-for-value lesson," he says. "If you're going to spend thirty minutes playing video games, are you gaining thirty minutes' worth of value? How's that helping you get to college? How's that helping you get that scholarship? I tell the kids, 'I love video games just as much as anybody else. But you have to have to have a balance in life. So why don't you just play for five or ten minutes? And when I explain it fully, the kids are like, 'I understand what you're saying.'"

JAWS AND COKE

I HAVE TWO PERSONAL STORIES that back up what Alex is saying. The first is about the dangers of sugar, and it happened during my second year in the NFL. The Steelers strength and conditioning coach, John Kolb, talked to me about sugar and told me that was what I needed to watch, if not eliminate from my diet, going forward.

Well, I completely cut it out of my diet the next day. I had scrambled egg whites and oatmeal with a little honey, and a grapefruit and blue berries. I felt better initially, but after a clean snack and lunch, my head started to pound. By noon I could barely stand the headache. My brain was craving sugar! Turns out that your brain uses about half the energy your body produces from sugar. Sugar is also addictive. Breakfast for me used to be a glass of orange juice along with some Cap'n Crunch and a few pieces of toast with peanut butter and raspberry jam. No wonder I was hurting! I'd gone cold turkey.

I weaned myself off sugar after that until I got rid of 90 percent of it, and now eating free of processed sugar is part of my lifestyle, and I've never felt better. That lifestyle change helped recover from head trauma, beat cancer, and get back to work ten days after open-heart surgery. Investing in your health is the most important investment you'll ever make.

The other story concerns balance and involves my old buddy Ron Jaworski. It was my first year at ESPN, and we were getting ready to do a show. Jaws is on the phone with former Eagles coach Dick Vermeil, laughing. Then all of a sudden, silence. He gets quiet, hangs up the phone. Then he says, "Hey, Hoge. Do I look like I'm gaining weight?" I say no and ask him why. "Well, Dick's concerned about me. He's seen me on TV, and he thinks I'm getting heavy."

Now we go do the show: me, Jaws, and Mark Malone. There's a term in television that, if you've got a three-minute segment and you go 3:20, you're "heavy." That day, every time we went to commercial break, I would say, "Mark, are we heavy there?" Mark would say, "I felt heavy there; did you feel heavy there?" Meanwhile, Jaws is losing his mind. "This is not funny!" Later, I was in the car headed to the airport, and Jaws called me.

"Hogey, I need to lose some weight. Can you help me?"

I said, "Jaws, here's what I'm going to have you do. All week, write down what you eat for breakfast, lunch, and dinner the best you can. Do that, and next week we'll look at it." The following week we met up, and before Jaws hands me the list he says, "Listen, you're not taking away my pizza or beer."

I said, "Jaws, first of all that's the last thing I ever want to do. We're not taking away anything. Because if you enjoy something, we're going to find out how we can manage it a little bit." So I looked at the list, and he was consuming four to eight Cokes a day.

I said, "Jaws, pizza and beer aren't your problem. Here's what we're going to do. We're going to substitute water for Coke, and we're going to keep doing that until you get down to one Coke a day. Because I'm not going to take that away from you, either. You like it—enjoy it. But here's what's going to happen. The more you get rid of Coke, the more you're going to wonder how you ever drank it."

He said okay and stuck to the plan. Six months later, he'd lost twenty pounds, and his Coke was the only thing we touched. To this day, he still can't drink a Coke.

Alex heard that story, and he confirmed that real wellness is holistic. It's about being happy, not just healthy. "Our method is based on a triangle of wellness," he says. "It's based on having a physical body and emotional body and a spiritual body. You can't be emotionally stable if you're not physically fit. If you're not emotionally stable, you won't be spiritually sound. If you're not spiritually sound, you can't be physically fit. We try to tap into what those three things mean to each client. When you're physically fit, you have a better absorption of certain hormones. You can be emotionally stable. Your adaptability to stress is a lot better. Then when you do that, if you're emotionally stable you're going to be more spiritually sound."

By the way, in his book *Square One: A Simple Guide to a Balanced Life*, Dr. Maroon echoes Alex's principles and provides a formula to avoid "burnout"—the state of being overworked, overcommitted, overwhelmed—that thousands have people have used successfully to attain work-life balance. Make it the next thing you read.

IT'S ABOUT LIFE, NOT FOOTBALL

IN THE END, THAT'S WHAT this is all about, really—being happy and healthy and living your best life, whether you're a youth football player, a pro, a parent, or just a weekend athlete. It's about the truth: we can prevent long-term damage from brain injury, make the body more resistant to inflammation, help people recover faster and more completely from all kinds of injury, make football safer in the future, and even recover after we have clinical symptoms of neurodegenerative disease.

Look past the bad information, conflicts of interest, hidden agendas, and egos, and you do find hope. A lot of hope. But I think by now I've said enough. So to wrap this up, I'd like to give the last words about football and all the rest to two guys I love and respect. First, Solomon Wilcots, whom you've heard from.

"Journalists don't know what to think about all this," he says. "They believe what they read, and Boston University was out in front with this stuff. So when they say ninety-nine of a hundred brains sampled had CTE, everyone is scared. Misinformation is the only thing worse than no information.

"When people ask me what do I think about the future of football, you know what I tell them?" Solomon says. "As long as there's some kid growing up in some urban center and he looks at this game as a way to change the trajectory of his life, the game will be fine. It's a way to make it the hell out of there and afford him an opportunity to get an education and provide him a platform to do whatever it is he wants to do with his life because that's what this game provides.

"From the time we first play, there's a chance to learn leadership, to learn how to work with others in a team environment," he concludes. "As long as there's some kid from the plains in Nebraska who wants off that farm and is tired of baling hay, and he's got the chance to change his life, own the farm, buy his own farm, and add to his parents' farm, the game is going to be great. As long as you've got some kid coming from Africa, or Samoa, or from some other country, and a football coach puts a helmet on him and asks if he wants to play the game, this game is going to be just fine."

You have to love the guy. Solly's got it right: youth football should be about having fun and developing life skills. It's an arena for helping kids realize their powers, develop good work habits, and set goals. It's about teammates, and your teammates are your teammates regardless of your background, race, gender, or religion.

Next, let's hear from David Baker, president of the Pro Football Hall of Fame in Canton, Ohio. He's an incredibly erudite, thoughtful guy who had a lot to say about the place of the game in our society.

"In 1905, the game was already under attack," he says. "There'd been nineteen deaths in college football alone that year and 179 serious injuries, and college presidents were going to terminate football. No less than Teddy Roosevelt got involved in saving it. He had been secretary of the navy so he prevailed upon Paul Dashiell, the head coach of Navy, to prevail upon Walter Camp, the keeper of the rules at Yale, to incorporate this thing called the forward pass, and today the game is all about the forward pass. Originally, it was meant to alleviate the battering ram that the game had become and make it safer.

"What's important about that is that thirty years later, we had seventeen-, eighteen-, nineteen-year-old young men in the Pacific, in Europe, on the beaches of Normandy, and in Africa, all before there were cell phones, before there was jet travel," David continues. "When they left, they left for two, three, four years, not knowing whether they'd ever come back. And yet, they knew not just from football but from a lot of sports that we competed in here in America that other cultures didn't have how to be part of a team, how to understand commitment, how to understand sacrifice and the greater overall good, how to surrender yourself to something that's bigger than you and how that makes you more relevant, not less relevant.

"That gave us what Tom Brokaw called the Greatest Generation, but that gave us a serious advantage that overcame Hitler and Japan at a time when the world needed it," he goes on. "It was those values that helped those guys, and so we're all about the character development and the values that come from this game.

"Taking it full circle in our discussion, the army is a big sponsor of ours. Let me tell you how important these values are in the US Army or the US Marines or the US Air Force or the US Navy," David says. "The army, navy, marine corps, air force, what they do and what they make out of those kids is incredible; it is heroic.

"It's because those kids understand all those values," he concludes. "What was it Wellington said? 'The British Empire was built on the playing fields of Eton years before.' MacArthur said, 'Upon the field of friendly strife, sowing the seeds on different days, on different fields, shall bear the fruit of victory.' Those are important fertile grounds for our character development for our first responders, policemen, firemen, for our soldiers, but more importantly for our fathers and our mothers."

Amen, David. But I want to finish with a story that illustrates perfectly what youth football really is to so many people. It's not about playing in the NFL. That only happens for a chosen few. Going to the NFL is not the only way to a better life. Getting an education, building relationships, and developing skills to help you build your best life— that's what youth football is about.

One day when Beau was twelve, he came home and asked if we could take his friend Josh Barajas and his sister to school and bring them home. No problem. I didn't know Josh's background, but I knew his dad was working multiple jobs, his mother no longer lived with them, and they did not have much. A few days later, Beau told me a story about walking home with Josh, and they were talking about what they wanted to do or be. According to Beau, Josh said, "I'll probably be a nothing." That really bothered me because I had dreams as a kid, and it was always the adults trying to tear them down. I guess that's why I still see things as much through a child's eyes as I do through an adult's.

I said, "Does Josh want to play football?" Beau asked him, and Josh said he would love to, but he could not afford cleats. I called my buddy Eddie White, who worked for Reebok, and asked him if he could sponsor my youth football team by providing cleats for all the kids. I didn't want Josh to be embarrassed, and I felt if everyone got a new pair, nobody would ask questions. Eddie did what he always did—said yes—and fired off twenty-five new pairs of cleats for my kids. It took only two practices for me to realize that Josh was a very good athlete and that with some coaching and support, he could do something with this game. I pulled him aside one day at practice and said, "Josh, if you work hard at this game, you could turn it into an education."

Josh was a beast as a linebacker, and he became the backbone of our defense as we developed as a team. He only played for me for one year, but Beau stayed in touch with him and kept me updated. I knew that he stayed with football, and I figured our paths would cross again. A few years later, my nephew Tristen was the best center in the country coming out of high school and signed with Notre Dame. When I went to see him play in a spring game, whom did I run into? Josh Barajas! The kid who thought he would be nothing had taken football and turned it into a college education.

That's what youth football is about. It helps us grow, develop, compete, and enjoy life. We owe it to ourselves and our kids to give them that precious gift of being the very best they can be.

THINGS TO KNOW ABOUT CTE AND QUESTIONS TO ASK ABOUT YOUTH FOOTBALL

THINGS TO KNOW ABOUT CTE

1. To date, rigorous scientific research tells us only that CTE leaves deposits of perivascular tau in the folds of the brain. It does not reveal conclusively what causes tau deposits to form or what clinical symptoms, if any, they cause.

2. CTE's true prevalence is unknown.

3. The role of genetics, mental illness, and other disease processes in the symptoms currently labeled as CTE is unknown.

4. The causal connection between brain trauma and brain pathology is unknown.

5. The association between brain pathology and mood, cognitive, or behavioral symptoms is unknown.

6. There is no evidence CTE causes any mood, behavior, or cognitive disorders; many neuropsychiatric conditions associated with CTE are also associated with other, more common neurodegenerative diseases.

7. The role of preexisting mental health issues in clinical symptoms currently assumed to be caused by CTE is unexplored.

8. Clinical and pathological staging of CTE has not been validated by the scientific community; "stage I CTE" is very likely a normal brain, not a diseased brain.

9. There is substantial evidence to suggest that CTE is caused by chronic inflammation.

10. All the brains in the infamous "110 out of 111" brains case were from players whose families reported that they had mental problems; there was no control group.

11. There is no agreed-upon definition of a subconcussive impact (SCI), so it is not a scientific concept.

12. There is no evidence that early childhood exposure to tackle football leads to neuropsychiatric problems later in life.

13. There is no evidence that CTE causes suicide.

QUESTIONS TO ASK YOUR YOUTH FOOTBALL LEAGUE

1. Do you have a head-trauma protocol? What is it?

2. How many days a week do you practice? (Note: My teams practiced three days a week until games started, and then we practiced two times a week, including the game.)

3. Do you know the proper way to fit helmets and shoulder pads?

4. How much live contact do you do in a typical week?

5. Do you adhere to Heads Up guidelines?

6. Do your games have a safety official or certified athletic trainer present?

7. How are your coaches trained and background-checked?

8. Are your coaches trained to detect symptoms of head trauma?

9. How do you match up kids during practice? Based on size?

10. How do you go about getting all kids in the game?

ACKNOWLEDGMENTS

FOOTBALL IS ONE OF MY greatest passions, and I'm proud to have written *Brainwashed* in the hopes of keeping the sport alive for future generations. But this book wouldn't have been possible without the help of my teammates:

To the trainers in my life—Rick Burkholder, John Norwig, Phil Lucky, Brent Faurè, Kevin Guskiewicz, Fred Caito, Tim Bream, and all the rest—thank you for taping me up, helping me recover, and teaching me how to take care of myself. You have my deepest thanks.

To the coaches who taught me everything—Chuck and Marianne Noll, two incredible people who supported me and taught me how to play the game of life right; Dirk Koetter, who believed in me; Jim Koetter, who was one of the greatest X's and O's coaches I've ever known; Dirk Hoak, my position coach for the Steelers who taught me how to be a pro; Bill Cowher; Tom Moore; Ron Erhardt; Marvin Lewis, who challenged me in college; Tony Dungy; John Fox; Dick LeBeau; Dom Capers; Bob Slowik; Mick McCall; Ron Turner; Mike Shula; Bart Haun; Brian Haun; Woody; and my many youth football coaches. You have all educated me on this great game, and I'm forever thankful.

To my former NFL teammates—Neil O'Donnell, Tunch Ilkin,

Craig Wolfley, Terry Long, Mike Webster, Justin Strzelczyk, Donnie Shell, John Stallworth, Rod Woodson, Carnell Lake, Greg Lloyd, Mike Tomczak, Louis Lipps, Mike Mularkey, Todd Blackledge, Dermontti Dawson, Duval Love, John Jackson, Erik Kramer, Tim Worley, Corky Federico, Troy Eastvold, Jeff Spadafore, and Bubby Brister.

To the Rooney family—Dan Rooney, Art "The Chief" Rooney, Dan Rooney Jr., John Rooney, and Jim Rooney. You've all had a significant impact on my life in one way or the other. Thank you for everything.

To those who helped get this book ready—Dr. Peter Cummings, Dr. Joseph Maroon, Dr. Julian Bailes, Dr. Rudy Castellani, Dr. Mark Lovell, Ben and Ashley Roethlisberger, Bruce and Christine Arians, David Baker, Paul Bright Sr., Bonnie Brister, Trent and Cassandra Dilfer, Mike Golic, Suzy Kolber, Debra Mirabile, Nicole Middendorf, Bill Polian, Mark Schlereth, Solomon Wilcots, and Kristen Willeumier.

To my wonderful family—my brother, Marty, who has been there from day one and always been my biggest fan; my amazing kids, Kori and Beau, who inspire me daily and who I love without end; and my wife, Angela, whose love for me proves love is the most powerful thing in the world.

To my editor, interviewer, and chief researcher, Tim Vandehey. *Brainwashed* wouldn't have happened without you.

And to the incredibly talented team at Amplify Publishing—Naren Aryal, Danny Moore, Ricky Frame, Kristin Perry, and Michelle Webber. Thanks for helping me get this book out there.

ABOUT THE AUTHORS

Merril Hoge is a former NFL running back who worked as an analyst at ESPN for twenty-one years, helping launch ESPN2, *NFL Live*, and *Fantasy Football*, along with being a part of the longest-running NFL show on television, *NFL Matchup*.

An eight-year National Football League veteran, Hoge spent 1987–1993 with the Pittsburgh Steelers and set the team record for most receptions by a running back, totaling fifty in 1988, and was one of only two Steelers to rush for more than one hundred yards in back-to-back playoff games. He concluded his career in 1994 with the Chicago Bears after suffering a series of concussions. At the time of his retirement, Hoge had played in one hundred twenty-two consecutive games, the longest streak in the NFL at that time.

A 1987 graduate of Idaho State University with a degree in education and minor in health and fitness, Hoge set eleven school records, including both single-season and career marks for rushing attempts, rushing yards, and all-purpose yards. He also scored forty-four touchdowns, a Big Sky Conference record.

Hoge is chairman of the board of the Highmark Caring Foundation, which has created four centers in Pennsylvania for children, adolescents, and families who have lost loved ones. He is also on the board of the Chuck Noll Foundation for Brain Injury Research and launched the Chuck Noll Hall of Fame "Game for Life" Award to honor outstanding youth football programs. After overcoming non-Hodgkin's lymphoma in 2003, he received the Chairman's Advocacy Award from the Leukemia & Lymphoma Society (LLS) in 2004 and 2008 for his outstanding participation in increasing public awareness of LLS.

Active in concussion research and in the prevention and treatment of brain injuries, Hoge testified at a congressional hearing on head injuries in football in the fall of 2009 and was appointed to the NFL Mild Traumatic Brain Injury Committee in January 2010, which initiates research and advises the NFL on best practices for concussion prevention and management. He also served on the NFL's Return-to-Play Subcommittee, which deals with head, neck, and spine cases.

In 2018, Hoge helped launch Your Call Football, a professional league in which fans call the play, and is the author of *Find a Way: Three Words That Changed My Life*. He lives in Fort Thomas, Kentucky.

DR. PETER CUMMINGS is board certified in anatomic pathology, neuropathology, and forensic pathology.
He earned his bachelor of arts from
the University of Maine, his medical degree from the Royal College of
Surgeons in Dublin, Ireland, and completed his pathology training at the
University of Virginia. He also earned
a master's degree in pathology from
Dalhousie University in Halifax, Nova Scotia.

Dr. Cummings worked as a medical examiner and the director
of forensic neuropathology at the Massachusetts Office of the Chief
Medical Examiner. He was a member of the SwissAir Flight 111 iden-
tification team in 1998. He has authored two textbooks: *The Atlas of
Forensic Histopathology* (Cambridge University Press, 2010) and *Pearls
and Pitfalls of Pediatric Death Investigation* (Cambridge University
Press, 2016). Dr. Cummings has also appeared in two NOVA television programs: "Can Science Stop Crime" (October 2012) and "Cold
Case JFK" (November 2013) and has been featured in *People* ("Cold
Case Comes to Life," April 2009). He lives outside Boston with his
wife, son, and dog.

REFERENCES

INTRODUCTION

1   Peter Cummings, "I'm a Brain Scientist and I Let My Son Play Football," Yahoo! Sports, September 19, 2017, accessed March 18, 2018, https://sports.yahoo.com/im-brain-scientist-let-son-play-football-135727314.html.

CHAPTER 2

1   Mark Fainaru-Wada and Steve Fainaru, *League of Denial: The NFL, Concussions, and the Battle for Truth* (New York: Three Rivers, 2013).

2   Elliott Almond, "Concussion' doctor: Youth football is child abuse," *The Mercury News*, August 8, 2017 accessed May 10, 2018, https://www.mercurynews.com/2017/08/09/concussion-doctor-youth-football-is-child-abuse/.

3   Peter Keating, "Doctor Yes," ABC News, July 21, 2016, accessed May 10, 2018, https://abcnews.go.com/Sports/doctor-/story?id=40772156.

4   Robert Fitzsimmons, "Dr. Joseph Maroon Is One of the Good Guys," *Pittsburgh Post-Gazette*, March 7, 2016, accessed April 4, 2018, http://www.post-gazette.com/opinion/2016/03/08/Dr-Joseph-Maroon-is-one-of-the-good-guys/stories/201603080035.

5   Alan Schwarz, "N.F.L. Picks New Chairmen for Panel on Concussions," *New York Times*, March 16, 2010, accessed May 16, 2018, https://www.nytimes.com/2010/03/17/sports/17concussions.html.

6   Mark Maske, "NFL's New Helmet-Hitting Rule Is in Place, but Will It Have the Desired Effect?" *Chicago Tribune*, March 29, 2018, accessed June 2, 2018, http://www.chicagotribune.com/sports/football/ct-spt-nfl-helmet-rule-instant-replay-20180329-story.html.

7   News Editorial Board, "Editorial: NFL Gets Proactive with New Rules on Kickoff Plays," *Buffalo News*, May 26, 2018, accessed June 1, 2018, http://buffalonews.com/2018/05/26/editorial-the-nfl-gets-proactive.

8   Interview, May 18, 2018.

9   Interview, June 15, 2018.

10   Daniel Flynn, *The War on Football: Saving America's Game* (Washington, DC: Regnery, 2014).

11   Thomas Vasquez, "NFL Concussion Liability Forecast," material provided by counsel to plaintiffs, Case 2:12-md-02323-AB Document 6167 Filed 09/12/14.

12   Bill Utterback, "NFL Life Signals Early Death," *Chicago Tribune*, March 4, 1988, accessed May 27, 2018, http://articles.chicagotribune.com/1988-03-04/sports/8804040445_1_life-expectancy-heart-attack-average-lifespan.

13   S. Baron and R. Rinsky, *Health Hazard Evaluation Report: HETA-88-085, National Football League Players Mortality Study*, US Department of Health and Human Services, Public Health Service, Centers for Disease Control and Prevention, National Institute for Occupational Safety and Health, HETA 88-085, January 1994.

14   A. S. Venkataramani, M. Gandhavadi, and A. B. Jena, "Association between Playing American Football in the National Football League and Long-Term Mortality," *JAMA* 319, no. 8 (2018): 800–6, doi:10.1001/jama.2018.0140.

15   E. J. Lehman, M. J. Hein, S. L. Baron, and C. M. Gersic, "Neurodegenerative Causes of Death among Retired National Football League Players," *Neurology* 79, no. 19 (2012): 1970–74, doi:10.1212/WNL.0b013e31826daf50.

16   David R. Weir, James S. Jackson, and Amanda Sonnega, "Study of Retired NFL Players," Institute for Social Research, University of Michigan, September 10, 2009, accessed May 24, 2018, http://ns.umich.edu/Releases/2009/Sep09/FinalReport.pdf.

17   N. Didehbani, C. Munro Cullum, S. Mansinghani, H. Conover, and J. Hart, "Depressive Symptoms and Concussions in Aging Retired NFL Players," *Archives of Clinical Neuropsychology* 28, no. 5 (2013): 418–24, doi:10.1093/arclin/act028.

18   Peter Cummings et al., "Homicidal Violence among National Football League Athletes," *Academic Forensic Pathology*, forthcoming.

19   Interview, June 15, 2018.

20   Mike Freeman, "New Helmet Rule Could Make NFL Unrecognizable," *Bleacher Report*, June 29, 2018, accessed June 29, 2018, https://bleacherreport.com/articles/2783289-new-helmet-rule-could-make-nfl-unrecognizable.

21   Cindy Boren, "Ben Roethlisberger Sends a Powerful Message about the NFL's Concussion Protocol," *Washington Post*, December 2, 2015, accessed April 29, 2018, https://www.washingtonpost.com/news/early-lead/wp/2015/12/02/ben-roethlisberger-sent-a-powerful-message-about-the-nfls-concussion-protocol/?utm_term=.abbfcf16f99c.

22   Interview, May 22, 2018.

CHAPTER 3

1   Associated Press, "Ex-Steeler Long Drank Antifreeze to Commit Suicide,"
     ESPN, January 26, 2006, accessed May 13, 2018, http://www.espn.com/nfl/news/
     story?id=2307003.

2   Associated Press, "Pro Football: Daily Report: Around the NFL: Terry Long Says He
     Attempted Suicide," *Los Angeles Times*, August 1, 1991, accessed April 30, 2018, http://
     articles.latimes.com/1991-08-01/sports/sp-224_1_terry-long.

3   Jane E. Brody, "After a Suicide Attempt, the Risk of Another Try," *New York Times*,
     November 7, 2016, accessed May 28, 2018, https://www.nytimes.com/2016/11/08/well/
     live/after-a-suicide-attempt-the-risk-of-another-try.html.

4   Alan Schwarz, "Expert Ties Ex-Player's Suicide to Brain Damage," *New York Times*,
     January 18, 2007, accessed March 29, 2018, https://www.nytimes.com/2007/01/18/
     sports/football/18waters.html.

5   "Know Your Brain—Reticular Formation," July 7, 2015, accessed May 20, 2018, https://
     www.neuroscientificallychallenged.com/blog/know-your-brain-reticular-formation.

6   Ben Kerchaval, "Washington State QB Tyler Hilinski Found to Have CTE, 'Brain of a
     65-Year-Old' after Suicide," CBS Sports, June 26, 2018, accessed June 30, 2018, https://
     www.cbssports.com/college-football/news/washington-state-qb-tyler-hilinski-found-to-
     have-cte-brain-of-a-65-year-old-after-suicide/.

7   Nancy Armour, "Why College Football Player's Death Should Terrify Parents," *USA
     Today*, June 26, 2018, accessed June 29, 2018, https://www.usatoday.com/story/sports/
     columnist/nancy-armour/2018/06/26/washington-state-qb-committed-suicide-but-
     football-killed-him/734604002/.

8   Associated Press and KOMO News Staff, "Doctors on CTE Research: 'We Still Don't
     Know as Much as We Think We Do," KOMO News, June 27, 2018, accessed June 29,
     2018, http://komonews.com/news/local/doctors-on-cte-research-we-still-dont-know-as-
     much-as-we-think-we-do.

9   D. M. Stone, T. R. Simon, K. A. Fowler et al., "Vital Signs: Trends in State Suicide
     Rates—United States, 1999–2016 and Circumstances Contributing to Suicide—27
     States, 2015," *Morbidity and Mortality Weekly Report* 67 (2018): 617–24, http://dx.doi.
     org/10.15585/mmwr.mm6722a1.

10   US Department of Health and Human Services, "What Is the U.S. Opioid Epidemic?,"
     accessed June 2, 2018, https://www.hhs.gov/opioids/about-the-epidemic/index.html.

11   L. B. Cottler, A. B. Abdallah, S. M. Cummings, J. Barr, R. Banks, and R. Forchheimer,
     "Injury, Pain, and Prescription Opioid Use among Former National Football League
     (NFL) Players," *Drug and Alcohol Dependence* 116, no. 1–3 (2011): 188-194, doi:10.1016/j.
     drugalcdep.2010.12.003.

12   G. G. Kovacs, M. C. Horvath, K. Majtenyi, M. I. Lutz, Y. L. Hurd, and E. Keller, "Heroin
     Abuse Exaggerates Age-Related Deposition of Hyperphosphorylated Tau and p62-
     Positive Inclusions," *Neurobiology of Aging* 36, no. 11 (2015): 3100–07, doi:10.1016/j.
     neurobiolaging.2015.07.018.

13   Ann C. McKee, Thor D. Stein, Christopher J. Nowinski, Robert A. Stern, Daniel H.
      Daneshvar, Victor E. Alvarez, Hyo-Soon Lee et al., "The Spectrum of Disease in Chronic
      Traumatic Encephalopathy," *Brain* 136, no. 1 (2013): 43–64, December 2, 2012, doi:
      10.1093/brain/aws307.

14   E. J. Lehman, M. J. Hein, and C. M. Gersic, "Suicide Mortality among Retired National
      Football League Players Who Played 5 or More Seasons," *American Journal of Sports
      Medicine* 44, no. 10 (2016): 2486–91, doi:10.1177/0363546516645093.

15   Grant L. Iverson, "Suicide and Chronic Traumatic Encephalopathy," *Journal of
      Neuropsychiatry and Clinical Neurosciences* 28, no. 1 (2016), 9–16.

16   Gary Solomon, "Chronic Traumatic Encephalopathy in Sports: A Historical and
      Narrative Review," *Developmental Neuropsychology* 43, no. 4, (2018): 279–311, doi:10.1080
      /87565641.2018.1447575.

17   Patrick H. F. Baillie, "Understanding Retirement from Sports: Therapeutic Ideas for
      Helping Athletes in Transition," *Counseling Psychologist* 21, no. 3 (1993): 399–410.

18   Jiri Kadlcik and Libor Flemr, "Athletic Career Termination Model in the Czech
      Republic: A Qualitative Exploration," *International Review for the Sociology of Sport* 43, no.
      3 (2008): 251–269.

19   Suzanne Cosh, Shona Crabb, and Amanda LeCouteur, "Elite Athletes and Retirement:
      Identity, Choice, and Agency," *Australian Journal of Psychology* (2012), https://doi.
      org/10.1111/j.1742-9536.2012.00060.x.

20   Luke Cooper, "Former Elite Athletes Reveal Mental Health Struggles after Retirement,"
      Huffington Post Australia, November 4, 2017, accessed April 17, 2018, https://www.
      huffingtonpost.com.au/2017/04/11/former-elite-athletes-reveal-mental-health-struggles-
      after-retir_a_22035114/.

21   Sugar Ray Leonard and Michael Arkush, *The Big Fight: My Life in and out of the Ring*
      (New York: Plume, 2012).

22   Flynn, *War on Football*.

23   Adam Kilgore, "Aaron Hernandez Suffered from Most Severe CTE Ever Found in a
      Person His Age," *Washington Post*, November 9, 2017, accessed April 22, 2018, https://
      www.washingtonpost.com/sports/aaron-hernandez-suffered-from-most-severe-cte-ever-
      found-in-a-person-his-age/2017/11/09/fa7cd204-c57b-11e7-afe9-4f60b5a6c4a0_story.
      html?utm_term=.fd896151cdf5.

24   World Health Organization, "Preventing Suicide: A Global Imperative," 2014, accessed
      May 14, 2018, http://apps.who.int/iris/bitstream/10665/131056/1/9789241564779_eng.
      pdf?ua=1&ua=1.

25   Louis Favril, Freya Vander Laenen, Christophe Vandeviver, and Kurt Audenaert, "Suicidal
      Ideation while Incarcerated: Prevalence and Correlates in a Large Sample of Male
      Prisoners in Flanders, Belgium," *International Journal of Law and Psychiatry*, 55 (2017):
      19–28, https://doi.org/10.1016/j.ijlp.2017.10.005.

26   Sean Coughlan, "Childhood in the US 'Safer than in the 1970s,'" BBC, December 23,
      2014, accessed June 5, 2018, https://www.bbc.com/news/education-30578830.

27   John Branch, "Autopsy Shows the N.H.L.'s Todd Ewen Did Not Have C.T.E.,"
      New York Times, February 10, 2016, accessed April 12, 2018, https://www.nytimes.
      com/2016/02/11/sports/hockey/autopsy-shows-the-nhls-todd-ewen-did-not-
      have-cte.html.

28   Eric Adelson, "Football and CTE: Fear Overshadows Facts," Yahoo! Sports, March 21,
      2016, accessed March 31, 2018, https://ca.sports.yahoo.com/news/football-and-cte--fear-
      has-overshadowed-facts-161625351.html.

29   Matt McCarthy, "The Hidden Victims of the NFL's Concussion Crisis," *Deadspin*,
      October 10, 2013, accessed April 20, 2018, https://deadspin.com/the-hidden-victims-of-
      the-nfls-concussion-crisis-1443101890.

30   Brooke De Lench, "CTE: Is the Media Scaring Young Athletes to Death?," *Huffington
      Post*, August 8, 2017, accessed April 13, 2018, https://www.huffingtonpost.com/entry/cte-
      is-the-media-scaring-young-athletes-to-death_us_5988d42de4b08a4c247f2503.

31   Joe Trinacria, "Eagles Safety Malcolm Jenkins Says He Doesn't Fear CTE," *Philadelphia
      Magazine*, March 16, 2018, accessed May 23, 2018, https://www.phillymag.com/
      news/2018/03/16/malcolm-jenkins-cte-gq/.

32   Tim Rohan, "A Calculated Decision: Why John Urschel Chose Math over Football,"
      Sports Illustrated, November 21, 2017, accessed February 13, 2018, https://www.si.com/
      nfl/2017/11/21/john-urschel-nfl-ravens-mit-mathematics.

CHAPTER 4

1   Joe Ward, Josh Williams, and Sam Manchester, "110 NFL Brains," *New York Times*, July
     25, 2017, accessed February 15, 2018, https://www.nytimes.com/interactive/2017/07/25/
     sports/football/nfl-cte.html.

2   K. M. Langa, E. B. Larson, E. M. Crimmins et al., "A Comparison of the Prevalence of
     Dementia in the United States in 2000 and 2012," *JAMA Internal Medicine* 177, no. 1
     (2017): 51–58, doi:10.1001/jamainternmed.2016.6807.

3   Gary Myers, "Game of Life and Death: As Concerns about CTE Grow and Players
     Suffer from Deadly Disease, Future of Football Looks Bleak," *New York Daily News*,
     November 5, 2017.

4   Kent Babb, "'The Demons' Are Always a Breath Away," *Washington Post*,
     December 12, 2017.

5   J. Mez, D. H. Daneshvar, P. T. Kiernan et al., "Clinicopathological Evaluation of Chronic
     Traumatic Encephalopathy in Players of American Football," *JAMA* 318, no. 4 (2017):
     360–70, doi:10.1001/jama.2017.8334.

6   UMass Lowell, "Poll: Majority of Americans Say Tackle Football Is Unsafe for Young
     Kids," 2017, accessed March 22, 2018, https://www.uml.edu/News/press-releases/2017/
     YouthConcussionPoll09122017.aspx.=.

7   B. Burnsed, "A Gray Matter," *Champion Magazine*, Spring 2015, accessed on May 8, 2018,
     at http://www.ncaa.org/static/champion/gray-matter/#sthash.fLCUdxnT.bLfliN0N.dpbs.

CHAPTER 5

1   Lisa Cosgrove, "Opinion: Bias Is Unavoidable," The Scientist, August 7, 2012, accessed May 15, 2018, https://www.the-scientist.com/?articles.view/articleNo/32462/title/Opinion--Bias-Is-Unavoidable/.

2   Carl Engelking, "What Are Woodpeckers Doing to Their Brains?" *Discover*, February 2, 2018, accessed April 28, 2018, http://blogs.discovermagazine.com/d-brief/2018/02/02/woodpeckers-brains/#.Wyq4bhJKjOQ.

3   Boston University School of Medicine, Twitter, June 27, 2018, 9:55 a.m., accessed June 27, 2018, https://twitter.com/BUMedicine/status/1012016590743883777.

4   Boston University School of Medicine, Twitter, May 1, 2018, 6:41 a.m., accessed June 27, 2018, https://twitter.com/BUMedicine/status/991311705262174208,

5   Boston University School of Medicine, Twitter, February 2, 2018, 10:24 a.m., accessed June 27, 2018, https://twitter.com/BUMedicine/status/959492854983921665.

6   Boston University School of Medicine, Twitter, January 29, 2018, 6:49 a.m., accessed June 27, 2018 https://twitter.com/BUMedicine/status/957989178930757633.

7   Boston University School of Medicine, Twitter, January 25, 2018, 11:35 a.m., accessed June 27, 2018, https://twitter.com/BUMedicine/status/956611553083740166.

8   Boston University School of Medicine, Twitter, November 13, 2017, 7:31 a.m., accessed June 27, 2018, https://twitter.com/BUMedicine/status/930095881323515904.

9   Boston University School of Medicine, Twitter, October 23, 2017, 6:16 a.m., accessed June 27, 2018, https://twitter.com/BUMedicine/status/922451749847388161.

10   Boston University CTE Center, "Former NHL Player Jeff Parker Has Been Diagnosed with Stage 3 (of 4) Chronic Traumatic Encephalopathy (CTE) by Researchers at the VA-BU-CLF Brain Bank," May 3, 2018, https://www.bu.edu/cte/2018/05/03/former-nhl-player-jeff-parker-has-been-diagnosed-with-stage-3-of-4-chronic-traumatic-encephalopathy-cte-by-researchers-at-the-va-bu-clf-brain-bank/.

11   Rick Westhead, "Scientist: NHL's Demand Would Harm All Ongoing CTE Research," TSN, February 7, 2017, accessed March 19, 2018, https://www.tsn.ca/scientist-nhl-s-demand-would-harm-all-ongoing-cte-research-1.666542.

12   Adam Kilgore, "Lawyers for Boston University Say NHL Request Will Slow Concussion Research," *Washington Post*, April 8, 2017, accessed May 18, 2018, https://www.washingtonpost.com/sports/capitals/lawyers-for-boston-university-say-nhl-request-will-slow-concussion-research/2017/04/08/6ab63464-1c64-11e7-bcc2-7d1a0973e7b2_story.html?utm_term=.200e2dab1ee3.

13   Rich Barlow, "Court Rules for BU, against NHL in CTE Case," BU Today, April 28, 2017, accessed May 14, 2018, http://www.bu.edu/today/2017/court-rules-for-bu-against-nhl-in-cte-case/.

14   Fainaru-Wada and Fainaru, *League of Denial*.

15   Brian Resnick, "One Reason Peer Review Is Broken: It's Biased in Favor of Prestigious Authors," Vox, November 29, 2016, accessed May 8, 2018, https://www.vox.com/science-and-health/2016/11/29/13770988/peer-review-bias-authors.

16   Branch, John, "Autopsy Shows the N.H.L.'s Todd Ewen Did Not Have C.T.E.,"
      New York Times, February 10, 2016, accessed April 12, 2018, https://www.nytimes.
      com/2016/02/11/sports/hockey/autopsy-shows-the-nhls-todd-ewen-did-not-
      have-cte.html.

17   "Todd Ewen," Hockey Fights http://www.hockeyfights.com/players/904.

18   The Canadian Press, "Toronto researchers find CTE in brain of patient with no
      concussion history," CTV News, March 2, 2017, accessed June 28, 2018, https://www.
      ctvnews.ca/health/toronto-researchers-find-cte-in-brain-of-patient-with-no-concussion-
      history-1.3308916.

CHAPTER 6

1   Richard Lovegrove, "Hard-Hitting Research," *Virginia Tech Magazine*, Winter 2016–17,
      accessed April 29, 2018, http://www.vtmag.vt.edu/winter17/helmet-research.html.

2   Jason Chung, Peter Cummings, and Uzma Samadani, "Does CTE Call for an End to
      Youth Tackle Football?" *Minneapolis Star Tribune*, February 10, 2018, accessed March
      21, 2018, http://www.startribune.com/does-cte-call-for-an-end-to-youth-tackle-
      football/473655913/.

3   American Psychological Association, "By the Numbers: Men and Depression," *Monitor
      on Psychology* 46, no. 11 (December 2015), accessed June 2, 2018, https://www.apa.org/
      monitor/2015/12/numbers.aspx.

4   P. R. Albert, "Why Is Depression More Prevalent in Women?" *Journal of Psychiatry &
      Neuroscience* 40, no. 4 (2015): 219–21, doi:10.1503/jpn.150205.

5   D. C. R. Kerr, L. D. Owen, K. C. Pears, and D. M. Capaldi, "Prevalence of Suicidal
      Ideation among Boys and Men Assessed Annually from Ages 9 to 29 Years," *Suicide
      & Life-Threatening Behavior* 38, no. 4 (2008): 390–402, http://doi.org/10.1521/
      suli.2008.38.4.390.

6   Megan Meyer, "Want to Fix Science's Replication Crisis? Then Replicate," *Wired*, April
      19, 2017, accessed May 10, 2018, https://www.wired.com/2017/04/want-fix-sciences-
      replication-crisis-replicate/.

7   Shawna Noy et al., "Chronic Traumatic Encephalopathy-Like Abnormalities in a Routine
      Neuropathology Service," *Journal of Neuropathology and Experimental Neurology* 75, no. 12
      (2016): 1145–54.

8   Mez, Daneshvar, Kiernan et al., "Clinicopathological Evaluation of Chronic Traumatic
      Encephalopathy."

9   Val J. Lowe, Heather J. Wiste, Matthew L. Senjem, Stephen D. Weigand, Terry M.
      Therneau, Bradley F. Boeve, Keith A. Josephs et al., "Widespread Brain Tau and Its
      Association with Ageing, Braak Stage and Alzheimer's Dementia," *Brain* 141, no. 1
      (January 2018): 271–87, published online December 8, 2017, doi: 10.1093/brain/awx320.

10   Michael S. Schallmo, Joseph Arnold Weiner, and Wellington Hsu, "Assessing Trends in
      the Epidemiology of Concussions among High School Athletes," *Orthopaedic Journal of
      Sports Medicine* 5, no. 7, supp. 6 (2017), http://doi.org/10.1177/2325967117S00439.

11   Schwartz, Peter. "From NFL to Youth Football, Females Are Showing That Football Has a Place for Them, Too." USA Football. August 11, 2015. Accessed August 26, 2018. https://blogs.usafootball.com/blog/1296/from-nfl-to-youth-football-females-are-showing-that-football-has-a-place-for-them-too.

12   Luther, Jessica. "There's a Rising Number of Girls Playing Football." Teen Vogue. February 1, 2017. Accessed August 26, 2018. https://www.teenvogue.com/story/girls-play-football-females-teams.

13   G. S. Solomon, A. W. Kuhn, S. L. Zuckerman et al., "Participation in Pre–High School Football and Neurological, Neuroradiological, and Neuropsychological Findings in Later Life: A Study of 45 Retired National Football League Players," *American Journal of Sports Medicine* 44 (2016): 1106–15; S. K. Deshpande, R. B. Hasegawa, A. R. Rabinowitz et al., "Association of Playing High School Football with Cognition and Mental Health Later in Life," *JAMA Neurology* 74 (2017): 909–19.

14   S. J. Kuzminski et al., "White Matter Changes Related to Subconcussive Impact Frequency during a Single Season of High School Football," *American Journal of Neuroradiology* 39, no. 2 (2018): 245–51.

15   Keisuke Kawata, Leah H. Rubin, Jong Hyun Lee, Thomas Sim, Masahiro Takahagi, Victor Szwanki, Al Bellamy et al., "Association of Football Subconcussive Head Impacts with Ocular Near Point of Convergence," *JAMA Ophthalmology* 134, no. 7 (2016): 763–69, doi: 10.1001/jamaophthalmol.2016.1085.

16   Lindsey Barton Straus, "Concussive and Subconcussive Blows May Speed Up Aging of Brain, Studies Suggest," MomsTEAM, accessed May 21, 2018, http://www.momsteam.com/concussive-and-subconcussive-blows-may-speed-up-brain-natural-aging-process-studies-suggest.

17   A. A. Tarnutzer, D. Straumann, P. Brugger et al., "Persistent Effects of Playing Football and Associated (Subconcussive) Head Trauma on Brain Structure and Function: A Systematic Review of the Literature," *British Journal of Sports Medicine* 51 (2017): 1592–1604.

18   Lynda Mainwaring, Kaleigh M. Ferdinand Pennock, Sandhya Mylabathula, and Benjamin Z. Alavie, "Subconcussive Head Impacts in Sport: A Systematic Review of the Evidence," *International Journal of Psychophysiology* (2018), published online February 2, 2018, doi: 10.1016/j.ijpsycho.2018.01.007.

19   Steven Kemp, Alistair Duff, and Natalie Hampson, "The Neurological, Neuroimaging and Neuropsychological Effects of Playing Professional Football: Results of the UK Five-Year Follow-Up Study," *Brain Injury* 30, no. 9 (2016): 1068–74, published online May 16, 2016, doi: 10.3109/02699052.2016.1148776.

20   M. L. Alosco, J. Mez, Y. Tripodis, P. T. Kiernan, B. Abdolmohammadi, L. Murphy, N. W. Kowall et al., "Age of First Exposure to Tackle Football and Chronic Traumatic Encephalopathy," *Annals of Neurology*, forthcoming, doi:10.1002/ana.25245.

21   Clara Passmann Carr, Camilla Maria Severi Martins, Ana Maria Stingel, Vera Braga Lemgruber, and Mario Francisco Juruena, "The Role of Early Life Stress in Adult Psychiatric Disorders: A Systematic Review According to Childhood Trauma Subtypes," *Journal of Nervous and Mental Disease* 201, no. 12 (December 2013): 1007–20, doi: 10.1097/NMD.0000000000000049.

22 Alice Lee, "7 Charts That Show the State of Youth Sports in the US and Why It Matters," Aspen Institute, February 24, 2015, accessed May 2, 2018, https://www. aspeninstitute.org/blog-posts/7-charts-that-show-the-state-of-youth-sports-in-the-us-and-why-it-matters/.

23 Scott Sleek, "How Poverty Affects the Brain and Behavior," *APS Observer*, September 2015, accessed May 2, 2018, https://www.psychologicalscience.org/observer/how-poverty-affects-the-brain-and-behavior.

24 Carol Joinson, Daphne Kounali, and Glyn Lewis. "Family Socioeconomic Position in Early Life and Onset of Depressive Symptoms and Depression: A Prospective Cohort Study," *Social Psychiatry and Psychiatric Epidemiology* 52, no. 1 (2017): 95–103. PubMed Central, May 22, 2018. https://www.ncbi.nlm.nih.gov/pubmed/27837235.

25 Shawna Noy et al., "Chronic Traumatic Encephalopathy-Like Abnormalities in a Routine Neuropathology Service," *Journal of Neuropathology and Experimental Neurology* 75, no. 12 (2016): 1145–54.

26 Gary Solomon, "Chronic Traumatic Encephalopathy in Sports: A Historical and Narrative Review," *Developmental Neuropsychology* 43, no. 4 (2018): 279–311, doi: 10.1080/87565641.2018.1447575.

CHAPTER 7

1 R. L. Blaylock and J. Maroon, "Immunoexcitotoxicity as a Central Mechanism in Chronic Traumatic Encephalopathy—A Unifying Hypothesis," *Surgical Neurology International* 2 (2011): 107, http://doi.org/10.4103/2152-7806.83391.

2 Blaylock and Maroon, "Immunoexcitotoxicity as a Central Mechanism."

3 Kristen C. Willeumier, Derek V. Taylor, and Daniel G. Amen, "Elevated BMI Is Associated with Decreased Blood Flow in the Prefrontal Cortex Using SPECT Imaging in Healthy Adults," *Obesity* 19 (2011): 1095–97, doi:10.1038/oby.2011.16.

4 Kristen C. Willeumier, Derek V. Taylor, and Daniel G. Amen, "Elevated Body Mass in National Football League Players Linked to Cognitive Impairment and Decreased Prefrontal Cortex and Temporal Pole Activity," *Translational Psychiatry* 2 (2012): e68, published online January 17, 2012, doi:10.1038/tp.2011.67.

5 Daniel G. Amen, Kristen Willeumier, Bennet Omalu, Andrew Newberg, Cauligi Raghavendrad, and Cyrus A. Raji, "Perfusion Neuroimaging Abnormalities Alone Distinguish National Football League Players from a Healthy Population," *Journal of Alzheimer's Disease*, March 2016, accessed May 1, 2018, https://www.ncbi.nlm.nih.gov/pubmed/27128374.

6 G. L. Iverson, C. D. Keene, G. Perry, and R. J. Castellani, "The Need to Separate Chronic Traumatic Encephalopathy Neuropathology from Clinical Features," *Journal of Alzheimer's Disease* 61, no. 1 (2017): 17–28, doi:10.3233/JAD-170654.

7 Fainaru and Fainaru-Wada, "NFL Backs Away from Funding."

8 "National Institutes of Health—What We Do," accessed June 12, 2018, https://www.nih.gov/about-nih/what-we-do/budget.

CHAPTER 8

1   Tod Leonard, "Youth Football Dilemma: Retaining Players amid Constant Concussion Talk," *San Diego Union-Tribune*, November 26, 2017, accessed May 30, 2018, http://www.sandiegouniontribune.com/sports/sd-sp-youth-football-declining-participation-and-concussions-20171123-story.html.

2   HBO Real Sports/Marist Poll, "Reports about Football-Related Head Injuries Impacting Youth Football," Marist College Institute for Public Opinion, November 22, 2016, accessed May 28, 2018, http://www.marist.edu/publicaffairs/realsportspoll2016.html.

3   Eric Sondheimer, "11-Man High School Football Participation Declines by More than 25,000 Nationally," *Los Angeles Times*, August 7, 2017, accessed May 26, 2018, http://www.latimes.com/sports/highschool/varsity-times/la-sp-high-school-sports-updates-11-man-high-school-football-1502127207-htmlstory.html.

4   The Aspen Institute Project Play, "State of Play 2017," accessed May 19, 2018, https://assets.aspeninstitute.org/content/uploads/2017/12/FINAL-SOP2017-report.pdf.

5   *Times* Editorial Board, "Banning tackle football for kids? There's nothing 'nanny state' about it if the science is sound," *Los Angeles Times*, February 2, 2018, accessed April 3, 2018, http://www.latimes.com/opinion/editorials/la-ed-football-concussions-youths-20180202-story.html.

6   Nadia Kounang, "Former NFLers call for end to tackle football for kids," CNN, March 1, 2018, accessed May 7, 2018, https://www.cnn.com/2018/01/18/health/nfl-no-tackle-football-kids/index.html.

7   Chris Nowinski, "It's Time To Ban Youth Tackle Football," *Huffington Post*, February 2, 2018, accessed March 22, 2018, https://www.huffingtonpost.com/entry/opinion-nowinski-ban-tackle_us_5a735bf7e4b0905433b23463.

8   *Mercury News* & *East Bay Times* Editorial Boards, "Editorial: Ban California kids from playing Pop Warner football," *San Jose Mercury-News*, February 15, 2018, accessed March 22, 2018, https://www.mercurynews.com/2018/02/15/editorial-ban-california-kids-from-playing-pop-warner-football/?utm_term=Autofeed&utm_campaign=Echobox&utm_medium=Social&utm_source=Twitter#link_time=1518714399.

9   Elliott Almond, "'Concussion' Doctor: Youth football is child abuse," *San Jose Mercury-News*, August 9, 2017, accessed March 23, 2018, https://www.mercurynews.com/2017/08/09/concussion-doctor-youth-football-is-child-abuse/.

10 Editorial Board, "Tackle football is not for children," *Washington Post*, September 26, 2017, accessed March 24, 2018, https://www.washingtonpost.com/opinions/tackle-football-is-not-for-children/2017/09/26/5959a0a8-9e40-11e7-9083-fbfddf6804c2_story.html?utm_term=.3def000b0bb8.

11 Nicole Wetsman, "We have no idea how dangerous football really is," *Popular Science*, February 2, 2018, accessed March 24, 2018, https://www.popsci.com/how-dangerous-is-football-cte#page-3.

12   Allen Raskin, "Children should not be playing tackle football, says Packers great Brett
      Favre as he fears HE may have C.T.E. after suffering 'thousands' of concussions,"
      Daily Mail, April 12, 2018, accessed May 2, 2018, http://www.dailymail.co.uk/news/
      article-5608231/Packers-great-Brett-Favre-opens-Megyn-Kelly-concussion-issues-
      dangers-football.html.

13   ProFootballDoc, "No Scientific Link between Youth Football and CTE," *San
      Diego Union-Tribune*, February 19, 2018, accessed April 4, 2018, http://www.
      sandiegouniontribune.com/sports/profootballdoc/sd-sp-pfd-youth-football-ban-bill-
      concussions-facts-0219-story.html.

14   Christine Organ, "I Know about Concussion Risks. Here's Why I Let My 8-Year-Old
      Play Tackle Football Anyway," *Washington Post*, January 7, 2016, accessed May 5, 2018,
      https://www.washingtonpost.com/news/to-your-health/wp/2016/01/07/i-know-about-
      concussion-risks-heres-why-i-let-my-8-year-old-play-tackle-football-anyway/?utm_
      term=.32195297ac40.

15   Wetsman, "We Have No Idea."

16   Chad A. Tagge, Andrew M. Fisher, Olga V. Minaeva, Amanda Gaudreau-Balderrama,
      Juliet A. Moncaster, Xiao-Lei Zhang, Mark W. Wojnarowicz et al., "Concussion,
      Microvascular Injury, and Early Tauopathy in Young Athletes after Impact Head Injury
      and an Impact Concussion Mouse Model," *Brain*, 141, no. 2, (February 2018): 422–58,
      https://doi.org/10.1093/brain/awx350.

17   Felice Freyer, "CTE Can Begin Soon after Head Injury, Even in Teens, BU Study Finds,"
      Boston Globe, January 18, 2018, accessed April 11, 2018, https://www.bostonglobe.com/
      metro/2018/01/18/cte-can-begin-soon-after-head-injury-even-teens-study-finds/
      yApExpCyyiESvgOYviI6NK/story.html.

18   Alosco et al., "Age of First Exposure."

19   Lynn O'Shaughnessy, "The Odds of Playing College Sports," *Money Watch*, April 4,
      2011, accessed March 31, 2018, https://www.cbsnews.com/news/the-odds-of-playing-
      college-sports/.

20   NCAA, "What Are Your Odds of Making the Pros?," accessed May 4, 2018, www.
      norwichcsd.org/Downloads/ProSportsOdds.doc.

21   Mike Oxendine, "Mom on a Mission," *Mail Tribune*, December 31, 2017, accessed May 7,
      2018, http://mailtribune.com/news/top-stories/mom-on-a-mission-04-24-2018.

22   Tod Leonard, "Moms take on football, suing Pop Warner for their sons' head trauma,
      deaths," *San Diego Union Tribune*, January 28, 2018, accessed April 27, 2018, http://
      www.sandiegouniontribune.com/sports/sd-sp-moms-sue-pop-warner-for-cte-damage-
      20180128-story.html.

23   Lindsey Adler, "Can Grieving Mothers Stop the Public from Forgetting the NFL's Brain-
      Trauma Crisis?," *Deadspin*, February 3, 2017, accessed April 15, 2018, https://deadspin.
      com/can-grieving-mothers-stop-the-public-from-forgetting-th-1791934820.

24   Kimberly Archie, "The NFL Must Listen to Football Moms if It Wants to Survive,"
      Huffington Post, January 30, 2018, accessed May 3, 2018, https://www.huffingtonpost.
      com/entry/opinion-archie-cte-football_us_5a6f87a2e4b00d0de222f3cc.

25   Tod Leonard, "California Bill to Ban Youth Tackle Football Pulled before Committee Vote," *San Diego Union-Tribune*, April 26, 2018, accessed April 27, 2018, http://www.sandiegouniontribune.com/sports/sd-sp-california-bill-to-ban-football-pulled-20180426-story.html.

26   Ken Belson, "Family Sues Pop Warner over Suicide of Player Who Had Brain Disease," *New York Times*, February 5, 2015, accessed May 11, 2018, https://www.nytimes.com/2015/02/06/sports/family-of-player-with-cte-who-killed-himself-sues-pop-warner.html.

27   Michael Martinez, "Pop Warner Settles Concussion Suit Filed by Former Player Who Committed Suicide," CNN, March 9, 2016, accessed May 11, 2018, https://www.cnn.com/2016/03/09/us/pop-warner-concussion-lawsuit-settlement-player-suicide/index.html.

28   Tod Leonard, "Moms Take On Football."

29   Tod Leonard, "Ohio Dad Is First to Sue Youth Helmet Makers for Death of Son," *San Diego Union-Tribune*, June 1, 2018, accessed June 8, 2018, http://www.sandiegouniontribune.com/sports/sd-sp-dad-suing-helmet-makers-over-sons-death-20180601-story.html.

30   Jeremy Bauer-Wolf, "College Football's Avalanche of Lawsuits," *Inside Higher Ed*, December 1, 2017, accessed June 6, 2018, https://www.insidehighered.com/news/2017/12/01/avalanche-football-related-concussion-lawsuits-against-ncaa-and-conferences-could.

31   DeKaro & Kaplan, LLP, "Youth Tackle Football—Proposed Legislation," accessed June 10, 2018, https://brainlaw.com/youth-tackle-football.

32   California Legislative Information, accessed June 11, 2018, https://leginfo.legislature.ca.gov/faces/billTextClient.xhtml?bill_id=201720180ACR156.

33   Chris Nowinski and Robert Cantu, "Flag Football under 14: An Education Campaign for Parents," white paper, updated January 17, 2018.

34   Andrew R. Peterson, Adam J. Kruse, Scott M. Meester, Tyler S. Olson, Benjamin N. Riedle, Tyler G. Slayman, Todd J. Domeyer, Joseph E. Cavanaugh, and M. Kyle Smoot, "Youth Football Injuries: A Prospective Cohort," *Orthopaedic Journal of Sports Medicine*, accessed May 3, 2018, https://www.ncbi.nlm.nih.gov/pubmed/28255566

35   https://www.change.org/p/save-youth-football-in-california, accessed June 14, 2018.

36   Alicia Robinson, "Bill to Ban Youth Tackle Football Is Government Overreach, Some Coaches Say," *OC Register*, February 24, 2018, accessed June 2, 2018, https://www.ocregister.com/2018/02/24/bill-to-ban-youth-tackle-football-is-government-overreach-some-coaches-say/.

37   Ann McKee, "Center for the Study of Traumatic Encephalopathy Neuropathology Report," accessed June 12, 2018, https://www.documentcloud.org/documents/4478840-Joseph-Chernach-Autopsy-Center-for-the-Study-of.html.

38   Scott Zuckerman, Zachary Y. Kerr, Aaron Yengo-Kahn, Erin Wasserman, Tracey Covassin, and Gary Solomon, "Epidemiology of Sports-Related Concussion in NCAA Athletes From 2009–2010 to 2013–2014: Incidence, Recurrence, and Mechanisms," *American Journal of Sports Medicine* 43 (2015), 10.1177/0363546515599634.

39   Cho Lwin, "Forensic Consultant's Report, Autopsy Report 2014-02378," County of Los Angeles, Department of Coroner, April 27, 2014, accessed June 1, 2018.

40   Surgical pathology report, OSU Histology Lab, LLC, medical record #40012-3008, March 2, 2015.

41   Pete Thamel and Michael McCann, "Complex Portrait of Ohio St.'s Kosta Karageorge Emerges after Death," *Sports Illustrated*, December 5, 2014, accessed May 26, 2018, https://www.si.com/college-football/2014/12/05/kosta-karageorge-ohio-state-death.

42   Tim Rohan, "A Young Athlete's World of Pain, and Where It Led," *New York Times*, June 22, 2016.

43   R. D. Rodriguez and L. T. Grinberg, "Argyrophilic Grain Disease: An Underestimated Tauopathy," *Dementia & Neuropsychologia* 9, no. 1 (2015): 2–8, http://doi.org/10.1590/S1980-57642015DN91000002.

44   Nik DeCosta-Klipa, "A Boston University Neurologist Is at Odds with His Own School's Conclusions about Youth Football and CTE," Boston.com, September 21, 2017, accessed March 29, 2018, https://www.boston.com/sports/sports-news/2017/09/21/a-boston-university-neurologist-is-at-odds-with-his-own-schools-conclusions-about-youth-football-and-cte.

45   Freyer, "CTE Can Begin Soon after Head Injury."

CHAPTER 9

1   Je Yeong Sone, S. Courtney-Kay Lamb, Kristina Techar, Vikalpa Dammavalam, Mohit Uppal, Cedric Williams, Thomas Bergman, David Tupper, Paul Ort, and Uzma Samadani, "High Prevalence of Prior Contact Sports Play and Concussion among Orthopedic and Neurosurgical Department Chairs," *Journal of Neurosurgery: Pediatrics* (2018): 1–8, doi: 10.3171/2018.1.PEDS17640.

2   Philip H. Montenigro, Michael L. Alosco, Brett M. Martin, Daniel H. Daneshvar, Jesse Mez, Christine E. Chaisson, Christopher J. Nowinski et al., "Cumulative Head Impact Exposure Predicts Later-Life Depression, Apathy, Executive Dysfunction, and Cognitive Impairment in Former High School and College Football Players," *Journal of Neurotrauma* (January 2017), accessed June 4, 2018, https://www.ncbi.nlm.nih.gov/pubmed/27029716.

3   Edward T. Riley, *Journal of Neurotrauma* (April 2017).

4   Ana Agustí, Maria P. García-Pardo, Inmaculada López-Almela, Isabel Campillo, Michael Maes, Marina Romaní-Pérez, and Yolanda Sanz, "Interplay between the Gut-Brain Axis, Obesity and Cognitive Function," *Frontiers in Neuroscience* 12 (2018): 155, https://www.frontiersin.org/article/10.3389/fnins.2018.00155.

5   Peterson et al., "Youth Football Injuries."

6   R. A. Campbell, S. A. Gorman, R. J. Thoma, R. D. Annett, C. A. McGrew, R. A. Yeo, A. R. Mayer, J. H. King, and A. S. Rowland, "Risk of Concussion during Sports versus Physical Education among New Mexico Middle and High School Students," *American Journal of Public Health* 108, no. 1 (January 2018): 93–95, Epub, November 21, 2017, doi: 10.2105/AJPH.2017.304107.

7   Deshpande et al., "Association of Playing High School Football."

8   *CDC Childhood Injury Report*, https://www.cdc.gov/safechild/child_injury_data.html.

9   Kids Safe Worldwide, *Bicycle, Skate and Skateboard Safety Fact Sheet*, 2016, accessed
       May 7, 2018, https://www.safekids.org/sites/default/files/documents/skw_bike_fact_
       sheet_2016.pdf.

10   Kristen L. Kucera, David Klossner, Bob Colgate, and Robert C. Cantu, "Annual Survey
       of Football Injury Research," National Center for Catastrophic Sport Injury Research,
       March 2015.

11   CDC MMWR, "Nonfatal Traumatic Brain Injuries Related to Sports and Recreation
       Activities among Persons Aged ≤19 Years—United States, 2001–2009," *Morbidity and
       Mortality Weekly Report* 60, no. 39 (2011): 1337–42.

12   Krushnapriya Sahoo et al., "Childhood Obesity: Causes and Consequences," *Journal
       of Family Medicine and Primary Care* 4, no. 2 (2015): 187–92. PubMed Central,
       May 25, 2018.

13   R. J. Johnson, M. S. Segal, Y. Sautin, T. Nakagawa, D. I. Feig, D. H. Kang, M. S. Gersch, S.
       Benner, and L. G. Sánchez-Lozada, "Potential Role of Sugar (Fructose) in the Epidemic
       of Hypertension, Obesity and the Metabolic Syndrome, Diabetes, Kidney Disease,
       and Cardiovascular Disease," *American Journal of Clinical Nutrition* 86, no. 4 (October
       2007): 899–906.

14   H. M. Francis and R. J. Stevenson, "Higher Reported Saturated Fat and Refined
       Sugar Intake Is Associated with Reduced Hippocampal-Dependent Memory and
       Sensitivity to Interoceptive Signals," *Behavioral Neuroscience* 125 (2011): 943–55, doi:
       10.1037/a0025998.

15   Miriam B. Vos et al., "Added Sugars and Cardiovascular Disease Risk in Children: A
       Scientific Statement from the American Heart Association," *Circulation* 135, no. 19
       (2017): e1017–e1034. PubMed Central, May 25, 2018.

16   F. W. Booth, C. K. Roberts, and M. J. Laye, "Lack of Exercise Is a Major Cause of
       Chronic Diseases," *Comprehensive Physiology* 2, no. 2 (2012): 1143–1211, doi:10.1002/
       cphy.c110025.

17   Y. M. Terry-McElrath and P. M. O'Malley, Substance Use and Exercise Participation
       among Young Adults: Parallel Trajectories in a National Cohort-Sequential Study,"
       Addiction 106 (2011): 1855–65, doi:10.1111/j.1360-0443.2011.03489.x.

18   Kevin M. Kniffin, Brian Wansink, and Mitsuru Shimizu, "Sports at Work: Anticipated
       and Persistent Correlates of Participation in High School Athletics," *Journal of Leadership
       & Organizational Studies* 22, no. 2 (2015): 217–30, first published June 16, 2014.

19   Rachel Jewett, Catherine M. Sabiston, Jennifer Brunet, Erin K. O'Loughlin, Tanya
       Scarapicchia, and Jennifer O'Loughlin, "School Sport Participation during Adolescence
       and Mental Health in Early Adulthood," *Journal of Adolescent Health* 55, no. 5 (2014):
       640–44, doi: 10.1016/j.jadohealth.2014.04.018.

CHAPTER 10

1   Tod Leonard, "At Seau Symposium, CTE Researcher Makes His Case against Youth Tackle Football," *San Diego Union-Tribune*, March 31, 2018, accessed April 11, 2018, http://www.sandiegouniontribune.com/sports/sd-sp-cte-symposium-chris-nowinski-junior-seau-20180331-story.html.

2   American Academy of Pediatrics Committee on School Health, "COMPETITIVE Athletics: A Statement of Policy: Report of the Committee on School Health," *Pennsylvania Medical Journal* 60 (1957): 627–62.

3   Thomas P. Dompier, "Replacing Youth Tackle Football with Flag Football Might Not Make Our Children Safer," *USA Today*, April 25, 2018, accessed May 4, 2018, https://www.usatoday.com/story/opinion/2018/04/25/youth-tackle-football-flag-football-column/543549002/.

4   USA Football commissioned research, accessed May 19, 2018, https://usafootball.com/resources-tools/research-library/.

5   Steve Alic, "USA Football's Practice Guidelines for Youth Tackle Football Define and Set Limits on Full Contact," USA Football, February 25, 2015, accessed April 28, 2018, https://blogs.usafootball.com/blog/1086/usa-football-s-practice-guidelines-for-youth-tackle-football-define-and-set-limits-on-full-contact.

6   Brain Injury Law Center, "Head Injuries in Rugby vs. Football," October 16, 2014, accessed May 20, 2018, https://www.brain-injury-law-center.com/blog/head-injuries-rugby-vs-football/.

7   Michelle A. King, Lisa R. Leon, Danielle L. Mustico, Joel M. Haines, and Thomas L. Clanton, "Biomarkers of Multiorgan Injury in a Preclinical Model of Exertional Heat Stroke," *Journal of Applied Physiology* 118 (2015): 1207–20, first published March 26, 2015, doi:10.1152/japplphysiol.01051.2014.

8   Don Rauf, "Guidelines Stop Heat Stroke Deaths in High School Athletes," University of Connecticut, Korey Stringer Institute, June 23, 2016, accessed May 3, 2018, https://ksi.uconn.edu/2016/06/23/guidelines-stop-heat-stroke-deaths-in-high-school-athletes-us-news-world-report/#.

9   Mark S. Link, Barry J. Maron, Paul J. Wang, Natesa G. Pandian, Brian A. VanderBrink, and N. A. Mark Estes III, "Reduced Risk of Sudden Death from Chest Wall Blows (Commotio Cordis) with Safety Baseballs," *Pediatrics* 109, no. 5 (May 2002): 873–77.

10 Richard Lovegrove, "Hard-Hitting Research," *Virginia Tech Magazine*, Winter 2016–17, accessed April 29, 2018, http://www.vtmag.vt.edu/winter17/helmet-research.html.

11 National Football League, "Helmet Laboratory Testing Performance Results," https://www.playsmartplaysafe.com/resource/helmet-laboratory-testing-performance-results/.

12 Alonzo Orozco, "Junior Warriors Seek Added Football Safety; Guardian Caps May Be the Answer," CoastalView.com, May 29, 2018, accessed May 30, 2018, http://www.coastalview.com/sports/junior-warriors-seek-added-football-safety-guardian-caps-may-be/article_35000a2c-6388-11e8-89a0-5f7cd2d96923.html.

CHAPTER II

1 Nadia Kounang, "Ex-NFL Player Confirmed as 1st Case of CTE in Living Patient," CNN, November 16, 2017, accessed June 5, 2018, https://www.cnn.com/2017/11/16/health/cte-confirmed-in-first-living-person-bn/index.html.

2 John Keilman, "CTE Confirmed for 1st Time in Live Person, according to Exam of Ex-NFL Player," *Chicago Tribune*, November 15, 2017, accessed May 1, 2018, http://www.chicagotribune.com/news/local/breaking/ct-met-concussions-cte-confirmed-in-living-person-20171115-story.html.

3 National Football League, 2018 Helmet Laboratory Testing Performance Results, accessed July 12, 2018, https://www.playsmartplaysafe.com/resource/helmet-laboratory-testing-performance-results.

4 NFL and NFL Players Association, "NFL And NFLPA Release 2018 Helmet Laboratory Testing Performance Results," April 16, 2018, accessed June 4, 2018, https://operations.nfl.com/updates/football-ops/nfl-and-nflpa-release-2018-helmet-laboratory-testing-performance-results/.

5 PR Newswire, "Riddell Kicks-Off Fourth-Annual Smarter Football Program." PR Newswire, June 5, 2018, www.prnewswire.com/news-releases/riddell-kicks-off-fourth-annual-smarter-football-program-300659934.html.

6 CU MR, "Colorado Football: CU Professor Aims to Improve Football Helmet Safety with New Polymer," KKTV 11 News, May 31, 2018, accessed June 11, 2018, http://www.kktv.com/content/sports/Colorado-Football-CU-Professor-Aims-To-Improve-Football-Helmet-Safety-With-New-Polymer-484233431.html.

7 Chris Gorski, "Will the NFL's Blitz for Position-Specific Helmets Pay Off?," *Inside Science*, November 17, 2017, accessed June 2, 2018, https://www.insidescience.org/news/will-nfls-blitz-position-specific-helmets-pay.

8 Associated Press, "Su'a Cravens Eager for a Do-Over in Denver after Missing Last Year," *Los Angeles Times*, April 2, 2018, accessed June 4, 2018, http://www.latimes.com/sports/nfl/la-sp-cravens-broncos-20180402-story.html.

9 Marjorie S. Miller, "Cooling Helmet, Supplement Show Potential as Concussion Healers," Medical Xpress, August 15, 2017, accessed April 20, 2018, https://medicalxpress.com/news/2017-08-cooling-helmet-supplement-potential-concussion.html.

10 Amir Hadanny and Shai Efrati, "Treatment of Persistent Post-Concussion Syndrome Due to Mild Traumatic Brain Injury: Current Status and Future Directions," *Expert Review of Neurotherapeutics* (2016), doi:10.1080/14737175.2016.1205487, accessed June 10, 2018, https://www.ncbi.nlm.nih.gov/pubmed/27337294.

11 Nina Mandell, "NFL Consultant: It's More Dangerous to Ride a Bike Than Play Youth Football," *USA Today*, March 18, 2015, accessed May 14 2018, https://ftw.usatoday.com/2015/03/nfl-medical-consultant-joseph-maroon-nfl-network.

12 Joseph C. Maroon and Jeffrey Bost, "Concussion Management at the NFL, College, High School, and Youth Sports Levels," *Clinical Neurosurgery* 58 (2011): 51–56.

13   R. L. Blaylock and J. Maroon, "Natural Plant Products and Extracts That Reduce Immunoexcitotoxicity-Associated Neurodegeneration and Promote Repair within the Central Nervous System," *Surgical Neurology International* 3 (2012): 19.

14   J. Maroon and J. Bost, "Review of the Neurological Benefits of Phytocannabinoids," *Surgical Neurology International* 9 (2018): 91, http://doi.org/10.4103/sni.sni_45_18.

15   CDC, "Traumatic Brain Injury & Concussion," accessed May 27, 2018, https://www.cdc.gov/traumaticbraininjury/get_the_facts.html.

16   Alex P. Di Battista, Nathan Churchill, Tom A. Schweizer, Shawn G. Rhind, Doug Richards, A. Jerry Baker, and Michael G. Hutchison, "Blood Biomarkers Are Associated with Brain Function and Blood Flow following Sport Concussion," *Journal of Neuroimmunology* 319 (2018): 1–8.

17   Jonathan D. Cherry et al., "Microglial Neuroinflammation Contributes to Tau Accumulation in Chronic Traumatic Encephalopathy," *Acta Neuropathologica Communications* 4 (2016): 112, doi:10.1186/s40478-016-0382-8.

18   Debra Goldschmidt, "Is Alzheimer's Disease Preventable?," CNN, June 19, 2018, accessed June 21, 2018, https://www.cnn.com/2015/06/23/health/alzheimers-early-intervention/index.html.

19   David Heim, "Bill Belichick Was Right to Distance Himself, Patriots from Alex Guerrero," Patriots Wire, June 8, 2018, accessed June 14, 2018, https://patriotswire.usatoday.com/2018/06/08/bill-belichick-was-right-to-distance-himself-patriots-from-alex-guerrero/.